Rendezvous with Life

A true story of a life uprooted & replanted

Uta Vessey

To the Glory of God

with thanks to my mother and grandmother who kept me safe

and

with love to Peter

© Uta Vessey, 2013

Published by Upper Springs Publishing

A CIP catalogue record for this book is available from the British Library.

ISBN 978-0-9575798-0-4

Book layout and cover design by Clare Brayshaw

Cover image courtesy of Photojohnic mrvessey@gmail.com

Prepared and printed by:

York Publishing Services Ltd
64 Hallfield Road
Layerthorpe
York YO31 7ZQ

Tel: 01904 431213

Website: www.yps-publishing.co.uk

This book is available from www.ypdbooks.com

"I have a rendezvous with Death...
at midnight in some flaming town,"
young Alan Seeger wrote - and died.
And I?
I had a rendezvous with Life,
fled flaming town and crushing tank
and found Life by a weathered cross
in sun-kissed dunes.

Contents

Book II: Islands in turbulent seas

Book III: Rendezvous with Life

My child,
you played in many places,
learnt war's language: terror
too great to feel and comprehend.
Kept silent.

Your story
is of no importance
because millions might
tell one more profound?
Keep silent?

Your voice
though small and reticent,
I promise, will not go unheard.
I write and let those judges be
Who read.

You, child,
and I will turn the pages
and we will cry and laugh together
and celebrate with joy that
you are here – alive.

War Generations

There was a time before two terrible wars swept across the world, when in the farthest eastern region of the Second German Reich Lithuanians, Germans and Jews and a few other nationalities lived peacefully side by side; when friendships and intermarriage were not unusual and most of the population was bilingual. The citizens of "Prussian Lithuania", the northern part of East Prussia, had developed their own unique culture where life was ordered, the roads cobbled and lined with trees. Human enmities as might occur in any community were not of an ethnic or ideological or religious nature.

My maternal grandmother, my Oma, Else Simoneit was born in Uszballen, a hamlet in that region north of the River Memel; one of five siblings. There she went to the one-class school and when needed helped her father on his smallholding. This little patch of land could not sustain seven adults and when, around the turn of the century a clarion call went out from the burgeoning industries of the Ruhr Region, the Great Spoon, which throughout the ages has stirred peoples from their homes and caused them to migrate, whisked my grandmother from one ethnic melting pot into another: Duisburg, city on Rhine and Ruhr. Here she went into service in a well-to-do family and was spared the indignity of having to cram into one of the *Mietskasernen* (literally 'rent barracks'), the overcrowded tenement blocks and small houses, purpose-built for the East European workers who lived in poor conditions on wages which necessitated sub-letting tiny rooms for extra income.

How she and my Opa, the Rhinelander Wilhelm Nehles, met, I have never been told. He, the son of an invalid miner, was born in Meiderich, a village soon to be given town rights and then to be incorporated into the city of Duisburg. The young man did not want to follow his father underground in pursuit of coal nor labour in the new steel works. No, he treasured independence and together with his East Prussian wife, who was used to deft work, he built up a dairy business – from handcart to horse-drawn wagon, to delivery van, to a shop and a stately house in which one day I would live and from where I would cut loose.

Oma never went back to her roots – until one day, four decades later. And when she travels I will go with her. And *her Heimat* will leave its indelible mark on me.

Meanwhile the First World War breaks over the land and at its end the Treaty of Versailles (1919) begins to make a tear in the finely-woven fabric of Prussian Lithuania, renames it Memel Region, severs it from Germany, its major market, and decrees that the area be controlled by French soldiers.

Memelland. Who knows of it today: that land strip along the river Memel in the south and stretching further north east along the Baltic, bordering on Lithuania Major? From 1871 until 1919 it belonged to East Prussia. Today, called the Klaipėda Region, it is part of independent Lithuania. In the 20th century its national borders changed four times.

The region's documented history takes us back to Roman times when it served as trade route for amber; and on to the Middle Ages when the Teutonic Knights subdued the Baltic tribes (Old Prussians) and colonized the region, founded Königsberg and built castles and other architectural monuments. For a long time the land remained their playing field until modern Prussia got possession of the ball, brought the Reformation, a sound economy and a flourishing culture. Since then other nationalities came to play, some treating it roughly, others caring for the field: Swedes and Russians; Prussians, the Poles and the French; Jews and Lithuanians.

When the plague ravaged central Europe at the beginning of the eighteenth century it raced to East Prussia and the Memelland and halved their population. So devastated was the region that the King of Prussia, Friedrich Wilhelm I, appealed to Protestant German-speakers throughout Western Europe to come and rebuild the land where they could live free from religious persecution. They trekked to the impoverished land from Salzburg and the Netherlands, from Switzerland and several German regions. At that time Lithuanian culture also flourished. French influence was exerted under Napoleonic rule at the beginning of the nineteenth century. The Prussian royal family made their residence in Memel (today Klaipėda), a commercial town, where later also Englishmen, Scots, Lithuanians, Russians, Jews and Poles lived at ease alongside the German population; where at times a distinctive English style prevailed and English was spoken everywhere. At the end of the nineteenth century a narrow-gauge railway was built to link the villages and small towns with the cities of Tilsit and Königsberg.

The victors of World War I, assembled in Versailles, and not understanding the delicate balance, took the region from Germany and placed it under English, American and French administration and made it a kind of French mandate. In 1923 a Lithuanian uprising annexed the yet again impoverished land, a move later sanctioned by the League of Nations. In Memelland, still bilingual and largely autonomous, the German population still outnumbered Lithuanians. Jews and Germans had high financial stakes in the region. Lithuanian culture blossomed.

In March 1939, three days before I was born, Hitler, amidst great jubilation, re-annexed the Memel Region, bringing it "back into the Reich". Under the Nazi regime everything pertaining to Lithuanian culture was closed down and Lithuanians fled over the border to their own country. The Jewish population had already left in a panic seeking asylum beyond the frontier.

Stalin had his eye on the area and claimed it for the Soviet Union while Hitler was busy conquering Western Europe. But not for long. The German invasion of Russia was already being planned.

Is there another place on earth where four huge 'ism'-waves of ideology crashed into one another with such devastating effect? In less than a decade, they destroyed each other and ravaged the land. Like four flashing sabres clashing against each other, so Judaism, Nationalism, Communism and National Socialism splintered on the impact. They left the land exhausted, its people driven out, uprooted, utterly spent or dead. Its towns and villages lay eerily quiet. Even today river and lagoon remain empty. But the wind of freedom blows once more. People can breathe, think for themselves and order their own lives in a free-market society that brings its own hardships. Cultures take time to form. To irretrievably destroy them takes no time at all.

~

Duisburg and the Vosges Mountains, Germany. 1914–1918.
Else Anna is born to Wilhelm and Else Nehles in Duisburg-Meiderich. She will become Ello to her friends and Mami to me. In her first year of life World War I breaks out. My mother is taking her first unsteady steps when her father receives marching orders to fight in France. The tasks of running a dairy business and caring for their little daughter fall on my grandmother's shoulders. On receiving news that her husband is wounded in the Vosges Mountains she gives birth prematurely. The twin boys live less than a day and my mother remains an only child.

Windsor, England, and Etaples, France. 1914–1918.
Soon after declaration of war, my husband's paternal grandfather, cavalryman in the Life Guards and veteran of the Boer War, embarks for Le Havre days before his third son is born. In London a young mother has to fend alone for three young boys. The mud in Flanders deepens. Trench warfare is not fought with horses. The regiment is soon dismounted and, as war nears its end, is converted into a machine gun battalion. The competent horseman must instruct his comrades in the deadly art of machine gun operation. His last letters to his mother have been preserved. They bear shocking witness of a man having lost his soul long before German bombs kill his body whilst he is asleep in his camp dormitory. They bed him down in another dormitory which he shares with thousands. The sleepers lie beneath a sea of identical white crosses. And within days the war is over.

Wuppertal, Germany. 1938.
My mother is lumbering under my weight when German soldiers enter Prague through streets lined with stunned faces and raised fists. All around the pregnant woman the atmosphere bristles with fear and the air crackles with propaganda. Fuel is being collected for a great blaze;

pokers are forged and bellows crafted: armaments; conscriptions; drills; weapon training; indoctrination. Soon a mighty fire will be kindled that will spread across the globe and devour all in its path. When, after hours of labour and weeks of loneliness, she suckles me and I dribble her milk, Britain is signing a treaty with Poland. When I can sit up in my cot and it is my mother alone who enjoys my smile, German troops invade Poland: Britain is committed to war. The land into which I am born is plunging deeper and deeper into a darkness that for me only the stars will penetrate. From now on, my father and the father of the man who will one day be my husband are obliged to become deadly enemies. As our grandfathers had been a generation earlier.

Surrey, England. 1940s.

My husband's mother leaves her home and takes her three young sons into the Scottish mountains to be safe from German rockets. Her father's toy factory, *Triang*, once the market leader in the production of prams and dolls' houses, rocking horses and tin toys has long been converted to manufacture armaments: millions of machine guns and rounds of ammunition.

Ruhr cities, Germany. 1942–44.

My father is helping to occupy France when Cologne burns. Even from the Dutch coast the glow of the city's inferno is visible. A column of smoke rises five kilometres high into the sky. From her bedroom window in nearby Wuppertal my mother, cradling her baby son, watches with terror the billows of smoke and the crimson sky whilst in Duisburg, on the Rhine, my maternal grandparents are only too aware that mortal danger is not far away: a few kilometres south on the same river. And before all the clouds over the Ruhr look "like cotton wool soaked in blood" my grandmother and my mother take my brother and me to safety. We board a train bound for Memelland. My grandfather chooses to stay behind under the bombs in Duisburg in order to secure house and business as long as he can. When he joins us in the East he is obliged to work on the land. He is too old to be a soldier. My paternal grandmother and a young cousin are found mangled in an air raid shelter in Duisburg.

Berlin, Germany. 1989.

Martin, our eldest son, having watched the news on German television races to Berlin to witness the breaching of the Wall. The Iron Curtain rises and soon opens the way to the former East Prussia which in the Potsdam Agreement (1946) had been divided between Lithuania (Memelland), Russia (the Kaliningrad Oblast) and Poland.

ISandlhwana, South Africa. 2007.

Leather hat pulled deep into his face, a raconteur recounts – blow by blow – the massacre of British soldiers in 1879. Waves of Zulu *impi* had swept over the ridge, crushing an ill-led and ill-prepared regiment. Their tunics had been red as their blood that soaked into the African earth. White boulders, piled into cairns, litter the cone-shaped hillside. The bones of 1369 men lie beneath them. A chill wind pierces our clothing. Perched on camp chairs, we listen to Robert Gerrard and then move among the eerie memorials.

This close encounter with a battlefield proves to be the experience that pushes open a locked inner door. From now on I want to read about war. Beginning with the Zulu conflict, I progress to the Boer War and finally to the scholarly researched accounts of World War II. Unbiased historians, having access to archives that had not opened before, knit together for me the few fragments I had gleaned first during childhood in post-war Germany and later as a British citizen. My ignorance which my reading reveals appals me. Sixty million human lives lost in less than a decade to a war that affected every corner of the globe! And each one was someone's son or daughter, or father or mother. How can a human heart envisage death on such a scale? How can it dare contemplate the many cruel modes of destruction? How can it endure the shame?

As for me, I had always maintained that the war had not harmed me. My reading confirmed that I had been spared the worst traumas. I had not choked in air raid shelters. I had not run through flames on melting asphalt. I had not trudged through snow and battled against icy winds. I had not known starvation or watched my mother being raped. The tanks I encountered had not crushed refugees beneath their tracks. Our houses had withstood the bombs and my father had not been held as a prisoner of war for long.

England. Late 1980s.

And then I find myself confronted with my Inner Child's terror, rage, abandonment, uprootedness and lack of healthy attachment. The problems I had caused for myself, and the neglected Child within, demanded that I face the universal trauma and the effect on me personally. Patiently and safely the Child had held my memories and I had to admit that I, too, had been a victim of war. I had to learn to handle a volcano of emotions and was compelled to revisit in my mind and in reality the places where the Child had lived. She had been washed across war-torn Germany: from Rhine, Ruhr and Wupper to the Memel; from the Memel to the Elbe; from the Elbe back to Rhine and Ruhr and Wupper. In the rubble of national guilt and national trauma and the bomb craters of painful personal need and crippling shame I discover treasure.

It is not uncommon for us humans to forget one of our highest values, our roots. Yet, warns the Viennese architect Hundertwasser, "if we do not honour our past, we lose our future and if we destroy our roots, we cannot grow". Our past makes us who we are today. No events that we as children *had* to split from consciousness because of their enormity at the time, should remain cut off but be integrated into our present life to make us whole. Not only war but many human experiences are caged up, and in the dungeons of our innermost being take on a life of their own over which we, the rational adults, have little control. Today, Attachment Theory heads up the list of psychological issues under discussion. In this book I show how healthy attachment for me came about in *practice* – by several different routes.

Book I

When the dams break

1955 – 1994

Wiederaufbau*
1945 ~ 1955

Grey slag, charred debris.
Rats and ruins.
Cellars are home to disillusioned people.
Secretive, sly, scrounging coal and
queuing for bread and fish.

The war's burnt out.
Black-out blinds discarded.
Sunshine and moonlight
pour again through broken panes,
promising Wiederaufbau.

Rebuilding of the ruined streets
and lives betrayed
will take my childhood's
last remaining years:
The German Miracle.

Meanwhile my heart
cowers beneath a pall of grey.
Grime, dust, billows of black.
Even the trees choke,
fight for air.

How can I live in starless night?

*Reconstruction and restoration

1

The Springboard

My life has ended. Flat-faced houses block my view. So much part of my childhood had been the undulating sea of rubble and dust outside our window. A war plane had crashed and flattened the smart houses with their stucco frontages. My open vista and the few blackened hollow teeth, the charred house walls that had remained standing, have been replaced by brand-new dentures: flats with nicely rendered and painted façades. These modern dwellings across the street bear witness to the ever rising living standard in Germany; *Phoenix*, like the reconstructed and renamed steelworks, has risen from the ashes. But the high walls not only eclipse my view, they also permit only a chink of the dust-laden and smoke-filled sky to penetrate down into our street. Net curtains forbid prying into private lives, yet the smooth rendered walls barely muffle the baby's endless crying nor the high-pitched screams of exasperated women and angry bellows of men at the end of their tether. Lace also veils our kitchen window. My grief cannot be seen. In clenched fist a handkerchief is being kneaded into a small sodden ball. Tears veil my eyes; walls bar my future. Next week I am sixteen. My life has ended. I howl like a wounded animal.

Last week we had all been together for the last time. We had dangled our legs from the parapet of the old castle bridge, had reminisced and laughed about our school days. We had celebrated six years of carefree comradeship. Everyone had plans and looked forward with great expectations to entering the world of work. Imagine, earning your own money! My fellow pupils knew that I had a contract with the Chamber of Industry and Commerce and they envied me my career prospects in such a prestigious organisation. But I had not shared my real feelings. Perhaps nobody had. Perhaps we had all been pretending. That was last week. Now it is all over. We are all heading into our own future, each one on their own lone path. Next week I will be an office apprentice.

We are living in Oma's house. Before the war, my grandmother had employed maids, and this narrow room had been a tiny bed chamber. Now it is our kitchen, further narrowed by cooker and table, kitchen cabinet and a hefty low cupboard that had been a part of Opa's grand oak desk. Could my grandparents have ever foreseen this chronic overcrowding when they ran their dairy business? True, they had suffered setbacks during the hyperinflation following the First World War, that carnage which had also cost my grandfather's health and the loss of two children. But would they have dreamt that Oma would live in just *one* room in her own house and that their daughter's family would squeeze into a kitchen no bigger than a cupboard? Yet it is here that my young brother Gert-Dieter and I live with our parents, here we listen to the radio or to our Papi grumbling and complaining about the bosses in the steelyard, where he works shifts. The table where Mami ladles out her cooking on to four plates becomes the tensest place on earth. My father looks grey and haggard; my mother tries to reduce her weight. Not far away the furnaces glow. Soot and grime settle on our window sill and my brother and I swallow our meals in silence.

My wailing by the kitchen window has summoned my mother. She is now standing behind me (there is no room beside me). My back jerks, my shoulders twitch.

"What is the matter with you?" Mami does not know what to do with me.

"My life's over," I sob. "I didn't want to leave school. You know that."

"Nonsense," she says and does not touch me. "Life is just beginning. The Chamber is a wonderful springboard from which to start your career.

Be sensible, child. You are so fortunate that Papi knows Dr. Schmidt and got you the apprenticeship."

I do not turn to face her. "It's an office!" I wail. "I want to go to university!"

I know. I know. Daughters of steelworkers do not go to university. It is not for us to become doctors, lawyers, scientists. Even if my parents believed in my academic ability, they had neither the money for school fees, books and stationery nor the incentive to let me cram Latin and catch up at the *Lyzeum*, the High School for girls. In any case my primary school teacher had assessed me to be of "average intelligence". So there would be no point in wasting money on letting me sit the *Abitur* that would open the door to higher education. Alas, I must set my eyes on becoming a municipal clerk, commanding a modest salary but securing a pension. Or even better: serve a two-year apprenticeship at the Chamber of Industry and Commerce.

"…an excellent opportunity," I hear my mother say but I have already decided that she does not understand me. Or perhaps she does…

Her parents *had* been able to afford to send her to the *Lyzeum*. Within three years she had become proficient in French and her English was already passable. But her parents' growing business had needed her help. So she never had the chance to "make her *Abitur*". Had *she* cried when she had to leave school at fourteen? Actually I don't care about my mother right now. It is *I* who am drowning in despair.

Often in my imagination I sweep into the large red-brick building through the mock-classical portico. Above me, golden letters blaze *Niederrheinische Industry und Handelskammer*. The regional Chamber of Industry and Commerce serves businesses from Duisburg to the Dutch border. The concierge in his glass booth nods at me; and from a glassed foyer, bedecked with huge rubber trees and cheese plants, I ascend the marble stairs like a royal personage, my hand gliding along the golden rail. Then I sail behind one of the many milky-glass doors where a desk and an old typewriter are awaiting me. Flanked by two stuffy clerks who have served the Chamber for centuries, I take my seat on the worn revolving typist's chair. My fingers press down hard on the keys, and ever so often I raise my dulled eyes from the typewriter and stare into the car repair yard below…the day is looming…

In my lower abdomen I feel a stabbing pain. On the first of April, the day my contract begins, I am not in the office but on the operating table in the local hospital. My inflamed appendix will certainly not accompany me into the Chamber. While for two weeks I am fighting to suppress coughs and sneezes, my parents are locked in battle with Herr Esser, the Chamber's Personnel Manager, who insists that I have broken my contract. I had failed to start my apprenticeship as agreed on the first of April! My parents win. Therefore I must board the tram into the city a fortnight later, dressed in my black skirt and white blouse. Today and every day I stand hanging on to the leather strap; others have a right to my seat: the old woman with burn-scarred face; the old man with watery eyes; the man wearing an armband with five black dots, indicating total blindness, who can only find his way on to the tram by wiggling his white stick; the man on crutches who has stumps where his legs should be. War-victims all. The tram sways and jerks and whines to a halt in front of the dreaded tax office, the *House of a Thousand Windows*. We cross many repaired bridges. Down below in the harbour basins the barges are having their empty bellies filled with coal, scrap metal and steel products. We are gliding past the City Hall. The *Salvatorkirche*, the Church of the Saviour, still bears the marks of war. The black roofless stump of the church tower announces that I am nearing my destination. We slither along the *Königstrasse*, the main thoroughfare, lined with leafy trees that have survived the bombing. Its once elegant look is returning. The shops display new designs in china, silverware and floral art. A music shop carries a large stock of old and new records and the art dealer's gallery is already getting busy. An Italian ice cream parlour has opened under the delicious name of *Panciera*, where the boys hang out and we girls mince unsteadily on our first high heels, swinging our wide 'plate skirts': layer upon layer of starched petticoats, stiff as meringue.

Set back from the main shopping street rises the theatre, flaunting its restored neo-classical columns. It casts a spell on our culture-hungry post-war society. The magical world on the darkened stage: *The Troubadour, Madame Butterfly, La Bohème...* On one enchanting evening each month I slip into my long pale-blue taffeta dress and pull the navy suede gloves up to my elbows. At the end of the performance my gloves sometimes leave blue streaks on my cheeks! Tragedy on the stage never leaves me unmoved.

The Chamber houses lack-lustre clerks and lascivious managers who complicate my life. Be grateful, girl. Be sensible. Take evening classes in shorthand and typing. Enrol in the *Berlitz* to improve your English, though you will probably never need it. Take the lift. Never mind the regal stairs. They are for show. The golden banister is only brass.

After the apprenticeship (during which you hardly count as a person) I rise to the position of departmental secretary (apparently the youngest in the Chamber's history) and am assigned to Herr Dr. Altmann, expert in finance and tax. His secretary has left him at short notice. My new boss is my father's age, and like my father's, his once red hair is greying. Someone has told me that he holds a doctorate from the University of Königsberg, Emmanuel Kant's alma mater, which strikes an unaccustomed resonance in me. Dr. Altmann, they also informed me, is a slave driver who works his secretaries hard. I am determined that I will manage the paper piles he daily unloads on our desks. Ursula, my colleague, is in her first year of apprenticeship. We laugh a lot and work from eight in the morning until five at night. At one o'clock we stop for half an hour's lunch break which barely gives me time to race to the park and eat my sandwiches in the open air.

Dr. Altmann wears many hats in the world of commerce – and one of them is that of a lecher. I soon sense his infatuation with me. Often he stands behind my chair brushing his body against mine. One evening, when finally I have toiled my way through the stack of correspondence, an hour after everyone has gone home, he traps me by the washbasin and kisses me so hard that his protruding teeth dig into my lips. His breath reeks of cigarettes.

In the morning a big blue bruise! My lip is swollen. I tell my mother that I had tripped and fallen face down on to the hole-puncher! I make out that I am not feeling very well. For days I stay locked in my bedroom until the swelling subsides. Back in the office, when Dr. Altmann calls me and the door shuts behind us, he presses hard against me, while dictating at speed. My hand races across the shorthand pad while *his* hands find their way into my underwear. And when after hours of typing I present him with a folder of error-free letters and reports for his signature, I have difficulty escaping from his hungry embrace. I feel ashamed but tell no one. After all I am working for one of the most respected members of management. Who has ever heard of sexual harassment in the workplace? Who would provoke a scandal? I would never be believed. No one knows that he writes poetry for me: about gales and hurricanes, all those tempestuous feelings he has to endure and which he hopes will one day abate. As my boss he can touch me with impunity but he does not succeed in evoking my affection. I need to play for time; fake interest in order to preserve my job. Somehow, somehow – I have to get away.

In the war Dr. Altmann had been an officer in the *Wehrmacht*; now he loves playing soldiers in the new *Bundeswehr* and takes a long period out of the office. During those weeks I can breathe freely, even though he has left mountains of work for Ursula, my colleague, and me to do. I still find time to transform his inefficient filing system and on his return he believes that it is my love for him that has prompted me to do it. I am living a double life.

And so is Ursula. For several weeks she has been off sick. I worry about her. I am also exhausted because all her tasks land on my desk. Guilt, shame and anxiety rob me of sleep. I decide to visit her unannounced. She opens the door. I am shocked. Her head is swathed in bandages.

"What's happened to you?" I gasp. She ushers me inside the hall and in hushed tones tells me that her boyfriend, a butcher by trade, had assaulted her with a cleaver. I listen to her story and feel nothing. On the tram home I catch my reflection in the window. Strange: something cracking inside me. Ursula's horror has caught up with me.

Shock and exhaustion make me an easy prey for a heavy cold. Like a zombie I sit in the tram, jerking, swaying, screeching to the office. I cannot leave Hans in the lurch! Dr. Altmann and I are now on Christian name terms. I feel so tired. Every hour I brew strong coffee. I get through the morning; work during the lunch break, nibbling at my sandwich, gulping down a bottle of coke and for dessert I swallow a large dose of quinine. Buoyed up on this cocktail I type furiously and fill the folder: original letter – carbon copy – original letter – carbon copy... Keep going. Keep going... My fingers race across the keyboard. Go on.

Finished! The correspondence lies ready in the folder for Dr. Altmann to sign. I swivel off my chair and knock. "Come in..." and the office spins...the lights go out....

When I come back into consciousness, faces hang suspended above me. My fingers and toes are tingling. Where am I? Have I said something I should not have? I hope I have given nothing away! They send me home.

My mind lives in the office, while I lie on my bed all day. I am filing and typing and answering a myriad of imaginary phone calls. Is Hans coping without me? I try not to think of his kissing and fondling. It pains me to see the concerned faces of my parents. Outside my bedroom the days are lengthening again. My meagre salary has stopped. In two weeks' time my private insurance grant will also no longer be paid. What is going to happen to this wonderful springboard? The Chamber's medical officer administers calcium injections; they burn my throat and weaken me further.

My mother hands me the inevitable letter: I am to collect my last sick pay. After that I will be stranded in a cul-de-sac: entirely dependent on my parents. I had dreamt of revisiting England which I had fallen in love with during last year's holiday and have been saving a few Deutschmark each month. Well, that dream has to die.

At the counter of the *Barmer Ersatzkasse*, my private insurance company. I linger for a moment, clutching my final benefit money. So, that's it.

"Where do I go from here?" I turn to the clerk behind her window, not expecting her to reply.

"Are you a Protestant?" I nod. What a strange question. "Have you tried the Church?"

"The Church?"

"The Rhenish Church makes grants to young people who are in need of a respite holiday. They run a convalescent home not so far from here. In the Eifel."

I make enquiries and find that I am eligible! I can go away for three long weeks! All expenses paid except for the train fare. My savings will not take me across the Channel but they will take me to the Belgian border. Stepping out of the station in *Monschau*, a watery March sun warms my face. Crisp, quite sharp, is the air here. I shall get well! I look for the bus that will take me to *Schleiden*; and then I ride high. Behind tall hedges lie ploughed fields ready for sowing, though patches of snow still nestle in the furrows and along the edges of the dark coniferous forest.

The driver stops, points to a large house among the spruces and heaves my suitcase on to the road. Before I pick it up to lumber to my destination, I inhale the hard air and drink in the stark beauty of the high plateau. I shall get well.

PLEASE, REMOVE YOUR SHOES. Obediently I slip off my high heels and dangle them on two fingers, feeling rather awkward now, standing there in my fur coat and stocking-ed feet! A friendly house: from white walls hang wooden balconies, and from somewhere inside spills the laughter of young voices. I press the bell.

"Hello, welcome, Uta. You *are* a good girl," the blond woman laughs, pointing at my unshod feet. "Come in, come in. My name is Christa. We've been expecting you. Someone would have met you at the station but we did not know which train you were coming on. Anyway, you've got yourself up here. Well done." Do I detect a Hamburg accent? I already like her, her open face and warm eyes.

"You are sharing a room with a girl from Lübeck. You two are our seniors. Leave your case here. Someone will bring it up." She leads the way.

Everything is beautiful: a flight of shiny pine stairs; a white fresh-smelling corridor; golden pine doors. Christa opens one. Dark spruces are waving through a large window. Snowy duvets sit piled high on two beds on opposite walls. One of them is mine – for a whole three weeks. I follow Christa out on to a balcony. A strong scent rises from the woodland floor, and as if riding above it, the aroma of an awakening forest.

"Here you will take your afternoon rest." She points to the two deckchairs on which blankets lie neatly folded. "Part of the treatment." Her laughter tinkles. Two young girls – pale and thin and giggly – are lugging my case into the room.

"Did you bring an anvil with you?"

"Sorry it's so heavy. I brought some books to read." They titter, shake my hand and tell me their names.

"How many girls are there in the house?"

"You are a group of twenty," says Christa. "Just make yourself at home. Unpack. Relax. Supper is at six. I hope you can wait until then? Come down into the games room on the ground floor when you are ready. There you will meet us all. Just follow the noise. You can't miss us."

Left to myself now, I feel apprehensive. My roommate from Lübeck – what will she be like? I want to stand outside again in that good air that promises spring. The mighty spruces sway to the music of the Eifel wind. They feel like old friends whom I have not seen for a very long time. Tears of happiness are welling up. I am so grateful to be here.

"Welcome!" Another northern accent. And there stands the girl who is everything I want to be: slim, beautiful, and self-assured, even wearing the navy blue knee socks I had always coveted. Elke shakes my hand. At night, snug under our duvets, we will share much of our lives. But of our war experiences as children and the bombing of our cities we will never speak.

Spring's light and smells invigorate us. On Sunday morning our little group traipses down the hill to church, all engaged in animated chatter.

My brief connection with the Reformed Church had been abruptly severed when Rolf, our bronzed lodger diverted my attentions. I had been a pagan girl throughout my childhood but when I was old enough to decide for myself, I asked to be baptized and confirmed. Two years' preparation classes had involved learning by rote Bible verses, chunks from the Heidelberg Catechism and long hymns from Reformation times. They instilled in me a rudimentary knowledge of the Christian faith. All this learning had culminated in a public examination in the sombre church, when Presbyters and congregation listened eagerly for any slip or forgotten line. For the 'sacred day' a black taffeta skirt and velvet top were ready waiting in the wardrobe. I also paid my very first visit to a hairdresser: long plaits chopped off, the rest permed. I looked really grown-up. And with that I had committed a heinous sin, broken an unwritten law. Girls must not cut their hair before they are confirmed! Now even my baptism is in jeopardy. But finally the blue-eyed missionary, who will perform the rites, relents and does sprinkle water on my new frizz. As he does so, I look up at him. Rivulets of tears are trickling down the deep furrows of his kind old face. Each one of us receives a Bible. On the fly-leaf, handwritten, these words: *"Fürchte dich nicht...*Fear not for I have redeemed you, I have called you by name; you are mine."

I am a member of the Church now and as such permitted to partake of the Last Supper. It is celebrated once a year and, so I discovered, only 'hypocrites' stay on to receive the bread and wine. After the main service has finished, most of the congregation file out, glancing back over their shoulders, recording who is staying behind, committing it to long-term memory, tut-tutting as they leave. So I have become a baptized, confirmed hypocrite. For one year I endure the dry and colourless services and the primness of the youth group where all that is enjoyable is *verboten*. Rolf leads me into 'freedom' from it all.

This morning the church in Schleiden is filled with sunlight. We settle in the choir stalls. I feel proud to know the tunes and words of the hymns we sing. For the recital of the creed we stand. I know I should shut my eyes while mumbling the words. But I keep them open because the way the shafts of light penetrate the windows and illuminate the sombre interior is just so beautiful. I see Christa opposite me. Her face is aglow. Her blond hair surrounds it like a halo. She stands erect; her hands behind her back; her eyes also open. Her voice rings out clearly above our mutterings. It sounds like a proclamation. "I believe in God the Father…and in his Son Jesus Christ…" I am spellbound.

Later that afternoon the young girls shriek over Monopoly and Ludo while we 'seniors' are getting seriously addicted to Canasta and Rummy. Play is essential to our cure. Only no one talks about 'cure'. We walk in the forest; rest on our balconies; eat food we like; amble to the cinema under a starry sky – and play. Sometimes Christa reads to us or tells us about her own life. Tonight she mentions a 'Christian Community' in England where she had worked for two years. Right now she is only deputizing as leader of the house. In two months' time she returns to Hamburg. England! My heart misses a beat. Would she tell me more? I ask to see her and later I emerge from her room with an address: The Lady Warden, Lee Abbey, Lynton, Devon, Great Britain. As I hold the precious slip of paper I know deep inside that my life will take a sharp turn. I will go back to the Chamber of Industry and Commerce at the end of this time, but tonight, in my best school and Berlitz English, I will pen a letter – and post it to England.

England is not entirely new to me. In the 1950s the municipal authorities launched initiatives to forge new friendships between the young people of England and Germany. My home city Duisburg was twinned with Portsmouth because of their importance as ports, and I became a pen friend to Joan from Waterlooville. Her parents invited me to their home. We clambered all over HMS *Victory*. Open-mouthed I watched the choreography of a naval tattoo and as 'giants' we carefully stepped through the tiny streets of a Model Village. I overfed on black-and-white television, Tommy Steele and Perry Como, pies and chips and tinned peas, greener than anything I had ever seen in nature. On a day trip to London we inched our way in long queues towards Madame Tussauds' and the Tower of London. In the New Forest I watched wild ponies through rain-misted car windows, while crunching S*mith's* crisps. Under a shy sun, soft damp turf beneath our feet, we had strolled down to the old wharf at Buckler's Hard. And on a visit to the Isle of Wight, amongst blue hydrangeas lining the cliff path, I vowed I would come back to England and not even the *lukewarm* coke served in the little café overlooking the Solent could change my mind.

Hundreds of young Germans are crossing the Channel: students, au-pairs, pen pals and adventurers. Once the crammed train leaves Aachen, conversations stumble into English. Perhaps we are just showing off our linguistic ability. But perhaps not. On the ferry, clusters of Dutch teenagers chat in Dutch; the Flemish students in Flemish; the Walloons in French. But we Germans speak English. Are we, from Ruhr and Rhine, trying to disguise our country of origin? Are we hiding behind the language we all want to master? No, of course not! What a thought! No, we are *Europeans*. We war children are not even *aware* that we are dissociating from our roots. Stigma and catastrophe are not ours to carry. Instinctively we have drawn a veil over our country's past as both aggressor and victim. We have bowed to the unspoken taboo. Being left ignorant, we see no reason to ask questions. We are not children of the former regime; we are democrats. A curtain has muffled the old drama. *We* are acting in a new play. And though in England the *past* meets us around every corner, yet more importantly, its life-style and language aid our dissociation and offer us a new identity.

My carefree, activity-filled holiday in Hampshire had not prepared me for the clouds gathering on the home horizon. Looking out over the busy Solent I had no inkling of the impending nervous collapse I would suffer a year later and that there would be no one to help me. After all, who could be counsellor or therapist to German people, since *every* adult and *every* child had lived through trauma and probably dissociated from truth and self? We were a land filled with survivors and everyone sought to escape from shame and guilt; loss and disillusionment; terror and pain. We were not looking for healing.

The postage stamp bears the profile of the English Queen. I tear open the envelope. I am invited to join the Lee Abbey Community! The first of October will see me back in England! An open vista lies before me: I will escape from the flat-faced houses, the Chamber and, above all, from Dr. Altmann. Let him play soldiers all through this summer! I will not have to find ways of avoiding him all the time. And when he is back in the office, let him dictate as fast as he likes: my fingers will fly across shorthand pad and keyboard. Let him write his poetry; I will smile indulgently. The secret I hold will strengthen me to survive the next six months and then I shall dismantle my golden springboard.

Shock waves ripple through the offices when I hand in my notice. Herr Esser makes every effort to intimidate me. He refuses to give me permission to leave two days early and even threatens me with prosecution through the youth courts should I try to flout his orders.

2

Lee Abbey – a fresh chapter

It is still dark when my parents see me off at Düsseldorf Airport. By the time the Lufthansa plane leaves the continental coast, the sky is ablaze. Engulfed in the glory of orange, magenta, red, crossing the Channel, I make a conscious decision: to sever myself from my past and my German roots.

London welcomes me with its hoardings: *You and Heinz together make salads really something* and *Guinness is good for you*. At Waterloo I board the mid-morning train to the West Country. My excitement grows as we emerge from the suburbs of the metropolis into an autumnal countryside. Only the railway stations repel me with their dirt and ugliness. On the last lap of the journey my sole travel companion is my own reflection in the window of a bus which eventually sets me down at Lynton. It is past ten, but Val and Christine have been waiting for me and are now loading my case into their van and I realize that my journey is not over yet.

"This is the Valley of Rocks," Val shouts from the driver's seat. I press my tired face against the glass, staring into a velvety darkness. In the beam of the headlights I notice with alarm that we have entered a roundabout – the wrong way! Questions are fired at me in English, and in English I have to answer them. This is for real, girl!

"You'll be working with us in the kitchen. Val here is our boss, aren't you, Val?" Christine laughs as the van turns into an archway. From enormous Gothic windows streams warm welcoming light. Val slows, and through a second archway we roll into a courtyard. The women carry my luggage up to my room and I follow in a daze. My bed is covered with a grey *blanket*. Instead of a duvet a small paisley-patterned silky eiderdown is balancing on the top of the narrow bed and is sure to slide off and spend the night on the floor. The two pillows (only half the size of ours in Germany) feel as if stuffed with concrete. A few wire hangers behind a faded flimsy flowery curtain serve as my wardrobe; an orange box as my bedside table.

"We'll go down into the kitchen and you can see where you are going to work." Val speaks slowly and very loudly. Corridors. A small courtyard. A hubbub of voices and laughter sounding from somewhere. The kitchen is not large. I have never met an Aga before but learn that these monster cookers will provide the meals for one hundred and sixty people every day. A large wooden table, scrubbed white, with a shelf at eye level, fills the centre of the kitchen. A larder bulges with huge tins and sacks. The *Red Devil* is an electric potato peeler! Two huge vegetable steamers have Biblical names...what did they say they were?

"You – could – do – with – a – drink, couldn't you?" shouts Val, spelling out each word slowly and deliberately.

"I would like some coffee, please," I say and feel quite proud to have managed the sentence but watch with horror Val pouring *milk* into a saucepan and stirring some brown powder into it. I see it boiling and forming a skin. That's coffee? By fixing my eyes hard on Val and Christine I manage to swallow the sickening liquid without retching.

"Let's introduce you to a few people." In a large octagonal lounge I float on a sea of faces. Voices rise and fall like waves. I answer smiles, move as in a dream. This long day is spanning two different worlds. Düsseldorf, my parents, my old life – I left them all behind this morning and now, close to midnight, I am playing a walk-on part in this extraordinary English scene. But I am not aware that I have attracted someone's attention. He is watching me and only he knows.

Pam and Anne, my roommates, tuck my blankets firmly around me. A straightjacket cannot feel more restricting than this. With great effort I kick myself free when they are asleep. In the morning Anne introduces herself as a Social Worker and launches into a lecture on Britain's class system. Wait, Anne, wait. My language school didn't teach that kind of vocabulary! But she means to educate this German ignoramus.

"Soon you will be the only girl from the Continent." (What 'continent'? I have not come from Africa or Asia!) The others are all leaving after the Valedictory. (Is that Val's proper name?) "You are not allowed to speak German at all."

"That is alright. I want to learn English properly." I do not yet have the words to convey how much I want to immerse myself in the British way of life. My candle flickers on the orange box.

"Lighting candles is a pagan practice," says Anne.

"At home we light candles all the time." She gives me a look that says, 'I am not surprised'. If giving up candles is part of the English lifestyle, I am not so sure that I want to immerse myself entirely in it. I decide that I shall enjoy the gentle flame whenever I am alone in the room.

Val has given me the day off to explore the place. It is the second of October. I wander into the courtyard. It is buzzing like a beehive. Young men in oily overalls, in shorts, ragged jumpers, flat caps, woollen hats and colourful neckerchiefs have congregated around a large teapot and trays of cold toast. Their laughter and banter becomes even louder when girls, in apron or overall, cross from one building to the other. To me they shout "hello" and "welcome".

"Good morning", I say shyly and walk briskly by, heading towards the stone archway. Hydrangeas call from the other side. In front of a high stone wall massive blue and pink lace balls bask in the sun. I smile at them, "I promised you that I would be back when I was on the Isle of Wight."

I have burnt my boats. My life is starting afresh. I breathe deeply, once, twice – the air smells so clean and good. Here it is not laden with coal dust and chemicals. My eyes glide across green cow-dotted fields... I gasp. Clasped in the green pasture land, framed by wind-slanted trees, lies a glistening jewel: the rippling waters of Lee Bay. Is such splendour really for me?

Lunch time. The large dining room is crowded and seems to be bursting with voices and laughter. At long tables, members of the Community ladle out stews and semolina puddings for the many guests who have come to Lee Abbey for rest and refreshment. Everyone talks; talks too fast; has a different accent. How little I understand! These mealtimes are fine for extroverts, but for shy German girls with only school English and *Berlitz* commercial English, listening is the easier option.

"How long have you been here?" and "Where are you from?" are questions I can now answer with some confidence. At this point the conversation usually ends, as nobody seems to know where Duisburg is. The questioner has already turned to someone else.

The lady next to me has read my name on my green label. "That's a German name, isn't it? *Bist Du deutsch?*" she asks in my forbidden language!

"It's good to meet you, Uta," she says and introduces herself. "My name is Vera. Where I work I meet many young people from Germany. I don't suppose you have heard of Capernwray yet? It's in Lancashire. In the north of England. I am Major Thomas' secretary. Since the war ended he had a vision to buy a large house and to bring together young people from all over Europe. To encourage friendships and reconciliation. Particularly between England and Germany. The war has caused so much damage, hasn't it?"

I start telling Vera of the twinning of my Ruhr city with Portsmouth and my visit to Joan. She wants to know what has brought me to Lee Abbey and asks me a strange and rather embarrassing question.

"Are you a Christian?" I blush. You don't talk about things like that.

"No, I don't think so," I mumble. Then I explain that in our Reformed Church Christian women wear dark clothes and buns". You see, here they dress colourfully. They wear their hair loose or short or permed, just as they like. Some put on lipstick and eye shadow. And they all laugh a lot. Here they are Christians as well. I don't feel I belong to either of them. Also: I burn candles."

She laughs, looking at me with warm eyes. As we rise from the table she says, "I shall pray for you."

Well, what do you make of that?

What is a *valedictory*?

"Oh, it happens every year. On the fourteenth of October you'll see for yourself."

That date is indelibly engrained in me. On that October day, in 1944, my paternal grandmother and my cousin Kriemhild (whom I had never met) were blown to pieces in an air raid shelter. The story of how they had been identified was always told in whispers, with certain pathos. Each Remembrance Day we used to assemble outside the sealed-up shelter: a sea of black coats and hats and sombre faces. The brass band, trombones muted, played in minor keys and the pastor's voice droned. Handkerchiefs. Nose blowing. Red eyes. A bitter wind sent the men into the pub after the ceremony, my father among them. We always ate our lunch without him.

And *this* fourteenth of October? Outside every bathroom a queue forms. The octagonal lounge is filling up with guests and Community members in their best clothes. An air of expectancy is palpable. Beyond the Gothic windows darkness hides fields and woodland; inside all lights are blazing. In the very centre of a row of chairs I feel safe, as if held by these kindly people. Tonight we will be bidding farewell to the last guests of 'the Season' and those temporary Community members who in the spring, had come from Holland and Switzerland. This much I have been told. As the meeting progresses individual people stand up and make little speeches. Sometimes they choke with tears; often their faces are aglow. Valedictory: it means goodbye and thankfulness.

A silver-haired old man finds it awkward to stand: Pop, the oldest member of the Community who had once been a farmer. Though his back is bent, he is still tall, and though his voice trembles with emotion, it sounds strong. A hush has fallen on the room. If only I could understand all that he is saying! I glean just enough: he had been "a very stubborn man" who only in his sixties had "finally surrendered to Jesus" who had changed his life. Pop totters back on to his chair. In the silence I sense a fierce burning behind my eyes. Don't cry! Not here! Not now! But my tears do not obey orders; they fall into my lap. I need to leave! How do I get out of this row? Squeeze by all these knees? I long for the final hymn. The Warden gives the blessing. I pass by a young man in my row. I am not aware that he had been watching me. Where do I go? I race up the wide staircase to the chapel where it is quiet and safe in its muted light. Sobs. They are mine.

Voices. Footsteps. The entire leadership team is filing into the chapel but before I can escape sliding by them all, the Lady Warden touches my arm and whispers,

"Go to my room and wait for me there. I'll not be long."

A fire leaps behind the guard. Flames are licking at logs. Outside a gale howls up from the bay, whistles around the house, rattles at the windows. Uneasily I perch on the edge of an armchair and wait. She is not coming. Oh good, then I can leave. In my own room I crouch on the bed, trying to make sense of my restlessness, these unaccustomed feelings. There is a gentle knock on the door.

"Oh, there you are." It is Madeleine, the Lady Warden. "I am sorry to have kept you waiting. Shall we go back to my room now?" I follow her. I feel so strange. A few minutes later I will have made the most important decision of my life. Madeleine asks me a few questions, and out spills the whole business with Dr. Altmann.

"You need to confess your sins. Kneel down, dear, and say after me…" I confess my feelings of guilt when I think about Dr. Altmann cheating his beautiful wife and children – with me. I echo her words in English, conscious of the crackling in the hearth.

"Do you want to give your life to Jesus?" I hear Madeleine ask. "You can do it in your own language." What was that German sentence I uttered, kneeling there by the armchair at an English fireside? All I know is that I feel calmer. I dimly understand that I have decided to commit my life to Jesus, Someone I do not yet know. Outside her door now, I feel light in my heart, but can't shake off the sense that 'they've got me.'

"You've changed!" says Anne in surprise. My new friends in the kitchen also notice it. Do I feel different? I am not sure. In my letters to my parents I am careful not to mention the event.

In November, at a special service in the chapel, my name tag, my green label is exchanged for a red one: I am now a fully-fledged member of the Community. I belong.

My first English Christmas is so unlike our German *Weihnachten*; not solemn and emotional, but creative, fun and very hard work in the kitchen. I have an audition and am allowed to sing the alto part of Christmas carols I had never heard before. On Christmas Eve I watch a beautiful Tableau: a handsome Joseph is bending over the crib. I have never spoken to him but I think his name is Peter.

Roast turkey, a dark heavy pudding, rapt attention to the English Queen's speech on the radio, and shiny paper rolls that look like giant marzipan fingers, beside each plate. They turn out to be Christmas crackers that are pulled apart and cause a small explosion, reveal silly party hats and everyone reads out a joke. There is so much laughter. And look! The festive tables are bathed in candle light! How pagan can it get? And the party that follows the meal is hilarious. On a long rope forty hot water bottles snake into the lounge: 'Joseph's' father, a guest, knowing how cold the bedrooms are, has cleared out the shops in Lynton and bought a comforting bottle for each girl on the Community. I shall meet this man again. Right now I am so excited to be part of all this English fun.

January brings a sprinkling of snow. I have found a friend in Megan from South Africa. For her this is a brand-new experience. Her red boots are jumping up and down in the soft white powder. What delight.

Pop is dying. I need to tell him about the effects his words have had on me. That he had sowed and reaped on the same night. He looks weak as I sit by his bed and I cannot be sure that he can take in my fumbling testimony. It is not long after that he leaves us for good. His triumphant funeral makes a deep impression on me. So this is how Christians die? How joy and sorrow mingle! Pop's trembling words have not only changed the significance of the fourteenth of October, they have changed the direction of my life.

Germany is far, far away. I think and dream and pray in English. I write long letters home and request my mother to keep them. When I read them years later I feel nauseated by the sugar-coated affection and the unfamiliar use of diminutives with which I address my parents. I also notice a *child's* handwriting, long after I had developed a more mature script.

Even community life does not alleviate a deep inner loneliness. Maybe it accentuates it. In my free time I roam the Estate, wailing for "Mami – Mummy". Why am I doing this? Madeleine had been the 'midwife' and Pop is dead. Who will nurture me? Despite the joy and warmth in my new world I feel strangely disconnected from it and myself. I decide to invite my parents to the International House Party. A flurry of cleaning begins: every item of clothing I possess is washed and meticulously ironed; all that can be wiped, swept, dusted, polished is wiped, swept, dusted and polished. Over and over again. Though I do not have a name for my obsessive-compulsive behaviour I am aware that it is crazy. I check timetables and in minutest detail I instruct my parents about their planned journey. By the time they arrive I am totally exhausted. Am I heading for another breakdown?

The Warden and his wife, Geoffrey and Dora, honour them by welcoming them to stay in their own house. When they have settled in, I introduce them to all that is precious to me and from an emotional distance I watch my parents respond to the Community's fun and affection. I so want to love them, too, but I cannot. I want to feel free and easy in their presence, but instead feel unwell inside. However hard I try to be warm and open, I find myself closing my heart towards them, finding no inner wellspring from which love flows naturally. It takes all my energy to make sure that I do not break down. I must not break down! I have to be a good witness to my new-found faith. But nothing seems to connect me with these two strangers I know so well. We have little to say to each other. I can read my parents' disappointment with me. I am responsible for causing them pain. Like a heavy weight this knowledge bears down on me, leaves me reeling with helplessness. I cannot prime the spring. I am counting the days and hours to their departure.

Today we are walking along the cliff path. Gulls are screeching and diving into the Bristol Channel. From the wind-stroked rocks peep fine grasses and tiny pink flowers nod in the breeze. My heart is hurting. Now we turn away from the sea and tramp through bracken into the Valley of Rocks where wild goats are eyeing us from the high crags. Insects hum in the heat. When we reach the road we meet *him*.

He is beautiful. His face is suntanned and alight. From his faded green jumper pokes an elbow. Wonderful hands rest on the wheel of the tractor he has driven up to the fence. He seems to have been waiting for us. Casually he asks whether my parents would like a trip on to Exmoor. Oh yes, they would love that! Good, he'll fix it. A warm smile for my parents and the tractor wheels round and rumbles away across the field.

"*Er heisst Peter.*"

Sun-kissed Exmoor. Peter has collected a small party for this trip in a minibus: a tiny Austrian 'herb woman', my pen friend Joan (whom I had also invited to Lee Abbey), a man from the Caribbean, my parents and me. He parks the vehicle and we start walking to the farm where a Devonshire cream tea awaits us. My skirt, in the colours of the Union

Jack, swings around my bare legs. At some point Peter comes alongside me and we talk. By the white farm gate, constructed from cart wheels, a group photo is taken. Can the fresh scones, filled with jam and clotted cream compete with German *Sahnekuchen*? It is still warm as we make our way back. Moor birds call; the Austrian lady discovers unusual plants; Peter is ambling by my side; and my mother senses something...

Why do I use the small photo taken by the farm gate as a book mark? Why do I keep losing the thread of what I am reading?

Back in Germany, my parents' lives change. Their marriage becomes warm, marking the beginning of many golden years. In England, a boat takes a small group of Lee Abbey Community members across the Bristol Channel to Tenby. On the bus returning us to Lynton I furtively glance at Peter's reflection in the window. Is he really asleep? We decline a lift and choose to walk together through the Valley of Rocks. Under the stars we draw closer. It is the beginning of a shared life. From that night on, long after everybody has gone to bed, two shadows entrust themselves to dark country lanes. Following Community Rules, they do not hold hands!

"I have a form to fill in. They want to know whether I am single, engaged or married?" Peter and I are leaning over a farm gate beneath untamed rhododendron bushes.

"Who wants to know?" I ask.

"The selection board of the Anglican Church. You see, I think I should be training for ordination. Would you rather marry a farmer or a clergyman?"

"I want to marry you," I hear myself say it without hesitation.

An English letter, accompanied by my translation, arrives in Duisburg. My mother already knows its content before she opens the envelope. Whether it was difficult for my parents to give their agreement to our marriage, I shall never know but they had shown that they liked Peter. And his parents? His father was the hot water bottle provider at the Christmas Party, but I had not spoken to him or his wife. Now I am to meet them at the Woody Bay Hotel on a night when Devon's lanes turn into raging rivers. How do they feel about their son wanting to marry me, a German girl? They give no indication. The Community is delighted when we announce our engagement. No longer do our walks have to be clandestine. We can spend our days off together. At Watersmeet we cross the footbridge where East and West Lyn converge: we, too, are building our own bridges of trust. Our shyness is waning.

Summer has given way to autumn. At the end of October it will be my turn to speak at the Valedictory before returning to Germany. Who would have thought it a year ago? One verse from Psalm 65 captures all I want to say. *"You have crowned the year with your goodness"*.

For our last outing Peter borrows a small car. Melancholy broods over Exmoor. In its very centre, at Pinkery Pond, where sedges are waving and dark waters ripple, in this sad and peaceful solitude, dusk is falling and we linger too long. Gently sways the ground, a deep-pile carpet under our boots. Hand in hand we pick our way across the heather, stepping from tuft to tuft, but when it gets too wet and muddy my chivalrous man lifts me off the bog. Two more steps and our combined weight breaks the surface and we drop a straight metre and stop suddenly. Peter's feet hit bottom, my back rests at ground level. I am still in his arms. He swings me sideways and somehow with my help he gets out but his boots stay buried in the bog. In a thousand years someone may find them preserved in dry peat. Covered from waist to feet in black smelly mud, Peter finds a stream, strips off his trousers and dips them into the ice cold water. We walk on across the moor to the car, his trousers drying draped over his shoulder. Clipped in the back window of the car, they flutter in the wind as we drive back to Lee Abbey. It would not look too good to be seen arriving in underpants with a girl in one hand and trousers in the other. Giggling we sneak – unnoticed – into the warmth and safety of his room. It is only then that the horror hits me. We could still be out there on the moor.

Peter is going forward to ordination. Next summer his three-year training course will begin at the London College of Divinity and our wedding will have to wait for several years as ordinands in the Church of England are not allowed to marry while studying. So I return to Germany, not knowing what I shall be doing there or when we shall see each other again. A long, long engagement is stretching out before us.

3

Waiting time

The very last passenger to jump on to the ferry is me. I wave to Peter. On the other side of the Channel, back in my Ruhr city, I am cast adrift. My love is in England. My life is in England. Only the love letters that cross the watery divide twice a week connect me with the self I have left behind.

On her small round rattan table Oma's black-leather-bound Luther Bible lies open. On Sundays she walks alone to church, which takes her thirty minutes. She has just learnt that the pastor's wife is suffering a breakdown.

"Couldn't you help out in the parsonage?"

Why would I want to do that? I remember the pastor as cold and aloof, with a voice that sounds like the grating of dry bread. I suppose it wouldn't hurt to visit her. At Frau Mull's bedside I tell her my story. She listens intently. 'Come and help us,' plead her troubled eyes. For several months I take over the family chores. The best time is sitting with her. Her husband and three teenage sons were evidently born without any sense of humour, so I love it when she laughs and her brown eyes shine with life. Do I want to become a pastor's wife?

Christmas is spent without Peter, but Megan comes to stay. She connects me with Lee Abbey, with England and also her own world in South Africa. When she leaves for her homeland and Frau Mull is able to lead the parsonage household again, I feel bereft. I long for Peter; yearn for England

My mother is watching my unhappiness with growing concern. "Why don't you go to the Harz Mountains and live with Tante Else? She is a good seamstress and will teach you to sew. Always a good skill to have. She never starved after the war."

I dislike sewing but the thought of living again in the countryside, among mountains and forests, appeals. And there my spirits revive. Never before has the village postman been so busy. The flow of letters into the seamstress' house! Correspondence with England and other parts of the world – they are my lifeline. This morning another bundle of letters. One carries an English stamp but I do not recognize the handwriting. I tear it open.

Dear Uta,

…Would you consider coming to au-pair for us during the summer?

We have two little girls and our third child is due in August. You would be closer to Peter – just across London – and learn the ropes of Anglican parish life.

I had met Ken and Margaret briefly at Lee Abbey. What is there to *consider*? Surely this is a gift.

All England is watching Wimbledon when Peter's father meets me off the ferry. In his lovely Somerset home my fiancé is waiting for me. The days we spend together fly like dreams. At bedtime he reads me stories he liked as a boy. Sometime these make me cry. But how to find a way into his parents' hearts?

I move into a modern brick Vicarage in a leafy sleepy London suburb where live two little girls with fine-spun golden hair. We 'sit comfortably' to *Listen With Mother,* create puppet shows, play games and I learn about three little pigs and a red hen and soon know many English nursery rhymes by heart. Evening classes prepare me for the Cambridge Certificate of Proficiency in English and I also join the parish youth club. Church is not as it was at Lee Abbey. The lustre of the Prayer Book services is dulling. In any case, I am not permitted to take Communion like everyone else.

"You need to be confirmed," says Ken.

"But I *have* been confirmed!" I remonstrate.

"Your confirmation is not valid in the Church of England. You need a bishop to lay hands on you. I think it would be wise for you to be prepared for confirmation now that you are going to be married to an Anglican clergyman." Well, at least my baptism is valid. Ken tutors me in church history, the sacraments and the Prayer Book and presents me for confirmation. I am reluctant though ready to 'wear the veil'. That silly white headdress keeps slipping from my head when I lean back in the pew. Sitting stiff and upright, it is difficult to concentrate on the procedures. Anyway, what is their significance for me? At the end of the ceremony we file towards the door where the Bishop stands, extending his ringed hand.

"Where are you from?" His eyes wander to the person behind me.

"From Germany."

"No, no, no. I mean which *parish* are you from?"

Is that important?

August is hot. Margaret, the children and I, scratched and purple, come back to the Vicarage laden with blackberries and Margaret announces that she is in labour. Will my first home-made jam set? The casserole dish should have gone into the oven, rather than on the hob. I clear the shards and beef stew from cooker and floor. How can I concentrate? I don a white apron and wait in my room until I am called and watch the downy head of a little boy pushing into life. My elation knows no bounds.

A few days later the news on the radio stuns us all: in Berlin they are building a concrete wall that will slice through the heart of the city. It turns East Berliners into prisoners, separates families and in a London suburb a mother's milk dries up.

The church youth club has congregated in a large Victorian house in Bromley where there are walls to paint and shabby old furniture to be sanded down. We meet Elly Jansen, an energetic young Dutch woman, who is creating here a safe half-way house for young people with mental health problems. These are the early days of the Richmond Fellowship. "As long as I have breath…," she later wrote, promoting her vision. I am inspired and, combined with my experience in the Eifel, a dream is born in me for a Christian therapeutic community. Best of all within the church. In Ken's church I find little interest in such a vision. But when Peter has his own church one day…

Meanwhile I follow someone else's vision for me. "Have you ever considered full-time Christian training?" asks P.D., Ken's Church Warden. He has in mind, of course, a certain Bible College on whose Board he serves. I had visited the establishment: two Victorian villas oozing old-fashioned English austerity. Not like Lee Abbey! I had met some of the young women who were preparing for the mission field. Am I going to be a missionary? I think not, but certainly the course would improve my English and give me a diploma and a University of London certificate. Best of all, Peter and I would not be separated by the Channel.

Eighteen dull months are eaten out of my young life. Indoctrination kills creative thinking and when I leave, I feel brainwashed and soul-dead. Our morality fixates on externals: forbidden is the wearing of trousers, make-up, sleeveless dresses, short skirts and even sandals. Dancing, the cinema, theatre, art gallery and novel are also *verboten*, and with a sweep of her hand my roommate clears the mantelpiece in our shared room of all objects that connect me with my culture. During my vacations in Germany, my parents are unhappy with my religious intensity, watching me add sleeves to dresses and inches to hemlines. They feel the pressure exerted on me to 'convert' them. In my own home I become an alien; I am in danger of losing myself. I see my mother cry for me. I notice something else, as I cross the channel back and forth during the vacations: on the way to Germany I feel anxiety, and on my return to England a strong sense of guilt.

The hardest winter since the end of the war grips the British Isles. Snow silences all traffic by land, air and sea. It extends our Christmas stay in the Channel Islands and further strands us in the Somerset countryside with Peter's parents. When I finally make it back to Bible College I discover that I have been chosen to address a large assembly of young people on the subject, '*Why I love the Bible*'. In vain I try to make Mrs. Lauderdale understand that I do not yet 'love the Bible', that my testimony would not be authentic. But instead of releasing me from the assignment, she cages me in a tiny room where I am to prepare my talk – prayerfully. Crouching by an ancient gas fire I pray, yes, I pray – that the snow may fall and fall and block the road to the venue. Hours go by and still I know that I have nothing inspiring or even truthful to say. My prayers go unanswered, it appears, and we make it to the large hall. It is already crowded. Here comes my turn to speak. Like in a dream I step to the edge of the stage. Eyes are riveted on me. What am I saying? I hear laughter. Have I perjured myself? Whatever I said must have touched the young people.

The highlight of the summer term is the Garden Party. In the weeks leading up to the event, we students are taught and practice how to sit, how we are to stand, what to say, how to sing. And most importantly: we are to wear *hats*. I do not possess one, but wear a headscarf when we file to the parish church while around me bob pillboxes, flowerpots and tea-cosies. They are called hats? No, girls, hats are those magnificent creations English ladies wear at the Queen's Garden Party at Buckingham Palace.

In the Easter holidays I tell Mami that I need a hat like the Queen's guests wear. My mother makes any milliner happy. From her favourite shop I emerge with a large box in which, wrapped in tissue paper, lies a wide-brimmed pink beauty decorated with a single rose delicately nestling in its brim. It is beautiful. And when I parade in front of my grandmother's tall mirror, I feel beautiful. Before I leave for England, Mami helps to lovingly pack the creation. At college I keep it wrapped in its tissue paper in a bottom drawer. I am not showing it to anybody, but imagine the "oohs" and "aahs" when I shall appear in it on the great day! Yet, as term progresses, I feel less and less comfortable. My hat is not holy. I have fancied myself in it. It's of the flesh. Or – more likely – of the devil.

I shall have to do it! No one is watching me stroke away the wrapping for the last time. My hat – it is so lovely. But it has to go. The pain of it! My foot kicks the drawer shut. Don't think. Just go! Outside the Principal's office I feel my heart thumping. You don't have to go through with it. Yes, I do.

I knock. Mrs. Lauderdale, upright at her desk, slowly turns her head. Her eyes meet mine.

"Yes?"

"I...I... mustn't wear this for the Garden Party. I want to give it to you." I hand over my mother's loving gift, still in its tissue paper. Mrs. Lauderdale inspects it.

"Are you sure, the Lord wants you to dispose of this hat?"

"Yes," I say as firmly as I dare.

"Sometimes the devil makes us sacrifice precious things."

"I am sure it's the *Lord* telling me to give it to you." I hope she will question my ability to hear God. I hope she will say that I am allowed to keep it. But then her voice slices through me:

"In that case I will put it into a jumble sale."

Following this heroic sacrifice I expect to be transported into heaven itself. Have I not demonstrated that I am a mature Christian? But nothing spectacular happens; no quantum leap into sainthood. Instead pain and sorrow burn and mingle with fear. I have betrayed my mother!

The rest of term I spend miserable and overloaded. A diver's helmet encases my head. Its name is Sound Doctrine. Peter and my friends are perturbed by the change they perceive in me. On top of the stress of these last remaining weeks at Bible College I am also preparing our wedding across the Channel.

Now it is here, that day for which I have waited so long. The open-top sky-blue Triumph Vitesse crunches to a halt on the gravel outside the college: our wedding present from Peter's parents. Laughing, Peter stows my luggage on the back seat. At last, at last, I can wave farewell. Several of my fellow students seeing me off will be embarking for the mission field on all the continents, while I am heading into a romantic sunset.

We plunge into the London traffic. Peter keeps his eyes on the congested road but ever so often turns to me with that warm wonderful smile that now threatens to make me cry out in agony. I am riding in this new beautiful car, close to the man I love. But my romantic sunset will not materialize. I half-listen to his reports: of the preparations he has been able to make for our honeymoon; of camping gear he has bought;

of wedding presents that have already arrived; of his parents' travel plans. He is not aware of my pain, knows nothing of the battle raging within me. All these preparations, all our waiting, three long years of waiting – it is all in vain. When is the right moment to tell him?

We reach the airport in good time. Peter is leaning back, folds his hands behind his head, letting the midday sun warm his face, his handsome face. He is aglow with happiness. I love you. I love you. And now, right here, it will all come to an end.

"Peter… I have something important to…"

"You love me?" he interrupts.

I nod. (How it hurts!) "Yes I do…very much… but you see…we…we… cannot get married." He laughs at the joke.

"I am serious."

He lets his arms sink, turns to me, scrutinizing my face.

"Why ever not?"

"Mrs. Lauderdale called me into her office the other day. 'Sit down, dear', she said. 'Tell me, does Peter believe in the inspiration of the Bible?'- 'I…I…don't know,' I said, 'we've never talked about it.' And then she warned me, 'If he does not believe in the inspiration of the Bible, you, my dear, are going to suffer a life-long heartache. You need to consider whether it is right for you to marry him.' She looked at me really hard…"

I dare not meet Peter's eyes. Everything feels unreal. Bizarre. "Perhaps God *is* warning us," I whisper, close to tears. Must I pay the ultimate sacrifice?

"Look at me!" Peter's face – his darling face – is close to mine and his voice is firm. "Listen to me. I am putting you on this plane right now and on Monday I shall drive to Germany and on Wednesday I shall marry you." And with that he twists himself out of the car, lifts my luggage on to the tarmac and starts off towards Departures. The sun dazzles me as my tears are falling. Like an automaton I hand over passport and ticket. My suitcases glide out of sight. Which gate?

Peter grabs my shoulders and his warm brown eyes search mine. "Will you marry me?"

"Yes, I will."

"That settles it then."

"Yes, that settles it." We laugh and kiss. It is not the end!

Two days later: our convertible draws up next to our house – here in Duisburg! It's for real! And just to make sure, we marry *twice* that Wednesday morning: first in the registry office and afterwards in the squat sombre church. The taxi delivers my parents-in-law to the central police station instead of the registry office. The hired interpreter decides after the church service that he cannot, after all, translate for us at the reception, so the bride will have to do it. My brother, one of the marriage witnesses, arrives at the church having forgotten to bring the vital papers. All that, but at last we are a married couple. From the reception hall we look out on the Rhine where the Ruhr joins it, and the new elegant bridge spans the busy river. At German weddings any guest may get up to make a speech. Herr and Frau Soyka, long-standing friends of my parents, are here too: erstwhile citizens of Königsberg and survivors of the flight from the Red Army. Herr Soyka likens us to a "double-span bridge between East and West", who will connect peoples and nations. On the barges below several national flags flutter in the breeze.

The cobbles relieve our car of the tin cans! Uncluttered we cross the Rhine and are on our way to *Nordcap* and a shared life. In Scandinavian forests, by lakes and rivers we camp and pick bilberries, wild raspberries and boletus. No romantic *sunset* for us, but in Finland days and nights are stitched together into seamless light.

"But, please, do not drive too close to the Russian border," I beg.

4

Flatlands: the Curate and I

A four-bedroom house at the northern edge of London, set in a spacious garden filled with rose bushes, crab-apple trees and nasturtiums, is our first home. The four bedrooms, however, are occupied by fellow students and we, their 'house-parents' live on the ground floor. The owners, medical missionaries in North Africa, have made The London College of Divinity the custodians, leaving all its contents for students' use. The chest of drawers on the landing is bulging with eiderdowns and blankets and the larder houses jars with flour, rice and sugar, and since previous house-parents have left these provisions undisturbed, moth, maggot and mealy bug are having the time of their lives.

From our own bedroom, through the hatch, we have a view of the kitchen. The kettle is in easy reach. That's handy. Now Peter can introduce that most excellent of English traditions into our home: the early-morning cuppa tea. Through the leaded window moonlight and thunderstorms light our marriage bed, actually two single 'boats' pushed together, creating a hard ridge up the middle. This house is a lovely place from which to launch our married life and romance is not seriously marred by a plague of flying ants, a flooded living room or the burglar who relieves us of our jewellery.

Peter's college is wonderfully free, so different to mine. Life's colours are returning. That 'diver's helmet' that had so tightly encased my head, has loosened and I can think freely again. I revel in the fun and banter between students and staff. College tutor Owen Brandon and his wife invite me for dinner every Thursday, and the College Registrar Michael Green allows me, a woman (probably the first in the history of the College) to sit in his New Testament lectures because I am still studying extramurally at London University. I type the manuscript of his first book *Called to Serve* (he gives me 10% of his £50 remuneration) and once a week I clean a neighbour's house. Fellow students join us for supper or breakfast and enrich our lives. Among them Amos Betunguru who later becomes a bishop in Kenya, and Janani Luwum, later Archbishop of Uganda, who was murdered by Idi Amin.

I have no interest in connecting with my language but almost on arrival I am asked to support the visiting Lutheran Bishop of Pomerania in translation should it prove necessary. A rumour circulates amongst the students who do not yet know me that the young blond woman in the front row is a member of the *Stazi*, the Secret Police, sent to accompany the Bishop, to vet his messages and inform on him to the authorities in East Germany!

Robert is a fellow student and married to Barbara. I am to meet her. Do I *have* to? She is *German*. (After many years of a solid fruitful friendship I am grateful that on meeting her, I had immediately overcome my initial reluctance.)

The Rector of a dormitory town parish has come to the College to look for a curate. Peter is the man. Should he follow the invitation? We shrug our shoulders. Why not? So much for prayerful consideration! This spells the end of our carefree living. Just one last fling before we move into the serious business of parish life: let's go camping. We borrow a tent and pitch it on the beach on the Gower Peninsula. All day the hills are clothed in autumn gold and by moonlight we walk the long beach hand in hand (while a roaming cow consumes our prepared supper.)

Before the removal lorry takes our few possessions there is one final task. The crab-apple trees groan under the weight of their shiny pink fruit pleading for us to pick as much as we can. On the final day in the student house juice drips through a muslin cloth suspended from an upturned chair and the first job of the *curate's wife* is making crab-apple jelly in a tiny empty kitchen!

What are we to do with these rough floor boards in the living room? Just look at those wide cracks. And that hideous fireplace. Which of these small rooms is to house Peter's many books? The master bedroom overlooks a pub. At the front of the house high grass and weeds threaten to strangle the solitary standard rose that is clearly quite unused to pruning. At the rear an outside toilet and a ramshackle shed have survived a century, during which nothing seems to have been planted in the clay soil of the narrow 'flower' bed. Perhaps our two gaudy red-and-yellow-flowered deckchairs will attract bees and butterflies!

Mrs. Fry, our neighbour on the left, scatters cotton wool all over her garden.

"It's for the birds," she explains. "They can make nice comfortable nests for themselves."

Joe and his Missis, whose house abuts ours on the other side, try to persuade us that everything printed in the newspapers is incontrovertibly true.

Peter's father has brought us a puce carpet, a throw-out from the house of a wealthy uncle. We have to *buy* it. It proves too small to cover the entire floor. Just add an off-cut of some other brown carpet. That'll have to do. At least in colour it matches our teak furniture and black-plastic-covered chairs. (That puce floor cover follows us to our next two homes and I shall loathe it for another decade.)

It takes a few days to settle in before Peter is ordained. In the cathedral I silently echo the vows he makes. We are in this together, commissioned into 'full-time Christian service'. As the weeks go by, my boredom increases, so does my sense of loneliness. Crouched on the edge of the bed I watch the shoppers returning from the Coop, lugging bags; women pushing prams; an elderly man shuffles by under the window. And Peter is out somewhere. He is always out. Or barricaded in his study. Had we undergone all the training, endured those long spells of separation – for this? On Sunday mornings I demurely take my seat in the pew assigned to me: next to the Rector's wife. Where is life going? I am to be 'light' and 'salt', but the dimmer switch has been turned down and someone has forgotten to fill up the cruet.

Winter reveals the true nature of the curate's house. A clammy cold clings to us in every room. The small coal fire in the living room is the only source of warmth. Upstairs not even our pink wedding-present blankets keep us warm in bed; beneath them we spend the night zipped up to our necks in single sleeping bags.

Only the lovely blue car allows us to flee and spend our one free day by the river, the sea or in the forest. In the evening Peter reaches for his German textbook, attends his class, and two hours later replaces it in the gap of the shelf. He wants to learn my language but cannot expect any help from me because I do not speak German or read a German book. The only concession I make to my culture is to celebrate Christmas Eve when I light real wax candles on a tiny spruce, hung with silver lametta and a few decorations I have brought with me from Germany. Our Christmas tree may be small, but I am growing bigger every day. Our baby is due in the summer.

Meanwhile winter drags on, cold and miserably. Even the few daffodils nodding in the back garden cannot evoke great expectations of the Christian life. Actually I am ready to walk out – out of this lonely, uncreative life. I sense Peter's disenchantment, too. Easter comes and goes. I look forward to friends from college days coming to visit us at Whitsun. I hunger for friendship, for stimulation, for hope. They bring news of unfamiliar yet biblical events taking place at the old college and in pockets of the Anglican Church. They speak of the Holy Spirit as I have never heard before and of spiritual gifts such as prophecy and healing and speaking in tongues. What is it all about?

Traditionally the curate preaches for the *Whitsun Offering*, a small boost to his meagre salary. The lesson set for the day is the second chapter of the Acts of the Apostles. As Peter speaks I sense his *yearning*, and I, having decided to forego my place at the side of the Rector's wife, find myself weeping, not knowing why.

Peter is carving the small chicken. "The Rector took me aside after the service," he says without looking up.

"To congratulate you on the freshness of your sermon?"

"No. He made a point of telling me that I had asked *thirty-two rhetorical questions*."

"Rhetorical?" I gasp. "You mean, he counted?"

"I asked him whether he knew the answers."

"And?"

"He just walked away."

On the coffee table lie two copies of *Trinity Magazine* which our friends John and Jenny have left behind. Idly I leaf through the glossy pages; put the magazine down; pick it up; read some more; walk about; read...Why this restlessness? It must be the baby.

The Holy Spirit? Nobody – as far as I can remember – has ever talked to me about the Holy Spirit. Not at Lee Abbey. Not at my Bible College. At Peter's College? It is time to find out for ourselves.

"Let's read a bit of Acts over breakfast every morning," Peter suggests.

"And make notes," I add.

They weren't a bit bored, those early Christians! And probably not lonely either. There was a lot of drama. A married couple deceive the Christian assembly and lie to them and they pay with their lives – instant and public! What about me? Am *I* not deceiving the people here by concealing my boredom and disillusionment?

Peter is at the church saying the office of Matins with the Rector and the Senior Curate. It is nine o'clock in the morning and I should be clearing the breakfast table. Instead I lumber myself off the chair and kneel on the puce carpet, my face resting on the black-plastic seat.

"Lord, I am so sorry for my pretence. My goodie-goodie mask hides my emptiness. I am really sorry about that." After this confession I try to push myself up again but find that I cannot move. Something akin to a warm shower is cascading all over me. I feel so clean and peaceful. For a few minutes I luxuriate in this outpouring until a strange sensation begins to play around my lips. Oh no! Tongues?! Please, no tongues! I pray aloud in English but the 'vibration' on my lips remains. I pray aloud in German – but it makes no difference. My lips tingle...

'Just let it happen'. Was that a voice? I obey. Listening to myself I have no idea of what I am saying, but the language I am speaking so fluently appears to be made up of proper words, phrases, syntax. Gosh, it sounds quite musical. I don't think I am going mad, am I? At least I feel sane and in control. I can actually stop this flow... and open my eyes. I clamber back on to my chair and look around. Nothing has changed here. The

breakfast debris still litters the table. While washing the dishes in the sink, I hear the front door opening … in the living room Peter is standing transfixed …

"What's happened here?"

Haltingly I tell him. We also need to inform the Rector who is on holiday. I will have to write to him about what happened in the curate's house. Much later his wife recounts to us that after hours of waiting, she had found him in their hotel room surrounded by screwed-up balls of writing paper. His response – when it finally comes – is terse, written on a postcard, instructing us not to speak about *this* to anyone. Yet all over the little town something amazing is happening: a new fellowship develops between Peter and leaders of some of the other denominations. With them he can share.

And I? I am learning how effective this strange kind of prayer is. Nothing has to be thought out or well formulated. Instantly I know myself in the presence of God, particularly in moments of danger and perplexity. Immediately I have access to His wisdom when I desperately need it. What a useful spiritual tool! And I discover that praying in tongues is like a *love language* between me and the living God! Now I have new energy and hope and I am certain that I shall manage to cope with parish life. But soon I will have to learn to manage something else: motherhood.

My baby and I together resist the resident midwife's wiles who wants the child to be born on his grandfather's birthday. Martin makes sure that he has his very own birthday by arriving after midnight! A year later, Kim-Allan also determines that no one is to induce him, thank you very much. The curate's house is now filled with noise. Little Kim is in pain and vomits a lot but no diagnosis is found for his condition. Peter (when he is at home) walks the house and writes his sermons with his baby draped over his shoulder. But domestic matters must not get in the way of parish affairs! At the Rector's wife's insistence I distribute 'baptism cards' to families up and down the treeless streets; Martin strapped to a seat on top of Kim's pram.

Since most of Peter's pastoral visits are made in the evening, I am often alone, the boys asleep upstairs. Then I scan the cracks between the floor boards to which the puce carpet does not stretch and I wait for the long black legs to emerge, followed by the massive black body of a rafter spider. And as soon as it exercises those long black legs, *I flee upstairs to bed.*

But on Sunday nights the walls of our living room are bulging. The whole youth group descends, each scrambling for the only armchair, making do with carpet and stairs. The young people want to know and they want to grow. Peter invites experienced Christians from all walks of life, be they a doctor, a Knight of the Realm, a shoe salesmen, a top model, or a Canadian businessman, and from them the young ones learn about Jesus. For me such fresh and honest encounters make parish life worthwhile.

After the statutory three years in this parish we move to Peter's second curacy: in a university city. Here the boys find play mates, go to nursery and start primary school. I had expected to have my thinking stimulated and to make friends. The lively youth group of this church does not meet in our house, but it devours Peter's hours. Yes, this city of clever men and beautiful women has much to offer; but the only thing it feeds in me is my sense of inferiority. The academic world as well as church life, barely brush me. At home I tune my guitar, sing Dylan songs and wait all week for Sunday evening's next episode of *The Forsythe Saga* and make sure that I have a packet of Marks & Spencer's roast-chicken-flavoured crisps to nibble. On weekdays the double pushchair, loaded with groceries from the supermarket a mile away, arrives back at the curate's house; and in the kitchen sink soak the nappies. My 'theatre', my 'opera house', my 'art gallery' – they are our garden turned into an adventure playground with climbing frame, swing and sandpit; the old family tent; a tricycle, a pushcart full of bricks and a wooden engine to share or to fight over. Beneath the canopy of the gnarled apple tree we have Easter egg hunts and birthday parties. I also know every swing, slide and roundabout on the public playgrounds and from the park bench watch my boys' growing courage.

In Biafra rages a civil war and through the television its horrors penetrate into our living room. I sometimes find myself 'playing' with unfamiliar suicidal thoughts. And then the door of my closed world opens a crack. We have the opportunity to attend *Clinical Theology* seminars. The subject matter and the ensuing discussions are stimulating and I am beginning to hope that at last we are moving in the direction of the healing of the mind and perhaps even a therapeutic community. The door opens further. We find spiritual food at 'charismatic' meetings held in the rooms of a university Dean. When he leaves the city these meetings move to our home where we cater for gown *and town*. Slowly they change in character and draw the depressed and the neurotic; those teetering on the brink of psychosis; the religious fanatic; the abuser; people who are inwardly alight and those tormented by evil. We witness dark hidden issues being washed up to the surface but to deal with them effectively, we feel out of our depth. Clinical Theology does not provide precisely the answers we need. Where else can we find help? Who will train us?

And wider opens the door. We hear of a conference during which an Episcopalian woman from the States is to give seminars on 'inner healing'. This is a term we have not heard in Britain before and we are hungry. The midweek sessions are designed for clergy, the weekend ones for lay people. Peter books us a place. When on the Thursday night he arrives home, I find him changed and feel shy in his presence. There is so much he wants to share, but I am keen to find out for myself. It's my turn this weekend.

The May sun is spinning gold from the hair of our sons. There are three of them now. In Peter's arms nestles little Christoph; he is almost eleven months old. The big boys are bouncing around on the pavement, eagerly anticipating having their Dad all to themselves. Kisses and hugs all round.

"Bye-bye, Mummy. Have a nice time."

I kiss my baby's forehead, "Hey, Toffee, you'll have learnt to stand all by yourself when I get back on Sunday!" He grins, screwing up his eyes against the bright light.

The conference hall is filling quickly and I find a seat at the back. Later arrivals crowd the window sills. A hush falls as a tall grey-haired lady enters. From the lapel of her jacket dangles a watch. She is American and Episcopalian. Her name is Anne White. Now she is scanning the room.

"Not *all* of you are called to this ministry," she drawls. "Some of you are here only out of curiosity. Ask the Lord whether you should not be at one of the alternative sessions."

No one stirs. You are in England, lady. You have something we all want. We are hungry for healing and the power to heal. But she is waiting for people to leave and when no one does, she herself heads for the door.

"I'll be back in a few minutes. Please, do go if you are not meant to be here."

A few people rise from their chairs, but I am clinging to mine. Healing of the inner being – through prayer and not psychiatry? This entirely new concept grips me.

Anne had made space in her schedule for a few personal *Prayer Counselling* appointments. I hear my name read out. Had Peter volunteered me to be prayed for?

Conference bedrooms are small and airless. I feel nervous as if awaiting an operation. The expected knock, Mary Clarke introduces herself and takes me to a counselling room where she and Anne White are giving me their full attention and asking me questions. I tell them of a mental picture I saw while waiting: of two little girls sitting on grey stone steps leading up to a light-coloured house... crowding around them was a group of older girls...'We are princesses!' I heard the small girls say...

The two women are now standing behind me, where I cannot see them. They have placed their hands gently on my head and shoulders. I understand little of what is going on. My picture finds no interpretation. (One day I will understand.) Anne leaves for another appointment and, alone with Mary, time now feels less rushed. I tell her about my strained relationship with Peter's father.

"He finds it so hard to accept me – because I am German." Mary prays. Back in my room, I feel strange and a little dazed. To clear my head I take a walk.

The last session is on *Commitment*. We are invited to write a "Letter to Jesus", to rededicate ourselves to him and relinquish our family to God's care.

"Hold them on open palms," Anne demonstrates, "and present them before the throne of God. Now take your hands away. Sit on them if you want to." One by one I 'commit' my family.

'What about Christoph?'

'Surely there is no need for that! He's had the operation. He is alright now."

'*Give him to me.*' Reluctantly yet obediently I 'commit' baby Christoph to Jesus.

The following day, Monday morning, I am frying bacon and eggs for Peter, his Vicar and the Parish Worker, who have come for breakfast. The Parish Worker sidles up to me in the kitchen, circling around me, giggling. This is ridiculous.

"What *are* you doing, Deirdre?" She cannot explain nor stop this silly dance around me, looking at me from all sides.

"What's happened to *you*?!" she blurts out

"What do you mean? Yesterday I was prayed for at the conference I went to. What's so funny?"

"You...well...you are *so* different... so *different*." All *I* feel is a deep inner calm.

Whatever the May sun caresses here in our garden, explodes into life. From the blossoming apple tree ring shrieks of laughter: Christoph, whom we all call Toffee ("because he is so sweet"!) is sitting in the swing. Kim is pushing him.

"Be careful, darling. Don't swing him too high."

"He loves it, Mummy."

Peter runs for his camera. Click.

"He's probably had enough now," I say, lifting the little one on to the warm grass. On chubby hands and knees Toffee speeds towards his Dad. Click. His little face is beaming; his eyes squinting in the brightness of that afternoon. Click.

When the film is developed, the images will tear our hearts.

It's Saturday afternoon and we have guests for tea. They want to stay on, want to talk, want to pray. I make a fresh pot but my mind is not with them. My baby is not well! When I hold him, his head lolls about. My guests stay on.

"I am sorry, but I *must* call our GP."

5

Toffee

On a cool June morning, before his brothers wake, Christoph utters his first cry. His skin is a delicate pink and he looks the most beautiful new-born I have seen.

"A healthy baby," announces the midwife and he proves her right as he sleeps and feeds well, gains weight and thrives. I put off taking him for his post-natal check-up, but on one sunny afternoon, having fetched the older boys from school, and for no apparent reason other than a slight urge to do so, I veer off the tow-path and push the pram towards the clinic. I leave that red-brick building in shock.

"Your child is severely anaemic," they had said. "You need to take him to hospital immediately." It takes a whole day before I allow myself to believe it: the blood test confirms anaemia. We are sent home with an enormous bottle of iron supplement. The phone rings as we unlock the front door.

It is the children's ward.

"Please, bring your baby back to us straight away. We have done further tests. The medication we gave you will be ineffective."

The car turns back into the city traffic. There is a more serious aspect to Christoph's anaemia. He needs an immediate transfusion.

A red balloon hangs suspended above his cot – filled with someone's precious life-blood. Awkwardly and dazed, I somehow manage to breastfeed him. The young registrar calls us into his office, offers us chairs and looks at us intently.

"Let me explain your child's condition to you. Spherocytosis is a serious disorder. Christoph's red blood corpuscles do not have the normal 'doughnut' shape but are spherical, which makes them very frail and susceptible to more rapid break down; in fact four times faster than normal cells. At such a rate of destruction, his bone marrow cannot reproduce cells fast enough. Hence the anaemia. Do you know of anyone in your family who suffers from anaemia?" We look at each other and shake our heads.

"There is a prevalence of your baby's condition in the Baltic countries."

"My maternal grandmother's family came from north of the Memel. But I know that she, her mother and three of her siblings lived to a ripe old age. There has never been any mention of anaemia."

He throws Christoph's medical file across his desk and sighs.

"This condition is normally congenital, but we might be looking at a mutation." His voice sounds tired. He leans back in his chair, folds his arms, stares at the wall. We sit in silence. Where to go from here? He turns to us:

"We are very close to perfecting bone marrow transplants. That would be the best way forward, but regrettably cannot offer them yet. So, we are left with two options. Either you bring your baby in for frequent blood transfusions, which are not without risk to life, or we perform a splenectomy. The organ responsible for the destruction of the red blood cells is the spleen. By removing it, we slow down the destruction rate of the red cells. But there is a problem. Removing the spleen in someone as young as your child robs him of his immunity. Up to the age of two this organ is vital to the functioning of the immune system. I must tell you that to my knowledge we have not performed this kind of surgery on a baby before. On the positive side, we are confident that with the help of antibiotics we can fight any infection until he is two. After that age the immune system no longer relies on the spleen alone. So, we are facing you with a decision: three-weekly blood transfusions or surgery. We consider the latter the better option."

Stunned, we sign the consent form.

After the operation I cycle across the city five times a day to breastfeed him. Our household is disrupted, but Toffee recovers quickly and we take home a *very pink* baby who smiles and thrives. We plan his baptism. And now he can sit unaided...he is crawling...now pulling himself up on the coffee table...not long before he can stand...and walk...just thirteen more months and everything will be normal.

An unexpected letter from the hospital:

Dear Mrs. Vessey,

I am sorry I forgot to write to you earlier and now that there is a postal strike on, I don't know when you will receive this. I have checked up on the inheritance of congenital spherocytosis and it is always dominant...

As your blood test has showed that the red cells were abnormally fragile, we think it must be assumed that you have the disease, though very mildly...

The disease does sometimes start de novo without a family history by mutation.

Yours sincerely,

Dr. H., Paediatric Registrar

Eight months later. Visitors have stayed all afternoon. If only they would leave! Toffee needs antibiotics.

"I am sorry but I *must* call the doctor."

Finally the front door clicks shut behind them. I race to the phone. Dr. Mansfield does not delay. He feels the heat on the baby's forehead.

"It might be a touch of gastroenteritis", he says. "Get antibiotics immediately."

But how? Peter is at a drama rehearsal in church a mile away and I have no means of contacting him. Our young neighbour fetches the medication and Christoph swallows his first dose. He should improve rapidly now, as he always does. I erect the playpen in our bedroom, so as not to disturb his sleeping brothers and crouch beside him. He seems to be in pain, throwing himself from side to side. I stroke him until he calms. I try to do some sewing. As I watch the child I feel so alone. Is there anyone I could call? Sheila. She has always been good to us. She crosses the city and I am relieved to see her. I lead her up the stairs. Toffee is awake again, moving restlessly in his make-shift cot, evidently in discomfort. I lift him up and hold him, while Sheila prays for him. He calms again. I gently lower him down into the playpen and we tiptoe from the room. We listen. Yes, all is quiet. I make us coffee...

...A piercing shriek! Eerie, spine-chilling, not like a baby's cry. I race up the stairs. He is writhing and even the dim light shows his face, blue and contorted with pain. Hurriedly I wrap him in his blanket and hand him to Sheila while my fingers fumble on the dial.

"Get him to the hospital as quickly as you can," Dr. Mansfield urges. "Don't bother with an ambulance. I will ring them and follow behind you."

Where is Peter?

Just then the key turns in the door.

It is just before midnight. Sheila stays in the house with the sleeping boys. The balmy May night has lured every student into the streets. Drunk and carefree they spill all over the city. Peter swerves. The tyres squeal. He disregards speed limit and red lights. The bundle in my arms emits rasping noises. 'Death rattle' – have I not read the expression somewhere? Peter accelerates. We must reach the hospital. Then all will be well. In the car park I clasp my bundle and tear along the corridor towards the children's ward. A nurse runs towards me, takes Toffee from my arms. We are ushered into the waiting room we know so well. The hands on the wall clock announce that it is now Sunday...Tick. Tick. Tick...frantic activity on the ward, but our room is so still. We pray silently. What need is there for words? All the time our eyes fix on the door. One o'clock. The registrar's face looks grave and I know. He takes our hands into his.

"I am so very sorry. We did all we could. There was so much fluid on his lungs. Would you like to see him?" Peter follows him onto the ward.

And the child's mother? She is sleepwalking...slowly along the corridor.. through the swing doors...to a car...somewhere...Dr.Mansfield...his mouth is moving...I can't hear. Peter's embrace secures me. He feels solid. Back in the car, hot drops are falling into my lap. We thread our way home through the revellers. My arms are empty and the journey home is slow. Sheila is waiting in the living room.

"We had to leave him behind. He is already…with Jesus." We fall into her open arms and her love penetrates my frozen state. Together we stand, sobbing. In the bedroom I deftly dismantle the playpen. 'All over the world thousands upon thousands of mothers are folding up blankets that are no longer needed', is all I can think.

Sleep will not come in those few remaining hours of the night, but I see beautiful pictures and hear Peter speaking words that do not seem his own. Dawn breaks. Martin and Kim are climbing into bed with us as they always do, warm and sleepy, and drink the milk their Daddy brings them. How hard it is to form the words.

"Toffee is no longer with *us*. He died in hospital in the night." Our eldest immediately understands and starts to cry; but Kim gives no sign of comprehension, shows no emotion at all. Peter leaves to take the eight o'clock Communion Service as arranged and only afterwards tells his Vicar of the night's events. Meanwhile I prepare the children's breakfast. Out of the corner of my eye, I see the feeding bottle in the sterilizer on the draining board. And the teat. That's no longer needed. Slowly my foot pushes the pedal of the kitchen bin. The lid flips open and I drop the rubber teat. My heart is cracking…it will surely shatter…suddenly from deep within…arises a swell of *joy*. 'Thank you, Jesus. You are here. You are holding my heart. It will not break. I will not go mad.' Later we all attend the Family Service, a depleted family. After the service, with a strangely numb and detached dignity, I receive many words from people: some comforting, some silly, some downright cruel. Invited to lunch in the Vicarage, only my body is present. My heart is in the hospital. I have not said good-bye to my baby. Left him behind last night. Left him with strangers. Never even looked at him. Did not kiss him good-bye. Please, don't engage me in your small-talk. I need to go home.

In the privacy of our bedroom, where Toffee was born, I wail. Primordial howls. Like a caged animal I pace back and forth, swaying. Then with a strange energy I go to the bathroom and wash my face.

"I am ready to go and see him." Peter shows relief. He calls the hospital where nobody had expected us. Hurriedly they lay out the little body in the chapel.

A white shroud. Only my baby's face is showing. His forehead feels so cold, so hard when I kiss it. I do not notice the flattened side of his face.

(Peter does and only tells me much later that this had been caused when after the autopsy the body had been left on some slab. How glad I was not to have noticed.) Holding me gently, Peter directs my eyes towards the crucifix on the plain wall. A broken body up there – in quiet agony – a small broken body down here. I am ready to leave.

"Good-bye, my little darling. We have enjoyed you so much. What fun you have been..." The chapel door snaps shut behind us.

Multitudes of cards arrive and so many flowers, I have not vases enough in which to arrange them. In the morning they lie strewn all over the carpet and there are spit marks on mirror and furniture. Martin's love for his baby brother had always been tender, now a six-year-old has vented his helpless rage. Kim, however, still shows no sign of grief or anger and lets nothing distract him from his play.

It is days later that screams shrill from the nursery. What is happening? Kim is lashing out at Martin, tearing frantically at his pyjamas to prevent him from climbing into the empty cot.

"No! No! No! It's Toffee's bed!" he yells desperately. The dam is finally broken: his tears flow and he releases his anger. We hold both mourning children.

There are few people gathered for the brief service at the crematorium. On outstretched arms Harry, the undertaker, carries a small white coffin into the chapel. Guard my heart. I am neither watching nor listening to the words. Behind closed eyes a scene unfolds and takes all my attention. There stands a little boy...Oh God, he can stand all by himself! Someone is with him: a tall Man whose hand lies on the child's downy head.

"Have you got him?" I whisper.

Yes, I have got him. You committed him to me.

Despite the assurance, no day goes without weeping and the nights drag on without sleep. My feet have to be actively instructed to move, because life must go on. The boys must go to school. Meals have to be prepared and cups of tea brewed for numerous visitors. Both our bishops call. For them to be able to talk to me I must make them feel at ease. My knees almost give way as one of them keeps me standing in the doorway for that last bit of conversation. Some people avoid us, crossing the street when they see us, afraid of not knowing what to say.

To a service of Thanksgiving for Christoph we invite friends, family, neighbours and the members of our church. Mr and Mrs Rutter, our next door neighbours are elderly. They do not have children but have always given us the impression that they loathe little ones. It must be unbearable for them to live adjacent to the curate's house where for years new babies were born and yelled in their prams and young children banged dustbin lids and shouted and threw toys over the fence! Mr and Mrs Rutter never return stray balls but push notes of complaint and threats through our letter box. Whenever I step out into the garden the curtain in their upstairs window twitches and I know that I am being watched, especially as pregnancy shows. Compulsively my eyes flick upwards towards the gable end and almost every time I see a face draw back from the window. I am developing a tic! When the woman's voice shrills as she berates her husband, I shiver. Now they have learnt of our baby's death, and we want to give them a personal invitation to the Thanksgiving. We dare to call at their house and are led into the front room. We decline a drink.

"I couldn't come to the service," wails Mrs Rutter. "No! No! I couldn't! I can't bear the thought of dead children!" She whimpers like a beaten dog. Only I seem to see the door opening and Someone tall filling the frame. She must have also sensed Him, because her wails and howls fade to a whimper and she suddenly grovels on the floor – before Him and falls silent. Before we leave the house, she offers to look after the baby clothes for me until I feel ready to discard them. For her sake I accept her offer.

As I write this, a light switches on. I understand something I had never seen before: Mrs Rutter had lost a child herself – her only child!

At the Thanksgiving only three members of our family are present. Peter's father has bought a turkey for me to cook before the service. When the bird is carved, out of its neck falls the little plastic bag with the giblets. Who cares? I am amazed that I have managed to prepare a meal at all and that Peter has the courage to preach. After the service I offer tea in our garden. Dad calls me aside, his eyes searching for mine. He keeps shaking his head.

"You look as if you are at a wedding! I don't understand."

"It's Jesus," I say without thought and know at that moment that I am no longer afraid of Dad. I love him. I feel his prejudice dissolving. Years later, shortly before his own death, we will exchange a couple of letters. They are love letters. My white-silken-haired patriotic English father-in-law has come to love the woman from the land he despised and feared.

Three weeks later a letter arrives from the hospital.

Dear Mr and Mrs Vessey

This is just a short note to tell you our final findings.

Christoph died from an overwhelming septicaemia (blood stream infection), this led to haemorrhage into both adrenal glands which is invariably fatal. I would guess that this disaster occurred in between the time that Dr. Mansfield saw you and the time he was brought up to the Children's Ward.

As has been said to you before, septicaemia does rarely occur following splenectomy in children. The risk was thought to be extremely small and justified especially as his severe anaemia repeatedly occurring was a threat to life...

Yours sincerely,

Dr. H., Paediatric Registrar

Though our grief has made us vulnerable we keep the door to our home wide open. Some visitors strengthen us; others deplete us; one or two accuse us. Like flies some feed on our open wound but some who come find healing for themselves.

We choose to visit places where Toffee had played, where he had licked his first ice cream and where we had fun as a whole family. Some revisiting is enforced on us.

"I don't want to worry you," Kim's grey-haired little headmistress begins cautiously, "especially not at this time. But I think your little boy is profoundly deaf." We had not noticed, rather we had thought that he naughtily ignored calls and orders. A hearing test confirms her observation and calls for surgery in his inner ear. We are back on the children's ward, walking the same corridor, passing through the same doors, meet with the same nurses. The Registrar, visibly shocked at seeing us, beats a hasty retreat. Dr. Mansfield also avoids any mention of the little patient he lost. A child's death disturbs everyone. Had the Consultant Paediatrician's decision been the right one? He writes:

We would never again perform a splenectomy on a child so young.

Earlier, in the spring, when Toffee was learning to crawl, we had visited the Vicarage where we would soon be living. While Peter and I measured up for carpets and curtains, the boys had explored the huge garden with its weeping willow and Toffee had slept peacefully in his carry-cot in the cubbyhole under the stairs, with the door slightly ajar; the only darkened space in the empty house. Now my dread is mounting as moving day approaches. The cubby-hole haunts me. I shall never be able to open that door!

6

Does a Living make for living?

It feels like a quantum leap: from curate to vicar; from a city culturally well endowed to one woefully deprived. Driving through its streets to *our* Vicarage, we experience a mild culture shock. Here and there the scars of war are still evident, and we notice poverty as we have not encountered it before. This city feels left behind. Without a specific purpose, no one visits it. It has taken us several hours to reach our new home, on small roads winding around ditch and dyke. I had once travelled to this city by train and had enquired from a fellow passenger where to alight.

"*Everything* ends here," he said with a wry smile.

"What have you *done* to be sent here," the undertaker asks Peter on the way to taking his first funeral in the parish.

"A dark cloud hangs over the city," announce the spiritually discerning.

"It's a hard place to work in," say his fellow ministers.

So what had brought us here? Pressure of time? Romantic idealism? A pinch of heroism? My affection for the people which sprang from my earlier visit to the city? The 'charismatic' aspects of the church? Or is it the call of God?

The red-brick Vicarage looks ostentatious in this artisan parish but belies its poorly designed interior where all heat generated on the ground floor is lost in the large stairwell, not reaching the unheated bedrooms. The huge uncultivated garden, however, promises to become paradise for the boys. I wonder whether house and garden seek privacy by hiding behind the high brick wall and the wild branches of the ornamental cherry.

Into our naked new home we carry four greasy, steaming packages from which waft the smell of fish, hot oil and vinegar. We are about to dig our fingers into the golden batter of the "best fish in England" when the verger arrives. I had avoided even a glance at that door under the stairs but Harry who cannot wait to show us the electrical miracle he has wrought jerks it open!

I gasp. Light floods the small space. And with it my dread evaporates. For the mourning to subside – that will take much longer.

At the end of our first Sunday service someone says that two women are waiting outside the church to speak to me. What about? They look me up and down.

"You are too young to be a vicar's wife." That's all they want to tell me.

Peter's study has just enough room for a desk and one chair. Where will he talk with his visitors? Anxiously he scans the few built-in shelves. There is barely space for his books. The essential grey metal filing cabinet just fits into the corner by the door. Martin comes bursting in.

"Dad, Dad. I have got new friends! They want to see my armour." Hurriedly he puts on the plastic breastplate and lets his Dad tie the sides together; dons his helmet; picks up the shield and wields his sword as he runs out into the street.

Within minutes he is back, sobbing.

"Dad, they pinched my sword!" His father is already on the pavement but there is no sign of the 'friends'. The city's first gifts: loss and betrayal.

Even before our arrival I had been designated leader of the women's group. At last a vicar's wife has arrived. From now on *she* will provide chairs from all the over house, serve tea and biscuits, give the address, steer the discussion through religious platitudes, wash up the cups and carry the chairs back to where they belong.

"Lord," I protest after a few meetings. "Does the growth of Your Kingdom really depend on just one woman? A woman in mourning at that? A pregnant woman?" I lay down my assigned role. No one is happy with me, no one takes my place and the group chooses to disband.

John Christian, our fourth son, is born and my mourning ends. He is a calm little boy who feeds well. But just before his next meal he spews out undigested milk. I hear him whimpering as if in pain: echoes of Kim's first year.

"All babies cry and spit a bit," comforts the Health Visitor without examining him, not sharing my concern. To be listened to by the medical profession I must speak the language of the scientist. I buy scales and weigh Johnny every day; keep a chart and draw a graph. There can be no doubt: Johnny is losing weight. The GP acts immediately and within hours our little son is in hospital. A diagnosis is swiftly made: pyloric spasm. The medication proves effective. If only Kim could have been helped in this way, how much suffering he might have been spared.

The depressed city incubates a great deal of mental anguish. Within a short time we encounter schizophrenia and depression; obsessive compulsive disorder and breakdown; kleptomania and alcoholism. The Vicarage door is ever open and where we can, we offer help and refuge. Except on Christmas Eve. Then we draw the curtains, light the candles and shut out the world with all its pain. For a few brief hours we are only present to our children and to each other.

Summer comes. On his weekly day off Peter mows the lawn and rakes the hay. In the evening Martin and Kim, bathed, snuggled into their towelling robes and hugging their mugs of cocoa are listening to their bedtime story on their Daddy's lap, when the doorbell rings. It's the verger who needs to speak urgently to the Vicar. I take him into the living room. As for the bedtime story? The end. I am furious with myself, loathe this whole lifestyle, this robbery of our time and privacy.

"We need a night as well as a day off! We have to get away," I demand.

It is a high bill we have to pay for a family room in the guest house by the sea. We get little sleep. One of the boys is sick and the baby keeps crying. Tired and unhappy, Peter runs the children back to the city to school, while I, barred from the B & B, feed Johnny on the beach in the lee of the cliffs.

Later we walk on the sands, thinking about our situation. A stiff sea wind tugs at our hair; waves form patterns in the sand; clouds race across an endless blue. Perhaps life is not so bad! We pass several caravan sites perched on the edge of the cliff. Wouldn't it be lovely…?

And then it happens. A family loan is unexpectedly repaid and we can buy our own four-berth static caravan. Now we have a *home* by the sea. No phone and no doorbell to interrupt the bedtime story. Every week we can escape for one night, and after the boys have been taken to school, the beach stretches out before us. Cliffs and clouds overhead, ammonites and pebbles at our feet and Johnny asleep in the papoose on Peter's back. We regain perspective.

I think I have found a friend in Samantha. She is a little older than I, an intelligent and creative person. I sense her frustrated untapped potential. We regularly meet for coffee and I watch a woman emerge from beneath debris of religious taboo and a stifling social class ethos. I see her blinking in the unaccustomed light of undreamed possibilities, and it thrills me. I want to help her into personal freedom. Secretly I wish we might achieve something together. A few church families have decided to go camping with us, while attending a Christian conference. Perhaps it is the intense atmosphere that makes Samantha uncomfortable. One night she tells us that she can hear heavenly music and angelic song. Though a little disquieted, I do not perceive that she is hallucinating. On our return to the parish Samantha becomes very agitated. She does not sleep and disturbs her household. Her husband brings her to the Vicarage and there she is, standing in my kitchen, looking wild and strange without the spectacles she has discarded.

"The Lord has healed my sight!" she declares, squinting at me, and I am frightend by these 'healed' eyes. In the living room I sit her down and her screams fill the house. I am concerned about the children. All I can do is to hold her and pray until she calms. Her doctor refers Samantha to a psychiatrist.

"A typical case of acute schizophrenia," is his diagnosis. That's impossible! We press for a second opinion which does not confirm the first diagnosis. Large doses of vitamin B and a change in diet improve her mental state. But whatever the experts' opinions and whatever the remedy: I have lost a friend and am banned from the new world that opens up to her.

Johnny's speech develops, but painfully slowly; and when eventually he strings words together to form his first sentences, these do not flow.

However hard he tries to push out sounds, be it by slapping his thighs or stamping his little feet, they do not obey. Speech therapy begins. Would it help if he was prayed for? An itinerant 'healer' with his wife come to hold a healing service in our church. People flock from all over the city. Johnny, on Peter's arm, wants nothing to do with it and clamours to be taken back to the babysitter. In the congregation is another young boy, probably autistic but also displaying other neurological dysfunction. His father, a pastor I know, has brought him for healing. As a queue of people moves slowly down the aisle, he asks me to accompany him and his son. Arriving at the front of the church, the healer's wife steps forward and, before I can explain my reason for being there, touches *my* forehead. Immediately I fall backwards. How long have I been lying on the church carpet? When I open my eyes, I see a smirking satisfaction all around me. 'The Vicar's wife was slain in the Spirit!' I feel tears spilling over and can't wait to reach the safety of our home. All through that night and the following day I weep without any means of stemming the flow and feel spent. What is happening to me? Is this a deep hidden sorrow breaking out?

The coal-fed paddle steamer chugs across the river and I feel Johnny's burning skin close to mine. Under the harbour lights I notice the spots.

"The little chap has rubella?" Dr. Holden laughs. "Nothing to worry about". I am about to leave his consulting room when I casually announce that I am pregnant. Dr. Holden's laugh turns to alarm.

"How far advanced are you?"

"About ten weeks." Now his face looks grave.

"Sit down. Have you had German measles as a child?"

"I don't know. German measles are not German measles in Germany. I have had measles, though." And from somewhere far away I hear the doctor's voice…"abortion…"

"That's out of the question."

"Then we must try a massive injection of gamma serum. I cannot guarantee…" and he lists the defects the baby may suffer.

How could I possibly think of aborting this baby? Quite clearly I remember the night. I was cleaning my teeth before bed when I heard the words, *'You shall have another child'*.

I had remonstrated, "Our family is complete." No, this baby I was *called* to bear. Abort? Never.

The October day had been rough and grey. Easterly gales are buffeting the cherry tree; its branches scratch at the bedroom window; the weeping willow is lashing the ground with long whips. Peter is in another part of the country and not due back until evening. The first contraction in the afternoon surprises me. Now dusk has fallen. Squalls of autumn rain bombard the city and halt the traffic. It is as if water is being flung from buckets. My own midwife is off duty and I have rung her deputy as well as Dr. Holden. I'd better ring Joyce, too.

The contractions are no longer the gentle warnings of the afternoon. At least Joyce is here to get the boys ready for bed. Vehicles slosh through puddles, but no familiar headlights illuminate our drive. I glance around the room. All is ready: a nice bassinet, the baby bath, towels and a huge cardboard box full of sterilized accoutrements that has been sitting in the corner of the bedroom for weeks. The branches of the cherry tree screech on the glass. Into the bedroom burst three boys with wet hair and pink faces; tumble on to my bed to kiss me goodnight.

"When you wake up in the morning we will have a new baby. How about that, eh?"

A fresh gust of sea gale buffets the cherry tree. The silly box over there in the corner keeps looking at me. I need a midwife to open it. Where is Peter? That flash of light? No, that was not him. No car door slamming. Obediently I go with every pain.

I hear familiar footsteps on the stairs. Peter pops his head around the door.

"Hi, darling I'm home. Bit later than I thought I'd be. Lousy weather out there. The roads are treacherous. I'll just nip over to church for the choir rehearsal. How are you?"

"The baby is coming!"

"Are you sure?" He throws off his jacket. I see him rolling up his sleeves…the pain is strong…he pulls away the duvet.

"The head is engaged."

Instinctively I bear down.

"Stop pushing! The cord is around the baby's neck. Don't worry. I am now going to loosen it. Ah…it's o.k." I push a last time. My midwife-husband lays the slimy bundle on my tummy and grins, "We have another boy."

I know his name: Patrick, son of a noble father. Neither of us hears the doorbell. The midwife bustles in, surveys the scene and, a little belatedly, rips open the sealed box.

"Well done," she says, somewhat reluctantly, and severs the cord.

"I've delivered *many* calves and lambs. And piglets, too," Peter informs her with that air of the expert. "It's not all that different."

"Well, really!!"

Boredom engendered by a world too small and too parochial catches me again and hangs its dark mantle on my shoulders. I am dragging the mop across the kitchen floor.

"I've got news for you." Peter stays by the door, so as not to leave footmarks on the wet vinyl. "A Christian community has just bought a large house in the city."

"This is the end of our isolation!" I stop mopping and cry – with relief.

Twelve young people make up the community and soon a steady traffic flows between our two houses. The children find new admirers. For me there is now a life beyond the parish. Linda, one of their members, introduced to me as "being good with depressed women", becomes a frequent visitor. One afternoon, as I squat on the floor, sewing knee patches on Johnny's trousers, we chat about this and that. Her question comes as a surprise.

"What is the desire of your heart?"

My response is immediate and the strength of feeling astonishes me even more.

"I would love to go to university and read psychology."

"Go for it then," says Linda.

"Put your feelers out. See what happens," Peter confirms.

Professor Clarke calls me for interview. I have no English qualifications, I tell him.

"What a pity," he responds when I say that in my school days it was deemed unnecessary to burden girls with science. He decides that an I.Q. test will show whether I have the necessary nous to take a degree course.

It is *above* average? That is not what my primary school teacher had told my parents. Suddenly everything moves fast. Linda comes to live with us. The freezer is filled to brimming. And here *I* am, sitting in a tiered lecture hall. Professor Clarke is teaching and it is *my* hand that is scribbling down notes on *Maternal Deprivation Reassessed*.

7

The pastures of the wilderness are green

The degree course is well manageable since Linda sees to the children and the household during the day and I spend quality time with the family in the early evening, studying in the early hours of the morning when the house is still. I miss the lack of therapeutic application, but am able to specialize in Abnormal Psychology. At least I learn about the theoretical aspects of the issues with which my heart wants to engage. And then I lay down my pen and hand in the final examination paper. I have finished the course. I have fulfilled my dream. As I walk out into a radiant spring day, the words of a hymn form in my mind: "I turn unfilled to Thee again."

At Professor Clarke's invitation I embark on a master's degree but after a year of literature research the subject proves dry and irrelevant to my quest. Instead I complete a teaching certificate (Slow Learners). For my teaching practice the authorities make up for me a class of four disenchanted and challenging teenagers. It proves a stressful endurance test, especially so as we have a schizophrenic lady living with us in the Vicarage at the same time who with her doctor's collaboration has come off all medication and is seriously suicidal. I work with her in my spare time and discover a history of war trauma in the Far East. Where is the Christian therapeutic community to hold and work with such a sufferer?

Nine years in the inner city have come to an end. Peter's workload as the new Vicar of several country parishes and as Chaplain to the County Police will be even greater. Will we see even less of him? When our belongings have found their place in the house, I explore our immediate surroundings. Stiles on footpaths are a new experience. I squeeze through upright stones or clamber over wooden steps. The Knoll is a peaceful place. Up here ancient footpaths converge and the fields are studded with black-and-white cattle. A copse grants shelter against the winds that use the bare hilltop as their playground. God's promise to me had been that the "pastures of the wilderness are green". Like the hub of a cart wheel the church squats in the centre of the village. A century of grime has blackened its stonework. Like spokes, brick-built housing estates fan out in all directions and I can clearly see our new home. It lacks an entrance porch and even casual visitors can see straight into the house. Peter had not taken to the Vicarage but I had been bidden to 'say yes to the house'.

The deep-sunken eyes of the lollipop-man at the cross roads bear witness to a time when coal mining put bread on the table, and hardship was the order of the day. Within one generation village life has changed. New houses have sprung up on the remaining pasture land and people live comfortably. Although industrial estates are close, they do not spoil the view from modern windows and nicely-tended gardens; they do not pollute the pure country air.

The sunsets are breathtaking and the landscape around us is beautiful. I am relieved to have left the city behind. Peter calls me a "city girl" but I do not feel like one in the least. Instead the rural scene below me gives me a deep sense of homecoming. Why should that be? Up here on the Knoll I wonder what this village has in store for us. Maybe it is here at last that my dream of a therapeutic community will be fulfilled. Look around: yes, the pastures of the wilderness are green. Will I be led into a wilderness?

"Can we now have a dog?" clamour the boys. As a Christmas present Topsy, a black-and-white springer spaniel pup joins the family. A reckless creature, she dives into water before she is supposed to, gets caught in waterfalls, scales rock faces too steep for her, chases low-flying teasing birds until she falls exhausted – and always, always she needs human rescue. She has fallen in love with Brandy, the multi-racial polygamist and Casanova who lives next door. Naively, I had opened the back door for her after midnight to stop her whining. Their tryst had been short, her litter too large for her. One morning, looking out of the kitchen window, I see her pups on our neighbour's terrace. No, they can't be hers, because they are here – with her. But they look the same! Brandy, you are a rascal. Twice in one night?

Long after Topsy's assorted offspring learnt to negotiate their own way around the house, she obeys her overdeveloped maternal instinct and carries the plump pups by the scruff of their necks until canine rebellion makes her drop her charges.

Recurring dreams of railway stations intrude into my sleep. I keep missing a train by a hair's breadth. Sometimes I find myself carrying an infant for whose life I am responsible. Sometimes I do not have enough milk, sometimes I cannot find a safe place to feed the child, sometimes I forget it altogether, sometimes I let it sleep too long and it misses all feeds. On waking I feel anxious and helpless and vaguely guilty about my neglectful behaviour. In one vivid dream the family has already left for the station and I have stayed behind because first I must dig up a small clump of violets growing in the Vicarage lawn. I need to remove every rootlet – intact.

To keep my brain 'oiled' I take an A-level course in *English* literature but have no yen for German writings. Unexpected doors open: I lecture on psychological issues in a male prison, join the National Schizophrenia Fellowship, Peter and I lead marriage retreats in Scotland and through the ministry *Wholeness Through Christ* we introduce *Prayer Counselling* into Holland, Austria and Switzerland as well as teach and minister on training schools all over the U.K. We are deeply committed to healing and restoration of soul and spirit and the renewal of the mind. Because of this, many people find their way to the Vicarage – in search of wholeness. Periodically we, too, are listened to and prayed for; a prerequisite for any counselling ministry to others. During one such session my counsellor draws my attention to the manner in which I wring my hands. Why am I doing this?

"Maybe it's grief?" I offer and tears begin to roll. "I have no home!"

"The Father will give you a home," my counsellor assures me.

A week later a cheque arrives. It is from Peter's Dad. And to our astonishment we hear, *'You may buy your own house.'* We scour the estate agents' notice boards, and there in the left-hand bottom corner is the picture of a tiny cottage, a Cinderella amongst houses. Close to woodland, at the edge of a village, it comes with a mossy lawn, a straggly rambling rose, a scrawny forsythia and a rhubarb patch. Scrub land and forest clamber down over crumbling dry-stone walls, threatening to devour the little garden. The inside of the cottage is rough and ready but – shout it from the roof tops – we have a home of our own! Peter carries me across the doorstep and in the years that follow his strong farmer's hands will saw and plane timber, rebuild dry-stone walls, move tons of rocks and improve the impoverished soil from which an army of self-sown trees have stolen water and nutrients.

Our new-found joy and freedom spill into the parishes. People are finding Life, marriages are renewed and we witness physical and emotional healings. Dormant plants awake and new seeds spring green shoots. The pastures of the wilderness *are* green. There is no *wilderness.* We give away our time, our space and our privacy. The Vicarage resembles a beehive. I have to undergo minor surgery and discomfort and do not recognize how vulnerable I have become. In Germany my father is dying.

8

Honour your Father

My father is a uniform, complete with jackboots. This is how I met him on four separate days in the first six years of my life. Throughout my school years I experienced him as a haggard lorry driver, later a discontented steelworker who drank too much, held monologues and fell into an occasional fit of rage. We never bonded. He did not know me and I did not know him. My Papi stayed a stranger. My brother and I tried not to listen to the war stories my uncle and his family and all his other friends always exchanged over coffee and cake, when the men's voices droned and the women's shrilled above them. My mother said little in those days. Perhaps she, too, was shutting her ears to the voices that reached a crescendo over beer and potato salad at supper time. All these oft-repeated accounts lacked personal reflection and sounded stereotyped. My father's world remained alien to us children. It never occurred to us get out an atlas and look up the places which Papi knew intimately, be they in France or Yugoslavia; and we never asked questions. We were all survivors of our own cataclysm, who though not crippled or blinded, had crept furtively from beneath the debris of years of delusion and violence. And because I never asked questions, I know little about his boyhood or teenage years in his Ruhr city Duisburg. Papi was only seventeen when his father died prematurely from the effects of gas poisoning. Whilst his mother had physically disciplined her youngest, she had spoilt her eldest son with all those enviable toys which the boy would not share with his two younger siblings. This brother made it in the world, but at a price. When I was a teenager he hanged himself from a tree in the garden of his villa.

My father became very knowledgeable about engines and dreamed of using this knowledge and his driving skills in the police. He fulfilled his dream before the war. In 1945 the door closed. Many years later, in his late forties he put himself through college again, joined the new Federal police and became a trainer. His self-esteem was restored and he became calm and dignified and creative. But by then I had already left home. Only during our family holidays with my parents did I glimpse Papi's personal fulfilment, the contentment in their marriage and his full engagement in village life and church activities. Our boys know him as a generous and caring grandfather. I had urged my parents to leave the city and retire to their country cottage. Thus they moved into their golden years. With professional help my father turned the run-down house into a small jewel and my mother a neglected piece of land into a paradise garden. I feel grateful that she had not listened to my earlier pleading during the grim times to divorce from my father in the hope of bringing peace into our household.

Yet even throughout these years, though filled with fun and creativity and love for his grandsons, I cannot bond with my father. I sense his longing for attachment but keep him locked out from my heart and my world. It is too late. War and post-war years have prevented him to be a father to me, and I have learnt to do without father love. During the years of his drinking my anxiety and shame increased and gave me further reason to defend myself against him. My rejection of him hurts him, I know.

In later years I glean more of a life humiliated by his teacher, his pastor (who once stood him against a hot stove in confirmation classes because he had not learnt the verse of a hymn), and the brutalization during his training under the Nazi regime. And then the war. My grandmother never accepted her son-in-law, leaving my mother (and later me) to straddle loyalties. And always that clammy fear: when will he get home from the pub? What state will he be in? I remember hiding in the bathroom while violent arguments raged in the living room and china shattered. My mind understands that drink anaesthetises pain and memories but my heart stays guarded. How can I trust him? Or respect him? How is he coping with my emerging womanhood? Is he afraid that his daughter is more intelligent than he? How could I turn to him when I am troubled about Dr. Altmann? Or find solace with him in the helplessness of breakdown? I choose avoidance rather than rebellion; withdrawn silence instead of confrontation.

We are nearing the end of a Prayer Counselling School. I am going to enjoy half an hour of free time before dinner and stretch out on my bed, languidly leafing through my Bible. A thunderbolt strikes me.

"He who hates, dissembles with his lips and harbours deceit in his heart…" The gong sounds but in that moment I realize that I *hate* my father.

Numbed I move into the dining room.

"What is the matter?" asks a friend. My voice sounds hollow as I tell her what I have just discovered.

"You can't stay under that condemnation. Let's talk about it after supper."

We go back to my room and I feel myself sliding downwards, into a dark warren of underground caves. And terror mounts.

"Don't take me there!" I scream. "Please, don't take me there!"

"Look at the cross," she says. That's what we *always* say. A kind of formula. But I do see an image: the *back* of the dying Christ. He does not turn towards me. I cannot make Him look at me! I feel in a Christ-less place. In the land of the damned. All through that night I am awake, engulfed in terror that does not loosen its grip at dawn. After breakfast everybody assembles for worship and someone announces the first song. '*Thank you, Lord, for the wonder of your healing.*' I am in a dark cave. '*You have turned my thorns to roses…*' I am going to faint. My head lolls against the shoulder of the man next to me.

"I have something to say to you", whispers the man, "I see you, bloodied and tattered, struggling out of a thicket. But you shall never have to go there again.'"

I silently release my father, my stricken, rejected father to his Creator. "Please, honour him." *'Thank you, Lord, you have turned my thorns to roses...'*

After this experience I do not see my father for a whole year.

On the hottest day of the summer we are driving from the Swiss Alps to the Dutch-German border, our two youngest sons, patient, in the back seat. All windows are wide open, but the wind is too hot to cool us, and the autobahn offers no shade. Yet a deep peace has settled on us all. Did we bring it with us from the stillness of the mountains? After hour upon hour of confinement in our metal capsule, we arrive in the cool of the evening in a garden and to a table laid for us. During supper my father touches my arm. I usually dislike physical contact from him, but I do not withdraw.

"I want you to know something," he says, visibly moved, "I want you to know that I am a Christian and I am a Christian because of you."

It is springtime, nine months after our evening shalom in my parents' garden, when I hear my mother's troubled voice on the phone, "I hand you straight over to Papi."

His raspy laboured breathing makes it difficult for him to talk. What am I to do? My head is spinning while stupid phrases travel down the line to the suffering man. What have I got to do? *'Read him a psalm.'* I have to translate! My glasses keep misting up. The letters blur. I am sweating. Psalm Ninety One. Oh gosh. What is the German word for 'refuge'? For 'deadly pestilence'? I cannot think clearly; my pulse is drumming in my temples; my hand leaves wet marks on the thin paper. There is silence at the other end of the line. My father listens patiently as I struggle. All he wants is to hear my voice. I catch the night ferry.

"Talk with him. Pray with him," my mother greets me at the door. But we've never done that together. How do I do it now? Can love grow in an instant when it has no seed? I will honour him. I will honour him. I will...

"Du bist ein gutes Mädchen." He has always wanted me to be a good girl. It has never been important to him that I might be beautiful, attractive, intelligent, competent, no, I must be a *good* girl. Obedient, like a child, he takes the medicine I give him and eats what I prepare for him.

"It's hard to be born," he rasps in staccato, "and it's hard to die." His night is torturous. The ambulance arrives in the early hours of the morning. They make him sit upright to ease his breathing. He is wearing his hat. A quick glance back at the house he helped to turn into an idyll. Now his eyes are seeking mine. "Do you love me?" they ask. I wish I could. I will honour you. Why is the ambulance so slow? I have never known the road to Emmerich to be so long? I smile at my father. I want him to be cared for by someone else. I can't bear this emotional responsibility. They operate on him.

"Things are worse than we expected," the surgeon says when we meet him in the corridor, "much worse". He explains but I do not comprehend. In the Intensive Care Unit, I think Papi recognizes me. I wish I could love you. I will honour you. What are his last words to me? I cannot remember. They keep him alive for another two days. My mother leans on me.

Sunday morning. We find him in a room of his own, tubes in and out of every orifice. Frosted glass obscures the view out of the window, only the top panes are clear glass. I fix my eyes on red roof tiles – against a leaden sky – shiny symmetrical patterns. Papi is restless, tears at his tubes. His growing agitation frightens me. I try to restrain him. My mother leaves it to me to soothe him. We need help. Two nurses tie down his wrists and pull up the bars. His bed becomes a cage. There he lies bound and gagged. The nurse pushes a needle into his fleshless thigh and an eerie quiet settles on the room. I am going to faint. Count the roof tiles! Look at the interesting patterns! I do not hit the lino.

"I am here, Papi." The monitor scribbles. Sometimes it halts and my heart, too, misses a beat. A pastor should come and give him Communion.

"I'll phone the chaplain," I say, moving towards the door.

"And Dieter, too." My mother's eyes plead. She wants her son to be here.

The phone booth is downstairs. I fumble through the directories. I just manage to speak to my brother…

"Come quickly", shouts the orderly, running towards me. I race up the stairs and along the corridor. The monitor is getting tired of scribbling, makes little effort. The spikes are small. I go over to my father. I pray silently. I will honour you, my poor imprisoned father. I will honour you to the end. There is no pastor, no Communion. It does not matter. "Jesus is here." And He holds the gossamer threads of this father-daughter relationship until the monitor records a fine green straight line. The bleeps stop. Silence. Lord Jesus, receive this man, my father, into your arms. Then I enfold my little mother in mine.

The coffin stands in the small church of the village where my father finally could love my mother and spoil her and reward her for her faithfulness; the village, a peaceful island, where he had blossomed after so many turbulent years.

"Is there a passage you would like me to speak about? Perhaps something that was important to your father?" asks the pastor.

"Psalm ninety-one," I say without hesitation.

From the pulpit he reads: "…I will rescue him; I will protect him, for he acknowledges my name…I will deliver him and honour him…and show him my salvation."

Even the "scourge" of the swastika and the personal oath he had sworn to his diabolical leader had been turned from curse to blessing when he renounced the beliefs of his unformed and unaffirmed youth. The little church is full. So many new friends and acquaintances! They have come to thank and honour my father.

The cortège glides along the autobahn: Papi is going home. We pass the stern squat church and the parish room where the young boy had experienced sadism and humiliation in the name of God. The coffin comes to rest in the cemetery chapel. The service is dignified. I will honour him.

I shovel soil on to the wooden box. Three thuds: 'I honour you, Papi. I tried to love you. Good bye.'

The police have sent a Guard of Honour. The uniformed officers click the heels of their black shoes and salute over the open grave.

I had not seen much of my cousin over the years. Now we are sitting in her house, reminiscing over apple cake and *Käsekuchen*. Karin was not born when her eight-year old sister with our grandmother had died together in the air raid shelter. She married Lothar, a high ranking police officer. He is a big man and his eyes fill with tears as he speaks about my father.

"As young cadets we all looked up to him," he recalls. "There was nothing he did not know about driving and vehicle maintenance. We loved his lectures. He sometimes mentioned you, his daughter."

"When we were troubled or needed to make decisions, we always went to see him," Karin adds. "Onkel Hein was always wise and helped us. I miss him." She wipes her eyes.

"He has always been quite somebody!" is Lothar's epitaph.

And I never knew.

9

Deep ploughing

God's plough gets to work soon after my father's death. The ploughshare is set low, churning over the green pasture, breaking up the familiar ground. Furrow by furrow. It lifts to the surface emotions I only know by their designation. Concealed in the muddy clods, it is not evident whether the finds will turn out to be treasures or treacherous bombs. If they are the latter, will I defuse them or will they detonate?

The doorbell rings and I make out two silhouettes.

"Meet Brian," says my friend John and pushes a young man towards me. "He needs to talk with you. I'll pick him up in half an hour's time".

Brian of slight build, a little bent, his hair unkempt. His watery pale eyes stare into the hallway, vacant, do not engage with me.

He is schizophrenic," John whispers, turns and disappears down the drive.

"Come in, Brian." I hold the door to the living room open. Awkward and limp like an uprooted plant, he follows my invitation, all the while wringing his hands. Slowly he lowers himself on to the edge of the armchair. He looks in my direction but his eyes do not meet with mine. He is a *something* in the room, flaccid and rigid simultaneously.

I have to start somewhere to make contact.

"Where do you live, Brian?" A monotone voice gives me an address: a small flat close to his parents' home. He is twenty years old and has never had a job.

"What would you like to do, if you could?"

Does his face brighten a little? "I would do an O-level in English." His answer is slurred, without the slightest inflection.

"You would." I try to disguise my surprise. "That's achievable, isn't it?"

As together we weigh up the practical possibilities, life seems to flow into him. He becomes quite animated. There is hope for this young man! Half an hour later the doorbell interrupts our conversation. John is back. Brian rises stiffly, shakes my hand limply and shuffles out on to the drive.

"Will I see you again?" I call after him. He nods.

How does he live? I want to know. A few days before Christmas I take a small present to him in his flat. Then the frantic season swallows my time. There are moments when Brian creeps into my mind and I wonder how he is doing. He will be with his parents. Now we have slipped into January. I am changing sheets when I hear Peter's footsteps on the stairs. Gently he opens the bedroom door.

"I have news for you. Sad news."

"What is it?"

"Brian is dead."

Ice packs around my heart. I begin to tremble, then shake violently and slip down on to the edge of the bed to steady myself.

"Dead?"

"They have just found him?"

"*Found* him? Where?"

"In his flat. He'd been dead three weeks, when they broke the door down."

Now it is white *heat* coursing through me. A cold burning.

"He took his life just before Christmas. Took an overdose."

"You mean, *nobody* missed him through the whole of the Christmas period?!"

"It seems not."

I rise from the bed – in slow motion. The room is spinning. Peter, the furniture, all becomes blurred. I grab a pillow – crunch it – wring it – throw it – trample it. I seem to have no words, only shrieks. I murder a second pillow. I want to destroy the bed, the room, I…I want to strangle the church, the whole world! Peter tries to hold me, to still me, but I wrench myself free and scream and stamp until my vision returns and I can see my husband, his arms hanging helplessly, the mangled pillow, the chaos I have caused! I slump on to the crumpled sheet and cry, "Where *is* that healing community?"

Brian is to be cremated. The chill wind makes me shiver as we wait amongst faded flowers and dishevelled wreaths. But the sun is shining in a clear winter sky and Brian's parents are easy to spot. They are not crying. They shake hands with the small group of mourners, mainly carers and nurses, and us.

I need to get back to the room where Peter had broken the news. In the stillness I can now name the powerful feeling that had threatened to consume me: rage. *Why* this murderous rage? Where does it come from? Is it the tragedy of this unnecessary death? This young man's unfulfilled dreams and potential? The injustice of it all? Yes, all of these. Suddenly I know the trigger. Brian had been abandoned.

The plough had unearthed a bomb and it had exploded. It had stayed hidden in the depth of my being. How long had it been buried there?

I have to write something.

In memoriam

Angular, awkward,
slow your gait,
slurred your speech,
you stood on my doorstep,

not of your own accord,
no: brought and dumped.
"Do something with him."
Do what?

Your eyes disturbed me.
I could not see *you*.
But a cavern
An empty nowhere nothingness.

It was *you* I wanted
to meet, to spur you on.
It would take time…
Time we did not have.

You caged in your solitude,
I trapped with my multitude.
Alone – both of us,
Helpless? That, too.

You died – alone,
Forgotten, left in the cold,
While I fanned the
family fire.

You were not my son but I
fostered you – just for Advent.
Abandoned! I rage.
Someone says,

"Welcome home, my boy."
You *there*. I *here*.
Two droplets
in God's waterfall.

Spring and summer have passed; autumn is shortening the days. My heavy cold is a good excuse to go to bed early. I close the curtains. The bedside lamp sheds a cosy glow. Before I tuck myself under the mound of German duck-down, I must dust my dressing table and buff its shiny surface. The mirror reflects my favourite vase, Peter's very first Christmas present to me: Swedish crystal; U-shaped; filled with the year's last roses. The scent is lovely. I shall need to light a candle and I want music. The choice of tape is quickly made. Harmonies and German lyrics enfold me, as soft as my duvet. A violin dances through the gaps left by the voices. I know Thomas, the bass, and Emanuel, the tenor, the altos and Erica's crystal soprano. They are my Swiss friends. At first I trace the paths the different parts travel, but then I allow the music simply to wash over me. I suspend thinking, analysis and memory. Indescribable well-being floods me. I drink in order and peace and beauty. Heaven…

The doorbell rings and I recognise Nicky's voice in the hallway. She slips into the room.

"Do you mind if I come in and see the invalid?"

"Hi. Nice to see you." I move my duvet-swaddled feet to the side and pat the mattress for her to sit down. The music stops but its echoes linger in the room. The chatter begins and my visitor releases her usual quantum of dreams and visions and Scripture verses she has scribbled down for me. I listen politely but find myself transported somewhere else. It seems that the music has opened a gate. The German words reverberate…

…a slight tremor. It starts in my feet, creeps up my calves. My knees are trembling. Something is lodging in the pit of my stomach. I am shaking all over now and the walls of the room are bearing down on me. An iron ring is squeezing my chest. I am being strangled! Nicky is watching my blanched face. I am no longer aware of her.

"What's the matter?" I can hear her words but cannot form my own, caged as I am inside a powerful nameless emotion.

"What's the matter?! Where are you?"

Where am I? I don't know. I don't know. Please, someone help me! Nicky feels torn between staying with me and fetching Peter. In the event she does not abandon me. Slowly, slowly I am being released to name the feeling that had taken me over.

"That was terror!" I say, exhausted.

"What was terrifying? Could you see anything?"

"At first it was all dark, and then I saw a tiny meadow... a green triangle...and my dolls..."

"Do you *know* such a place?"

"Yes... I think I do."

"Where have you seen it?"

"A...long way...away...a long time ago."

"Where?" she persists.

Now I know. "In a little village in East Prussia."

"How old were you?"

"Three or four."

"That would have been in the war?" she works out.

"Yes...but the *war* never harmed me."

The plough has unearthed the buried feelings of a little girl. From now on this Child will intrude into my adult life – with all her needs and emotions. She will no longer rest until I understand the language of these overwhelming feelings and the meaning of my insistent dreams. I had not been submerged under debris and dust after an air raid; I had buried *myself*, had split off from the formative period of my life. The unaccustomed rage and terror have torn the grey curtain, the ever-present backcloth of my inner life. Now that the veil is rent, I will have to walk through it, back into my past and all I had left behind. The green grassy triangle has become a marker. I have not yet faced my own abandonment nor the Child's emotional deprivation.

10

The enabler

There they are sitting in our living room, the two women, and what they are telling me with great seriousness is that people in the parish don't think that I am really "human"! What? Is this true? I want to be personable and I certainly want to be *human*. Could they pray with me, they ask. I feel somewhat reluctant, not least because I am aware that neither has managed to form a deep relationship with anyone. Nevertheless I give them permission, because what harm can it do? I shut my eyes and almost immediately see in an inner picture a woman in the apse of the church – behind a high glass panel. It is me, cocooned in a spiritual 'sanctuary' where I feel safe.

"Come out of your isolation," the two women urge. Do they know what they are asking of me? I will lose the security I have. But because I want to be obedient to God and because I want to be thought 'human', I decide to leave the safety of 'holiness' and step down into the congregation, to be one with the people. I have made a dangerous decision.

The long corridor in the local hospital displays a poster which reads CAREeR (with the second 'E' crossed out). Yes. That's me. That's my career: to care for people. This is my identity. Now I know where I am going. Years ago, someone had called me "a mother in Israel". How I had laughed then at the absurdity? Am I now to take this designation seriously? Aha, now I seem to understand: I am to be a mother figure for Christians. And when from the States a new therapeutic approach to abandonment and non-attachment in infancy is introduced, I feel confirmed in my calling. John and Paula Sandford advocate *reparenting*, i.e. substitute parenting of adults who had been deprived of adequate emotional nurture as children. And the glimmering wick, the dream of a therapeutic community, is also reignited.

My own recurring nightmares of railway stations and missed trains, of unfed and neglected babies now haunt me into the daylight hours as does a new dream: we bought a house, very dark and so cluttered with the former owner's possessions that there is no room left for our own.

In the particular Christian culture in which we are moving, 'words' and 'pictures' (from the Lord) abound. So it comes as no surprise when Dorothy, who lives in our village, tells me she has such a picture for me. The primitive pencil drawing she has made of her vision, however, amazes me. Harassed women in head-scarves and small children are pulling handcarts loaded high with belongings. They look like refugees from Eastern Europe. The scene is familiar. Dorothy knows nothing of my past. But *I* know.

"Mum, phone for you!" I push my chair back and jump up from the supper table.

"Hello, Denise…" Forty minutes later I leave Peter's study and rejoin the family for the dessert. In those forty minutes Denise has poured out her troubles, her anxieties, her complaints. She has whined and wept and aired her resentments: I have listened and empathized and encouraged. And from now on, nearly every evening around six o'clock the phone rings and the boys shout, "Mum, Denise…" and sigh as again I leave them to eat supper without me. Denise is unhappy living with Tom and Sarah. Relational conflicts in their home and the demands of her own professional life have worn her down. Denise is crying. She is always crying and declaring that she "cannot go on like this any longer". I hang on to the receiver until my ear burns and she has cried enough. It is up to me to find the solution for her unhappiness.

It is Saturday evening and she knows that Peter is away. On the phone a small voice. "I wondered whether I could come over tonight and play a game with the boys?"

I had looked forward to an evening with the boys myself, but since she has no children of her own, why shouldn't she enjoy being with ours? Denise deals the cards. The mantel clock shows midnight, the boys have gone to bed but Denise "would like some prayer". I am exhausted, but Denise is hurting, crying, needing. At one o'clock I offer her one of my nightdresses and make up the bed in the spare room.

"Your home is so conducive for my healing", she says over breakfast and spends the whole Sunday with us. Yet she is not feeling any better and looks as if she might be heading for a breakdown.

"You'd better come and stay with us for a while." Did I say that? I have not even discussed the possibility with Peter and the boys. But she will be an asset to the family, won't she?

"Well, at least the long phone calls will stop," Peter says with his mind already on tonight's Parochial Church Council meeting.

The spare room is filling up. Papers, books, clothes are strewn everywhere and, look, there is her dear little sewing basket and her flute and pot plants. Denise is making a home. What have I done? The new member of our family takes all and gives little. Since the question of a financial contribution was not raised at the onset, it is certainly not mentioned now. A heavy cloud shrouds me, growing inescapably denser with every day. Denise has taken sick leave and from now on all my spare moments are crammed with her sadnesses. A little talk here, a little prayer there, and always "another important-issue-has-come-up". The hugs she needs are getting longer and her tear-tap could do with a plumber. Why don't I tell myself the truth? We have a child-woman from a comfortable background living with us who still loves to be dependent. I am "a mother in Israel" and she and I play an elaborate game: I am convinced that when she has regressed back to babyhood, a new foundation can be laid on which to build a healthy and responsible life. Yes, that's how it will be! But in this game Denise appears to be always on the losing as well as on the winning side. How long will her healing take? My arms feel leaden, so heavy, that I can barely lift them. When I describe my symptoms to her, she is quick with her diagnosis: "You are mourning your father."

"I need to go to the cottage by myself for a day or two," I face Peter across his desk. "Could you manage without me?" Of course, no problem for him but for Denise it is. She will be left with some responsibility for the household and this is bound to interfere with her healing. I give her no choice. When *she* wants to take a "long break" and go on holiday abroad, we gladly take her to the airport. And I can lift my arms! I can swing them freely.

"We must detonate the bridge. She is not to come back."

"You bet."

Learnt our lesson? Far from it. We collect 'children in need'. Hurting people find their way to a church that is alive; even buy homes close-by. They buzz around the Vicarage like bees around blossoms: professionals in breakdown; the depressed and suicidal; addicts and those traumatized by life's events; those adorned with a necklace of psychiatric labels; victims of child sexual abuse and neglect. A kaleidoscope of human affliction. More and more serious issues come creeping up from under the 'floorboards' like the black rafter spiders in the curate's house long ago.

We hold many confidentialities; many secrets.

Around us grows an illusionary family, probably no less dysfunctional than their families of origin. Boundaries between professional and family life become blurred. The door to our home and family is always open. We deceive ourselves that we have become a therapeutic community, that our long-held dream of the local church as a city of refuge, asylum and sanctuary has come true. How we could do with a white-haired sage to guide us, challenge us, warn us – but where to find one? Clergy and their spouses generally have no objective supervisors. That I am getting more and more depleted is obvious to no one, least of all to me. Our children graciously accommodate the influx of needy people into their home. Peter and I often feel alone.

"Fiona's family is wonderful," a parishioner enthuses to me and I become curious to meet this Fiona and her wonderful family. When Peter has a vivid dream in which he is told that Fiona will work with him in the church and she invites us to dinner, the die is cast.

We meet a gregarious and talented woman, 'a big fish in a small pond'. The broccoli is cooked to perfection, but while she is serving us our hostess strikes me as somewhat preoccupied, as if something is sapping her energy. After dinner over coffee she confides in me that she is "near a breakdown". My lights are flashing: I have a task in front of me. Fiona clearly needs to come into the Vicarage for a rest. Sometimes I creep into her room when she is asleep, crouch by her bed and pray for her recovery. How precious and vulnerable she looks. When her laughter peals from the spare room at something funny she is reading it makes me happy. When on her return to her family she feels worse, I am disappointed. And when she releases to me her long-held secret, it shocks me more than I dare to admit.

How can *a woman* have done this to her? *Female sexual abuse* – who has ever heard of such a thing? Fiona swears me to silence. Child sexual abuse is still a taboo subject. No law has been passed to protect children; no directives are given; as yet I have seen no books published that deal which such an issue; child witnesses are not readily believed. Such secrets are kept hidden but I have been handed such a secret and have been forbidden to expose it. The door to justice is firmly locked.

Only the door of mercy stands ajar. I decide to go through it and walk alongside Fiona into her healing from abuse. An image appears before my inner eye: a hook tearing into bloody meat; a flesh hook. I disregard the warning but commit myself to my self-appointed task with renewed determination. In fact, I become more and more obsessed with her healing; I want to see this young mother restored to her "wonderful family". But something has happened to me. It has a name. I do not know that name nor do I perceive that my condition requires objective intervention. I have been *vicariously traumatised*. Instead of looking for appropriate support for myself (where would I find it?), I set myself to do all in my power to see Fiona free. But *she* knows what is best for her...

"May I have your wife, Peter? I *need* her for my healing." Peter, feeling safe in our marriage, 'gives me away'. She looks elated and I pay no attention to my disquiet.

Her depression deepens. She speaks of feeling trapped in a narrow place, unable to escape from her emotional imprisonment. I decide to descend into her cage. Still the woman in her past is holding her captive in the present. Why is Fiona so fiercely protecting her? Why? I figure that she must *love* her. An idea forms. I am convinced by some logic that one cannot love *two* people at the same time and devise a plan that I am sure will work therapeutically. It is a risk I am about to take and I feel scared.

"You are allowed to fall in love with *me*," I offer her. Now *she* looks scared.

When Fiona appears to sink yet deeper into depression, I know what I must do: I need to take her away for a rest, away from all her responsibilities, away from the triggers, into a beautiful world I know. High in the mountains nestles a cluster of chalets and I have had an invitation to bring my family for a holiday. So I gather from the church a small group of people whom I consider in need of refreshment and take them up into that magnificent mountain world – and enter a drama which revolves particularly around three women.

11

Mountain ridges, mountain valleys

On the last leg of the journey our train snakes upwards and a new grand vista opens at every bend. Slate-grey walls end raggedly in a deep blue sky and the meadows are dotted with picture-book chalets. While such glory unfolds outside the window, inwardly I am worried and trying hard not to show it. How will I manage? The women and I are alone in the compartment. I vaguely hear Laura relating an incident from a story she has just read. I catch the one phrase:

"…then she had her heart ripped out…"

"What a bloody mess!" Pauline remarks with a serious face. Fiona is convulsed and then the other two burst into hysterical laughter. Pauline rolls off the wooden seat and writhes on the carriage floor. Such loss of emotional control! 'Insecure children,' I think, 'and I have brought them here to be healed'. But in these frenzied minutes I sense that all authority has been wrested from me. The sun turns the peaks blood-red. The summer is burning itself out.

"We have arrived, folks." I try to sound cheery and relaxed.

"Have we?" There is defiance in Fiona's voice. For a brief moment she looks at me; then averts her eyes.

On reaching our goal I am told that our group has been split up between two chalets. Fiona decides to be with Laura and Pauline is to share a room with me. During the first night my overstuffed duvet feels too short and is weighing heavily on top of my weary body. The church clocks strikes every quarter. What have I done?

In the morning Fiona suggests a climb to the waterfall which is clearly visible from the dining room. Good idea. Over root and rock we clamber towards the white wall of water roaring from a great height; the noise drowns our chatter and banter. Fiona and Pauline dare each other and move perilously close to the torrent. Laura is standing back. I think she is afraid – and possibly in pain. If only I could be a droplet in this cascade and simply be absorbed.

In the cool of the evening we climb to a shepherd's hut – again Fiona's decision. She decides most things these days. The mountain crags are aglow. Under the single window is fixed a small wooden bench. There is something familiar about it. What is it? Sun-warmed rocks lie strewn in the grass and we each find our own to sit on. The silence that hangs heavy between us is not only due to the majesty around. We all sense the tension. My responsibility for these women threatens to crush me. Please, I want to go home. All of a sudden the glass cracks and shatters. No, look, the window is not broken but the sound of splintering glass is very real. Something within me has splintered! The jagged shards hurt. Fiona has noticed.

Each day, minute by minute, my attention is divided between 'my charges'. From my balcony I watch with alarm how Laura is limping along the path by herself, a white shawl shrouding her head against the sun. Is she not acting strangely? Something is wrong. I race down the slope to catch up with her.

"How are you?" I am trying to recover my breath and she is too disturbed to answer.

"Are you sleeping alright?" She shakes her head. Gently I take her arm, steer her towards the chalet and open the door to her room. Has there been a burglary? Bedding, books and clothes are scattered everywhere. I hide my shock.

"Get into bed, Laura. I'll do a bit of tidying while you get some rest." I pick up the duvet and the pillow with which she covers her head. Soon her books are safely back on the shelf. I fold up her clothes. When I think that all is peaceful, she suddenly sits up and with fists clenched, beats the wooden panelling. The drumming continues until I prise her fists open and can hold her hands in mine. If this is a psychotic episode, then who is there to help us? I speak to her slowly and calmly until she finds release in tearless sobs.

"Can we go for a walk? Just the two of us."

"Yes, Pauline, of course." I lay down my book. I have read no more than two pages and cannot concentrate anyway. We set off briskly; it is strenuous to keep up with the young one. Our conversation is stilted at first. I can barely hear her; her voice almost a whisper. Soon the beauty all around us relaxes us. "I am like a polo mint inside," she says.

"That empty?" How can she be filled?

The valley has filled with engine noise which the mountains echo back and forth. A loud harsh rattle – very close. Instinctively we start to run. A helicopter swings low and hovers above the chalets. A red cross is clearly visible. There must have been an accident! Someone is injured. Or worse? Laura? My lungs ache. Pauline outruns me. A stretcher is being winched up.

"Laura! Laura! Laura!" I scream.

The air ambulance disappears into the valley and the watching crowd disperses.

"Did you call me?" Laura touches my arm. "You thought it was me, didn't you?"

"Am I glad to see you!" I squeeze her hand hard. Fiona is watching.

"What happened?" Now I dare to ask.

"It's one of the staff. I noticed they were giving her oxygen. I have such a strange feeling about her." At lunch the atmosphere in the dining room is subdued but outside the air feels good. The ancient rocks stand high and solid and from the flowerbed below wafts sweetness.

In the far corner of the terrace Fiona lies stretched out in a deck-chair, reading. Huge sunglasses shield her from the world. And from herself? I really should go and ask how she is.

"Do you mind if I sit with you?"

"No, do."

I ask inane questions which Fiona answers politely, never once taking her eyes off the panorama. How can I break into this fortress? Will she ever let down her drawbridge?

A new morning promises glory. "Let's all go down to the wooden bridge and play Pooh Sticks." It is Fiona's idea, but I lead the way. Intent faces drape across the sun-bleached railings. Our twigs get entangled and diverted from their course.

"The water is too turbulent. Let's go on." I say, still in charge, happy to see us all so relaxed with each another. Fiona points up to a low rocky outcrop, surrounded by young spruces and we scramble up the scree. A green velvety blanket woven from moss and soft grass covers the rock. Butterflies we do not know flit between flowers we cannot name. The late summer air is heavy and intoxicating. Jagged walls like ziggurats stand naked against the sky. We choose our own place on the warm matting. Fiona slips between Laura and me. She begins to sing and when her rich soprano soars, I weave, timidly at first, my alto voice with hers, gaining confidence all the while. Our duet draws in the others and soon "the hills are alive with the sound..." of worship. Even Pauline, who believes herself to be tone-deaf, cradled here in this accepting group, begins to sing as she has never sung before. This is how I have always wanted it to be! A healing environment, full of beauty and harmony, open to God. I feel elated and Fiona opens her arms wide and clasps Laura's and my shoulders. Her bare flesh feels warm and I melt into it. I close my eyes. Heaven itself is holding me, enveloping me in peace. Oh, that this would never end.

It has to. I glance at my wrist. "Hey folks, we'll be late for lunch!"

Slowly, as if waking from a dream, I rise, brushing the grass off my skirt. Fiona is the first to slither down the scree and I follow close behind her. Before we reach the bridge – I have shrunk to the size of a child. In the short shadow Fiona casts, trots a very small 'I'.

And in the dining room, humming with animated voices, there now sits a Child at the table, demure and silent, poking at the contents of her plate, heaping the mashed potato into a castle and in the 'moat' flows the gravy.

"I need to do some shopping. Who's coming with me?" Fiona's voice rings strong. We all go. A Child stomps into the village, in boots too big for her. All the while she wants to stop and be hugged. In the grocery shop, so familiar a few days ago, I can no longer find my bearings. Fiona has to point to the crate I am looking for. I pay for my apples and rush outside. What is happening to me? Neither the effort of the steep climb back to the chalet nor the cool breeze has the power to bring 'me' back to 'myself'. The silver crags of the morning have turned to pewter; on me they bear down like lead. We pant up the incline, walking in pairs; Fiona stays close by my side and does all the talking. I need her to do so. Does she know that her listener is a five year old? The night's sleep brings me back into the adult.

Soon after our arrival I had explored the chalets on my own and had found myself outside tall wooden doors. They opened into a chapel: high-roofed; pine-panelled; beautiful in its simplicity. Tall windows invited mountains and trees into the space. Honey-coloured pews were arranged in a V-form, and at the front of the chapel gleamed a wooden table, supporting a single container aflame with summer flowers. In Gothic script a verse from the Psalms: painted in red and gold across the wall above the table. The sun had turned the room to gold.

I need to tell the others about my discovery, this jewel of a sanctuary, and I will have to seek permission for us to use it for ourselves. And when our group enters, a hush falls. Laura strokes the smooth polished pews. From now on every day the lofty room fills with our singing; it divides into a delta of harmonies; I sing an alto line I have never learnt; forget the others; forget myself; am transported…a soft hand rests on my shoulder.

"I just *had* to come to the singing," whispers Fiona.

Laura has always longed to dance. Now she is holding hands with the others and they dance around the altar-table. I could burst with happiness to see this.

One morning Fiona jumps up from the breakfast table. As she passes me, she hisses, "I am *so angry*." Oh, so she does have feelings! Good. I leave my coffee and run after her up the path to find her kicking stones; her knuckles white.

"What's up?" I pant.

"I don't know! I am absolutely bursting!" She kicks a large rock and sends up clouds of dust.

"Don't do that. Don't hurt yourself."

Fuelled by rage she charges off. I must stay with her. By the time we reach the open meadow she is calmer.

"Let's sit down here," I point to a tree trunk. Butterflies dance, bees hang on open flowers. Cowbells tinkle close by.

"I love you," she says, not looking at me. I feel a shock wave passing through me, a bolt of fright and delicious excitement.

She loves me. She loves me! sings the Child.

Good, finally we have transference, exults the would-be therapist.

This is scary, winces the adult.

The morning has lost its innocence. Shadows race across the mountain, carrying a sense of foreboding. But the Child within dances: She loves me. She loves me. She loves me.

Steam rises from a huge cauldron. The valley boils, brewing a grey soup into which mountains and trees and houses are being stirred.

"Pauline has gone," Laura tells me calmly but I detect her alarm.

"Gone where?" I make my voice sound light.

"Don't know. She just said, 'I'm going' and disappeared into the fog."

"She'll be back soon, she won't go far."

"She'll be lost in minutes in this." Fiona has overheard and pushes me to take responsibility.

"In which direction did she go?"

"Difficult to say."

"We must go and find her," urges Fiona.

It is *I* who must take charge. Firmly I say, "That wouldn't help. We'd all get lost."

"She could miss her footing and fall down a ravine," Fiona warns.

"We'll have to *trust* that she will be kept safe. Let's go into the chapel and ask for her protection. Let's sing as we always do. She'll be back, you'll see." Inwardly I am shaking but resolutely lead the way. This is absurd...you should be out there in the mist, looking for her...you are being irresponsible...

"Don't you think we should alert Mountain Rescue?" Fiona' eyes pierce mine.

Our golden room has turned grey. The summer flowers have been removed from the altar. When I switch on the lights we feel a little better but our singing sounds turgid. My own voice feels unsteady as my throat is constricted by fear. We take it in turns to pray for Pauline's safe return. And after a while our voices blend as they had always done. I close my eyes and allow myself to be carried on the harmonies as if floating. From deep inside me I 'see' a flower growing: ever taller and stronger. What am I watching? Dimly I perceive that it is my *soul* coming to life! When I open my eyes, the chapel is beautiful and there – in the doorframe – stands Pauline: her hair dripping; her clothes clinging to her shivering body; her face white as chalk.

"Pauline! Where have you been?" We cluster around her. Her hands are ice-cold. I gratefully hug her sodden frame. "Oh you are back! Thank God, you are back!"

Upstairs we help her change into dry clothes. Laura brings blankets and wraps her. Pauline is shaking but a smile plays around her lips. We wait until she can speak.

"A black dog…led me back here. I had just decided not to top myself. I wanted to come back to you. But I didn't know where I was. Then this dog appeared out of nowhere. It walked steadily and I followed it until I recognized the chalet."

"Where is the dog now?"

"I don't know. As soon as I reached the house, it disappeared into the mist. It just went. " Her mischievous grin is back and her cheeks are rosy.

"You've got to do something about Laura," Fiona keeps urging me. "She has not slept for three nights now. You've no idea how restless she is. She just wanders about in her room. Then at times she acts really odd. I am worried about her."

"I think we need to let things take their course," I say calmly though I do not feel at ease. Stress and lack of sleep can trigger psychosis. I know that.

It is dark when I knock at Laura's door. No answer. I turn on the light. Laura is staring into the chaos she has again created.

"How are you?"

"Terrible. I am caged in. There are bars across the window and the door is locked."

I thrust open door and window. A cool breeze rushes in, leafing through her scattered notebooks.

"There are no bars now, see? You are not in hospital. Would you like to go for a walk?"

"I want to throw myself off a cliff." I feel her despair.

"Come on, let's walk a bit." Am I not taking a huge risk? Should I not rather put her to bed? Can I really handle this? It's dangerous to be outside. Laura tries to pull her hand out of mine. I grip it more tightly. She tries to shake herself loose but I manage to hold on. *I need help.* The deep purple sky is crowded with lights.

"Look up, Laura! Look up into that sky. It's endless and it's not black."

Her head tilts back. "Abraham would have seen the same stars," she murmurs, "and...he was...given a...vision..."

"Yes, yes, that's right, Laura. And there is a future and a hope for you, too!"

We stand silently beneath the star-spangled canopy. Her damp face is leaning against my cheek. The first tears! The air has grown cold when I take her back to her chalet. I know she will be safe.

"Let's take the cable car up this afternoon. A path runs to a river." Fiona has already perused the map and enquired the times of the *Gondelbahn*'s ascents and descents. Donned with rucksacks, shod with hiking boots, we climb into the red bubble. The cows shrink to toy size. We glide above the mighty spruces and the world falls silent except for the whirring of the cables. Our world is contained in a tiny cabin. High rock faces drift by. Pauline is clutching her seat, her knuckles white, and she keeps her eyes glued to her boots. Fiona's face is aglow. The red capsule becomes a glasshouse.

It is wonderful to inhale the thin still air up here. Someone produces a carton of cherry juice. As I push in the straw, the red liquid spills on to my white T-shirt. Everyone laughs and the Child feels burning shame. An indelible red stain...blood...a bloody mess...

Laura and Pauline have brought pads and pencils, prepared to sketch the mountains, and have ensconced themselves on a shady mossy hillock. The broad shady path to the river is clearly marked. Fiona and I start our walk.

"We will be back in time for the last descent," I shout and feel strangely liberated as I stomp along, happy to be alone with Fiona. My new hiking boots rub against my ankles. The wind carries the scent of the spruces. They become ever smaller, ever sparser as we climb, and we are learning about each other's lives.

"The river is further away than I thought," Fiona says. I don't mind. The trees have stopped altogether now and a wide vista opens before us; bleached rocks lie scattered amongst the gravel. And there – the mountain stream glistens under a low sun. The anxiety I feel, I dismiss immediately. Of course we will be back in time. It is hard going through this rough and dazzling terrain. My hiking boots keep rubbing against my ankles. I try not to feel the pain. When we reach the river we are as excited as if we had reached the North Pole. We are alone. The slanting sun transforms the clear waters into liquid silver. Fiona pulls her boots and socks off and plunges her feet into the fast flow. When *my* bright red socks are shed, my ankles are covered in angry pink blotches and I have several blisters on my feet. The icy water numbs the pain and we are hypnotised, suspended in time.

"Are you glad that we are here?" I dare to ask.

"Yes. This is bliss." Fiona's face is upturned, her eyes closed. She has taken off her dark glasses.

"Do you miss your family?" I ask, hoping for a negative answer to ease my own guilty feeling about having wrenched her away from them.

"I do a bit," Fiona says, "but not so much when I am with you. Wouldn't it be wonderful if we were all of the same family? A community where you share everything...?"

This is music to my ears. "Sounds like the early church..." I say.

"It could be the present church..."

"Mm. Do you know, I have always dreamt of such a community. The church as a healing community. So far it has never really worked out and I've always been disappointed."

"Maybe this time. Are we not living it in miniature here? We could ignite such love back in England...in the church...the parish...the village..."

Ideas tumble out and the sun is sinking. Reluctantly we put on socks and boots. Fiona pulls me up and we hurry along the darkening path. Our artists are waving frantically. The *Gondelbahn* has already returned to the valley – on time. Empty.

Pauline is angry. "Where have you *been?*"

"By the river. It was wonderful!" I can't believe I have been that irresponsible.

"I am very sorry but we shall have to foot it," I say cheerfully. The path falls away steeply.

"I can't make it!"

"We'll help you down, Laura. Hook your arms around our necks." Fiona organizes the descent. "Pauline, you go that side, I'll take Laura's weight."

I am not assigned any responsibility. My ankles throb. Every step on the near vertical path is agony. Pauline is telling jokes at which we all laugh excessively. Fiona begins a song, and breathlessly we join in. Frequently the bearers have to take a rest. I insist on taking over from Pauline. How good it feels when Fiona and I half-carry our friend together! The sun has disappeared behind the summits and dusk is falling when the roof tops of the chalets come into view. Of course, we have missed supper.

Fiona gently helps me out of my boots. "Ouch!" My ankles are on fire; friction has burnt crimson patches from foot to calf. She fills a bowl with tepid water, bathes and dries my feet with a tenderness that touches me deeply. "Greater love has no one..." Laura produces a soothing lotion which Fiona applies. Then we share, divide and sacrifice the snacks we had hoarded. The healing community is starting right here. I am convinced that this small 'pebble' will cause every-increasing rings in a bigger pond. The love we share must be contagious.

"We have not been up on the chairlift," says Fiona.

"I am *scared* of heights," Pauline objects.

"We could pray for your fear to go." I must not lose sight of the *purpose* of our time here: it is for healing. Eyes closed, Laura and I lay our hands on Pauline's soft hair. A warm fleshy arm curls itself around my waist. Fiona had crawled across the parquet and is now clinging to me. I feel scared but do not shake her off.

"Now let's see how you fare, Pauline? I'll travel with you in the chairlift." We fasten our safety chains and settle ourselves under the blankets provided. There is a metallic clatter and then we swing upwards into silence.

"Look at the mountains all around. Don't look down."

"How lovely!" she cries. "Oh, it's awesome!" At the terminal, as if to demonstrate to us her new-found freedom, she scampers along the ridge like a mountain goat.

We follow a little more sedately. Laura cautiously lowers herself on to a grassy patch amongst rocks. Fiona and I join her. How the subject started I do not know, but we are analysing the difference between self-acceptance and self-esteem.

"You have got to be *yourself*," Fiona lectures Laura.

"And what exactly does that mean, may I ask? Do you know what you are talking about?" Laura is angry and rams her foot against the nearest boulder. It starts to roll! We watch it gather momentum... faster...faster... oh gosh... It hits the flank of a chocolate-brown cow... and lies still. We hold our breath... The cow continues to graze unperturbed.

The slow descent in the chairlift does not cause Pauline anxiety either. From the station we amble towards the village.

"Don't you ever get tired? I mean, tired of life?" Pauline asks.

"Oh no. Life is so good."

"Of course, you have a family."

"Yes, but that is not the only reason why I think that life is good. I see it as a gift. I mean, look where we are right now." I stop walking. "Isn't this paradise?" And while I am drinking in the beauty *I* become aware – ever so faintly – of a gnawing painful loneliness. It is as if I have been left behind...somewhere... For a brief moment I am the Child again, but then the adult 'me' points to the café.

"We deserve an *Eiskaffee*, don't you think?" Huge chalices of ice cream floating in coffee appear on the red-and-white gingham table cloth, each topped with a Matterhorn of whipped cream. We slurp like naughty children.

Two long weeks are drawing to a close and I feel spent. But it is essential to end this time together peacefully and positively. How? My mind is refusing to plan; my imagination has taken a break; my emotions are muffled by cotton-wool; my body is craving sleep. The would-be therapist congratulates herself on work done well. The Child just wants to pick flowers.

"How do you want to spend the last evening?" I ask as I know I must.

"We'll have a feast, shall we?" Pauline suggests.

"We'll sing." That's what Fiona does best.

"…and pray!" Laura dreads going home.

"I am just going to say 'good-bye' to Ruth," I say.

When I arrive at the manager's office, Ruth is still engaged. While I wait, I leaf through a book of fine charcoal sketches of the area and my attention is captured: "Our life today stands under the dictate of powerful dangerous influences that threaten to alienate man from himself," I read in the foreword.

Ruth's face lights up when she sees me. "I suppose you have come to say good-bye. I shall miss you. You have brought life into this mausoleum and I know how much you have enjoyed our wonderful chapel."

"I hope we weren't too much of a nuisance. Things have not always been easy. We are leaving tomorrow morning early. Just one more night to go…"

"You're glad it's over?"

"Yes, I am quite looking forward to shedding the responsibility."

"You've looked after them well."

"It was successful," says the would-be therapist. "How is the lady who was taken to hospital?"

"It is not the first time she has tried to take her life," Ruth sighs. "Tomorrow she will back with us and we shall have to watch her more closely."

"I wonder why she wants to kill herself?"

"She feels caged here. It is all service. Serving others. All the time. We all do it. We do not give any heed to *just being*. If not in theory, in practice we live by the Rule of St Francis: we labour, do not ask for any reward and do not count the cost, as Jesus said we should."

"I suppose, that's what I am doing. I serve others but fail to give enough time and care to myself."

"You need to remedy that," she smiles.

I hold out my hand. "Thank you for everything," says the adult.

"I want my Mummy," whines the Child.

Peals of laughter are ringing from the chalet. Cushions are spread on the floor and a banquet laid out. I feel thankful. It really has worked...it's turned out well after all...

Banter flies back and forth as we feast. Pauline is shaking.

"I am frightened." Her voice is barely audible.

"Of what?"

"Don't know."

"You'd better calm her." I obey Fiona and hold the shaking child-woman but the Child longs to be in Pauline's place.

That last night I sleep fitfully. I must not miss the alarm. Every time I wake an owl hoots and Pauline stirs restlessly. The dining room is only partly lit; mountains, spruces and waterfall are still shrouded in darkness. Breakfast is lovingly set out for us but we barely touch it. Our luggage is waiting for us at the station. We walk unencumbered – in single file: neither connected nor entirely free. I bring up the rear, feeling very old. I stagger like a drunk. I feel cold. The summer has burnt itself out.

The stars look down.

12

Depersonalisation

Our shared experience of worship and mutual caring does not touch the church back home as we had hoped and our dream of a healing community remains – a dream. Fiona and I meet on occasions. Today we have planned to walk in a beautiful river valley and somewhere there Fiona wants to read to me. The rain has washed the limestone crags and strewn silver on to the dry-stone walls. Steam is rising from the tarmac like windblown tattered veils.

"I'll get the parking ticket," I hear myself say, extracting my rubber boots from the sea of sweet wrappers.

"No, I'll get it," says Fiona. And although I am adamant, she insists on pushing coins into my jacket pocket. The dispenser seems miles away. Right foot…left foot… The sun reflects off the asphalt and dazzles me; the air smells of wet earth; gusts of wind blow my hair into my eyes and balloon my long muslin skirt. Waddle. Waddle. I waddle like a duck. I try to put spring into my steps. I swirl my skirt; it brushes against my calves and that feels good. I am young…I am playful…I am clumsy…I am old… my feet are made of lead…she is watching me…I feel exposed.

Faced with the ticket dispenser, I panic. I struggle to make sense of the instructions. The sun reflects off the metal. I fumble for the coins. Which buttons? Which slots? To my surprise and relief the machine spews out a white slip of paper. Now back to the car...look carefree...swing your hips...the colours of my skirt are merging ... how lovely ...

Fiona is not looking up as I approach the car. All her attention is focussed on dragging her boots over thick grey-mottled socks. Perhaps she hasn't been watching me at all. Did I want her to? I lift the wiper and snap it down on the ticket. Not such a big deal, was it? Keep your voice steady and don't cry. Fiona removes the ticket and puts it on the dashboard.

"Shall we take the thermos?" I ask.

"No. We'll have our coffee when we get back to the car. Don't fancy carrying all that stuff." There is no argument. I am tuned to her every movement, to the nuances in her voice, the slightest expression on her face, the look in her eyes. My own words and my behaviours I also subject to scrutiny. Fiona slips her book into a small rucksack and I watch how she swings it over one shoulder; the way she hooks her powerful arms through the looped straps. There was no point in offering to carry it, I know, because she is the strong one, the one who cares for me. A fine mist still hovers above the surface when she takes my hand. When we get to the first stile, I let go and I thread myself through the narrow opening, close behind her. We begin our descent into the green bowl of the river valley.

Countless hikers before us have polished the rocks that stud the footpath and the recent rain has made them slippery. Walk carefully and stay in her shadow. I no longer swing my hips but the brambles grab fiercely at my skirt. I am grateful I can walk unobserved. The next wooden stile is high and Fiona offers her hand to help me over. Her hand and smile are warm.

The splashing and gurgling of the weir sound closer. Glistening branches bend over the river. Birds are giving a springtime concert. Our shoulders touch as from the little wooden bridge we watch the cascading waters: twirling ballerinas, performing complicated dance patterns, leaping, catching crystals...

...a teenage girl in a Sixth Form blazer is standing on the bridge. Who's that? It is me! Don't be silly! You have never worn an English school uniform. *But I am wearing one!* You've not gone to school in England. *But I am a Sixth Former.* No, you are leaning over the handrail of a bridge watching a river fall over a weir... *Who is this? Who is me?*

Beyond the bridge the meadow opens wide and the rain has spangled it with a million diamonds. It is achingly beautiful. We are alone in all this glory. I touch my cheeks and am surprised that they are wet. They must be my tears. A tree trunk lies where a gale had felled it. I lean against its rough bark and a loud wailing emanates from that woman by the slain tree. With astonishment I watch dark patches on my blue jacket growing larger. Something uncontrollable is bursting from a great darkness within and its vehemence frightens me. I am afraid of myself! I am face to face with a stranger. I see Fiona. She can do nothing. Does she know that I have lost *myself*? Our walk had been planned to aid *her* healing. I was trying to help her to find *her* true identity, that, stolen from her when *she* was a school girl wearing a Sixth Form blazer. Now I am wearing her uniform. Have I become *her*?

A story floats into my mind of a man who had found a costume and mask in someone's deep wardrobe, had donned the attire and enjoyed his reflection in the mirror. But to his horror he was no longer recognizable, not even by himself...

I don't know anything anymore. I am going mad. Who will give me back My-Self?

"Shall we go on?" Fiona asks quietly.

Go on? Go where? She offers me her arm, I hook mine into hers and we rejoin the footpath. The little river, unimpeded now, runs happily down the valley. Along its course it has left a shallow bank of warm and dry sand. Fiona spreads out her anorak, takes the book from her rucksack and motions me to sit down. I hear her voice, but the words wash over me, finding no comprehension. All I want is to snuggle up to her and seek oblivion. The final sentence hangs in the air: "the mother, the child and the friend". There is no oblivion. I am confused: old enough to be her mother...supposed to be her friend...a child in need of succour and protection.

"I want to go home". I struggle to stand up, dust the sand from my skirt and automatically slip my arm back through hers. I walk in a daze.

I really need to see this woman who had captured Fiona's schoolgirl body and soul. How? I know where she works. Her organisation is holding an open meeting. I will go to the hall and get a good look at her. Nervously

I fidget on my chair. The officials file in. There she comes. She is fat. She swings her hips. She waddles. *Am I her as* well?

Psychological terminology helps me make sense of what is going on: over-identification with both victim and offender; substitution; depersonalization. This painful relationship with Fiona is threatening my sanity. I want to wear my own clothes ... I want to live in my own skin ... I want to be again the person I thought I knew.

13

Hope

In the small Alpine town of Altdorf on the southern shores of Lake Lucerne, near to the statue of Wilhelm Tell, the old barracks are hosting an exhibition of works by the Swiss sculptor Bettina Eichin. Grey stone steps, ground down by thousands of army boots, lead up into a rough loft where a soft glow greets the visitor: muted sunlight is reflected in dark copper-coloured bronzes. Fashioned in russet metal are tiny books, diaries, leaves and insects; collections in small showcases; the artist's own memorabilia. I sense my irritation at these objects: they are personal to *her* and so meaningless to *me*. I am about to leave, disappointed. Then I see *her*: a life-size sculpture of a woman, crouching, knees drawn up to the chin, her head cradled in her arms. Eichin has created her as one of *Nine Muses*. Like a river, issuing from the *Copper Woman* (as I come to call her), flows her long garment. I move towards the figure, stand close to her, fascinated. Her face is hidden, only the crown of her head is showing. She is no longer deeply asleep. Energy, dynamism, concentrated power emanate from her. I want to wait for her to wake. It will not be long now before she will lift that powerful head, slowly emerging from her inertia. She will be born. She will break out. Come forth. Be fully alive. And she will inspire and create. It is just a matter of time. The more I watch the sculpture, lit by the sunbeams piercing through dusty windows, the more hope is being fanned in my distraught deprived soul. I, too, shall lift my head.

In England dawn is breaking and promising a golden summer day. I am awake, and, unseen, I sneak into the wild garden I had once known as an ordered and fruitful space. Now it lies neglected and denuded of its fruit-bearing bushes. No annuals light the once stunning flowerbeds; the neat little lawn has grown into an untidy dandelion meadow. Old stone steps, now greened with moss, lead to the lower level of the garden. They are still cold from the night. The sun is rising and I am in pain.

On the other side of the brick wall live Patrick and Diane. Yesterday I had seen them, hugging mugs of coffee and discussing the next planting project in their beautiful garden. Our conversation had been so easy and natural, showing me that there lies outside my self-imposed prison another world, beyond the wall which I, the enabler, have built for myself. I glimpsed a new realm free of neediness and manipulation; a life-style other than parish and church. To live such a life! I had already taken a stand, had refused to be part of the church contingent who had travelled the country for a training weekend in someone else's parish. It had struck me as irrelevant and I had stayed behind, looking after some of the children. It had felt good to see that Patrick and Diane, although members of the church, had not joined the group either.

The stone step feels cold, but I want to sit down and think. My head rests in cupped hands. The rising sun slowly warms my bare arms and toes. I peruse the poor garden and feel sorry for it and for the previous owners who had lavished such care on it and had gathered a plentiful harvest. Why let it become such a mess?

Suddenly an explosion!

Not a detonation but a silent explosion of light. A tiny dew jewel had nestled against a blade of grass and in a moment the sun has woken it. The water droplet bursts into dazzling colours. A tiny rainbow! Emblem of promise. As I watch the tiny firework, my clouded thinking clears and I am able to make a decision. I will extricate myself from all this dysfunction around me and I shall heal. "By my God I will leap over the wall."

I muse that if anything is ever again to grow in the field of my life, the ploughed-up ground will have to be harrowed. Dormant as well as fresh seeds will have to be coaxed from the ground. To get out of the wasted years, I need a controlling purpose, some practical steps and just a few guidelines for action. I need direction from the past, guidance from the present and hope for the future.

In the afternoon the church group returns.

"How did it go, darling?" I ask Peter who looks tired rather than enervated.

"They were rather put out that I had come without you. They insisted that a vicar and his wife needed to work together."

"Indeed? And who gives them jurisdiction over us?"

"They had also wanted to prayer counsel me but I declined the offer and reminded them that it had been *us* who had taught them this ministry in the first place."

I had followed my inner leading and I had not been wrong.

"One man had a word for you. He said you would have a very special ministry." Oh, really?

Sometime I will tell Peter about the exploding jewel but not yet.

Later, much later, by the light of a candle over a meal for two, I share my discovery.

"You know," he says, gently caressing my hand, "when cows graze they twist their tongues around the blades and tear them. The blades feel very bruised indeed. Even when a scythe makes a clean cut, the grass is injured. And yet: when grass is mowed it gives off a wonderful fragrance and in turn it is given a new incentive to shoot up again into new life." My eyes fill up.

"Yes," I say, "the first dew drop has fallen on torn and bruised grass."

Meanwhile, church vision statements are rolling off the press and are debated like marketing strategies. Our time is eaten up by a multitude of meetings: large meetings, small meetings, early morning-prayer meetings, fellowship meetings, home meetings, strategy meetings, planning meetings, all humming with enthusiasm. But where are people's hearts? And where is healing for mine? No help is going to come to me through all these parish activities. Fiona and I book into an international conference on healing and deliverance.

Anxious and tense throughout, I try to subdue my conscience. The auditorium is packed for the evening lecture and our seats are in the centre of the row. Unexpectedly the speaker challenges our motives for being here. Terror grips my heart. The hall suddenly turns black. When I regain consciousness, both of us are led out and separated. In the corridor

I collapse again. No one brings a glass of water; no one thinks of taking me out into the fresh air.

"Should we get the paramedics?" I hear a voice say.

"No, she is under the judgement of God," replies another.

I do not know how long I lie there exposed in the corridor. Four faces are bent over me: a man and three women.

"Come to the small room over there," orders the man and one of the women supports me. I collapse again. Sick with terror I vomit. Steel-blue eyes bore into me; the man, a well-known musician rather than a counsellor, evidently has already been briefed: he interrogates me; does not connect with me; has no idea where I am. I cannot respond and I cannot correct his wrong assumptions.

It seems ages before I am released from the room. Fiona is waiting for me. On my behalf she asks for a woman counsellor. The steward looks at his watch. No, they have to clear the hall now. I take her arm and she threads me through the excited crowds to the entrance. I am grateful for the night breeze. On the way to our lodgings I spot a friend from Lee Abbey days and she, a nurse, recognises that I could do with some care. In her flat she invites me to rest on her bed. Thankfully I drink the hot tea she brews and feel better. But at night the terror again engulfs me. We choose not to return to the conference and leave for home. The drive is long and silent.

Terror has become my daily companion; everywhere, any time, it threatens to overwhelm me. In the local supermarket I am pushing the shopping trolley. By the delicatessen counter I feel myself sliding to the floor. Through the haze, out of the jumble of concerned voices, I hear someone ask,

"Are you all right to stand up?"

"I think so."

"Open the doors!" a woman calls to the shop assistants. The service doors are unbolted and a whoosh of cool air hits me. They bring a chair for me and a glass of cold water. The store manageress never leaves my side, all the while speaking softly and encouragingly, making little jokes until she has me smiling. When the faint has entirely worn off, she supports me to the car, settles me into my seat, carefully tucks my skirt in and gently closes the door.

Who do you think was neighbour to me?

My addiction to Fiona is not broken; rather her kindness and loyalty have re-cemented it. The 'flesh hook' I had seen in a warning vision is deeply imbedded. She still has power to rule my emotions, dominate my thinking and influence my plans. I want to see *her* healed and keep deluding myself with rational and spiritual explanations. I pen letters, sent and unsent, search for parallels in our backgrounds, try to make sense of this blissful/painful attachment, believe our basic issues to be congruent. It takes months and much courage to admit to myself that, through her transference and my substitution for her abuser, I have become emotionally dependent on her. And she on me.

At a teaching and healing seminar on gender-confusion I watch Fiona speak to one of the team. Evidently she is talking about me.

Then comes the dressing down.

"You as the older woman should know better," the young woman says sternly. "*You* have status. *You* have power." Have I really? That had never occurred to me. To the contrary, I had always felt the disempowered one in the relationship.

"You and your husband had better talk to our leader."

His room is small and stuffy and he half our age. I describe our situation as honestly as I can. He ignores me and turns to Peter, lectures him on his failing as pastor, husband and father and lays all responsibility for this mutual dependency on him. I am outraged. This is my husband you are laying into! This is my best friend. You don't know him at all. He is a good father and pastor. Why don't you talk to me? This situation is incongruous. But terror is stalking. Don't faint here, I tell myself. Not now. Fix your eyes on the roof tiles like you did in Papi's hospital room. You must stay conscious. I pray for wisdom. How do we get out of here? And suddenly I know.

"We will speak to our bishop," I say. My voice sounds firm and decisive. And at that we are allowed to leave. I wail even before we reach our room.

I have reached my nadir. I pick up the book I had brought with me because its title sums up my pain. I have a wounded heart and the author seems to understand.

During broken sleep I remember *Topsy*, our dog. Why could I not have learnt from watching her absurd behaviour, when she insisted on carrying her puppies by the scruff of their necks long after they had needed or wanted her maternal care? Funny. I smile into the dark and promise myself that I will lay down my assumed over-responsibility. Comforted, I go to sleep and wake just after sunrise. A beautiful morning beckons. Quietly I leave the house and as I round the corner of the building, I gasp. A crystal carpet! A glassy ocean! Dew: glistening; refracting; exploding. That dewdrop in the neglected garden, that single jewel has multiplied. Thousands upon thousands. Hope is rekindled. Joy and gratitude rise as I allow the damp grass to wet my shoes. I can still lead a fruitful life? Life will not flow from attachment figures, or from 'successful' ministries, or from acclaimed Christian 'heroes'. We are all fallible, however high our calling. Jesus is the only source of Life. The myriad of dewdrops on this fresh morning assure me that my long nightmare will come to an end. It is just a matter of time.

God's plough has reached the end of my field. It has come to rest facing the black rock face of *despair*, the place where helplessness and hopelessness converge and the only exit left is a cold desire for oblivion.

"I want to die. I want to die," I wail in Peter's study when he tries to work. Each time we go out in the car, I am hoping for an oncoming lorry to crush us.

No lorry does, but church members do. They throw fistfuls of discontent into the church. Letters of resignation are delivered under the cover of night, even on our day off. Now that the enabler has become herself disabled, well, let's go somewhere else. Fiona is the first to leave, and after her the church progressively empties. Friends abandon us. Every kind word, every sane conversation I encounter, I treasure for its rarity. We had laid down all extra-parochial work to commit ourselves entirely to the parishes and thereby cut off *outside* stimulation, encouragement and challenge to growth. I am left a prisoner in the parochial ministry and even in the Vicarage, bound by the silent vows of allegiance I had made at

Peter's ordination. Our marriage has become strained, as active attempts had been made to weaken it.

"You two are too strong together," I was told.

A black river is oozing through the villages, full of poison. It is flowing from home to home, engulfing Christians. Those we sought to help; those to whom we extended hospitality; those to whom we gave of ourselves, they inject yet more poison into that stream and no one understands its source or its nature and no one knows how to dam it. The dark waters propel sludge of rumour and slander. Accusations are levelled at us and outrageous stories circulate through the villages, continuing to pollute relationships and end long-standing friendships. I observe one of the Church Wardens circling around my car parked on a private drive, peering inside. What is he looking for? What new rumours does he want to start or feed? A prowling informer in our midst? Oh, what has become of this living and loving church community? Can anything be salvaged?

Why did I step out of my sanctuary? Why did I allow my personal boundaries to be broken? Why did I abandon myself in order to affirm and free others? There are bound to be reasons for it all and I need to discover them.

And then He allows some of us to fall more severely and distressingly than before – at least that is how we see it. And then it seems to us, who are always wise, that all we set our hands to is lost. But it is not so. We need to fall; we need to see that we have done so. For if we never fall we should not know how weak and pitiable we are in ourselves. Nor should we know the wonderful love of our Maker.

Julian of Norwich

14

Informing the mind

Several years before the onset of my psychological chaos I had met Dr. Elizabeth Moberley and (more out of politeness than interest) had read her then newly published book *Psychogenesis*. At that time the concept of *defensive detachment from the love-source* in infancy had not seemed relevant. But now that I am seeking to make sense of my emotional dependency, I return to her research findings. On re-opening her book my eye is drawn to the chapter *Towards the Healing of the Deeply Wounded*, and am surprised to see how many sentences I had underlined at my initial reading. The author makes a connection between real (or perceived) betrayal and abandonment by the mother and a defensive cutting off from her, thereby closing off any further possibility for receiving nurture from her. Moberley's research proffers the hypothesis that a same-gender relationship is part of the solution: a drive within a detached person to repair the break and to restore attachment. Such statements, imbibed years earlier and lodged in my unconscious, had evidently strengthened my resolve not to cut loose but to stay attached to Fiona for as long as was needed for her sake and mine. But would I ever have outgrown my neediness? Would the emotional hold have lessened over time? Would the push-me-pull-me agony, my powerlessness and burdened conscience have ever ceased?

The time has come to veer off the 'healing' path Moberley outlines. I believe that the attachment to Fiona has lasted long enough, has done its job of drawing up the buried infantile emotions of terror, rage and despair. Now that they are no longer unconscious, I do not have to defend myself against them. I no longer need to skate on thin ice. These strong feelings are now out in the open; I no longer have to repress them but am learning to handle them. Yet without the uninvited touch and the ensuing attachment, would I ever have found my abandoned Inner Child? Certainly that unexpected hug which Fiona spontaneously gave, was the prelude to change and healing, propelling me to seek truth about myself and the country of my birth. The whole episode had been revelatory. Even essential?

Despite attending seminars based on Dr. Frank Lake's discoveries for four years, my knowledge had remained theoretical. His weighty work *Clinical Theology* had been a church leaving gift (along with the carpeting for our first Vicarage). Since then the book has languished on Peter's shelf, opened only occasionally. It is a cool dark autumn evening as I walk alone, my mind in turmoil, my heart in agony. What shall I do? *Find that book and read the longest chapter it contains.* God's voice is clear and in Frank Lake I find an ally who describes the realities of dread.

Disciplining myself to read daily a section of the chapter *The Understanding and Care of Schizoid Personalities* and to make notes, prove to be instrumental in objectifying my condition. Confusion unravels. My mind cooperates. The symptoms the author outlines match mine: the need for privacy and to be out of reach for a long time; the difficulty of establishing a routine in my life; introversion to such an extent that the outer reality appears secondary; the quest for wisdom and understanding; the numbing of emotions; a sense of inferiority sometimes coupled with an imagined superiority; affliction; the torment of despair; the somatic symptom of dread as painful genital tension; fainting; regression and the sense of disintegration. My cosmos had become chaos and my ability to trust had shattered. Depersonalisation and the inability to perceive appropriate boundaries apparently are also part of the condition. Dr. Lake understands isolation, impoverishment and 'nothingness'. Fiona's *eros* had threatened my personality to the core: I had fallen into the *abyss of non-being*. To escape from this deep sludge-filled bomb crater, I really must tackle the addiction. I need to walk on a different path.

I have to make a one hundred and eighty degree turn. My school teacher, Herr Betten, during his last year of sanity before the bullet embedded in his temple addled his brain, had instilled in us a love for the German language and a basic understanding of the Christian faith. We ten-year-olds had ignored the indentation in his head, hung on his softly-spoken words and the kind eyes in his warm ageing face. I remember the day he called me to the front of the class and ordered me to walk away from him into the furthest corner of the classroom (usually the place of shame and punishment). My face was pressed against the wall.

"Now turn round," he had called and I had swung round in relief. "Come, walk towards me." I obeyed until I had stood right in front of him.

"That," Herr Betten addressed the class, "is repentance. You see? A complete turnabout."

Now is the time to put into practice what I had learnt so long ago. Not once, but again and again I have to deliberately face into the opposite direction: away from Fiona. I cut loose by moving into our cottage. I call it my exile and do not know how long it will last.

Someone else has to cut loose. A car pulls to a halt outside the cottage. Pauline has come for her hug, the last vestige of my ill-conceived reparenting. There she sits in the corner of my room but I do not move towards her or encourage her to come over to me. She sulks; becomes angry; baits me; hurls insults at me. When nothing works, she bursts into tears. When her sobbing elicits no hug either, she storms out of the house. A car engine roars. Crunch. I hear the shattering of glass. I think the low garden wall is the culprit but I do not go out to investigate. She's gone. A delicious silence settles over the room. I get up and lock the door, draw the curtains, settle myself on a cushion by the radiator and begin to read the book that has long and patiently waited for me and confirms my decision to be *Codependent No More* (by Melody Beattie). I will heed Jesus' injunction to love my neighbour *as* myself and not exclude myself from my love nor negate myself in the service for others. I want to learn to live a healthy lifestyle. I must find the reason for my dams having been so weak that they could be breached so easily. I hope to discover the antecedents, the beginnings of my habitually seeking out the needy and offering them my space, my time, my very life. I determine to erect stable boundaries between others and myself. Beattie's analysis of the concept of co-dependency - along with those of Moberley and Lake - becomes the third tributary to swell my river of conscious learning.

A fourth stream brings pragmatic aspects which contribute to my healing. A paper written jointly by two Dutch psychiatrists proposes a new diagnostic category: *Deprivation Neurosis.* Its symptoms include altered reality and altered perception, separation anxiety and immaturity, inner pain and terror, the need for a sanctuary and the need for flight. I tick all the boxes. Anna Terruwe, a practitioner in the Netherlands and Conrad Baars from the States (where he had emigrated after two years in a German concentration camp, something I learn later) advocate that this dysfunction be treated differently from other neuroses. Its cause, they argue, does not lie in repression but rather in the fact that emotional growth, halted in infancy, calls to be reactivated and to proceed from one developmental phase to the next, each stage to be completed before moving on.

"A child," they state, "must have had the chance to feel and live as a child if he is to be fit to experience fully the disintegration and reintegration of puberty. The adolescent cannot attain normal adulthood unless he had the opportunity to be an adolescent." The co-authors assert that the child's emotions continue to search restlessly for the gratifications that had been rightfully his and that without such, progression to a higher stage of maturity becomes impossible. The kind of therapy Baar and Terruwe deem essential for the healing of the emotionally deprived - begins with touch, since the tactile sense is the first to develop. I had never liked touching things or felt the need to do so. If I stroked an animal I did it for the pet's pleasure, never mine. It had to be a woman's touch to wake up the deprivation. Fiona's had been the trigger I needed to make contact with my own tactile needs.

I had long known about the importance of mother-child eye-contact. My own mother's warm brown eyes I had always perceived as reproachful, rather than accepting - as if I never measured up to her expectations. When Fiona's eyes had sometimes almost bored into mine with that silent demand "fill me", they had always scared me.

Each developmental phase - the Dutch therapists insist - must be treated 'age-appropriately', i.e. cuddles at the 'baby' stage; for the 'young child stage' dolls, teddies and train sets; chewy sweets; play and creative pursuits. And above all: genuine love from an older mature woman. I had tried to provide for others from an empty container, attempted to give what I had not first received for myself. Thus I breached my own dams and lost even the identity I had known.

I think I understand: defensively detached from my parents and their affection had made me seek refuge and strength behind a spiritual glass wall. When challenged, I had left my self-made sanctuary and become vulnerable. Fiona's affection had been strong enough to draw me back to the margin of the 'Schizoid Position' where trust might again become possible, but then left me floundering in the 'Hysterical Position' of need and clinginess.

Though my mind is finding clarity, my emotions are trailing behind. I keep listening for Fiona's car. I scan the path. She does not come. Not yesterday, not today. As the weeks go by the longing becomes less intense and slowly the pain turns to relief, then to gratitude. On my daily walks by the river my boots stomp: 'no more' - 'no more' - 'no more'. My brain and my heart are recording the message. The spiritual and emotional battles subside. People greet me as I walk and it strangely nourishes me. I belong to the human race. Stomp. Stomp. Stomp. I observe creatures and touch plants and tree bark as I have never done before and write poetry about my discoveries. I look forward to the evenings, when Peter and the boys join me for supper in the cottage. When they leave and I am alone again, I light candles and sit in the stillness of the night in gratitude and adoration of the One who knows how to heal me. Memories of childhood flood back and find their way on to the word-processor. Through inner visions I learn how far I have progressed on the road to recovery. I see an inner picture of the ruin of what had been a sanctuary, roofless and open to the sky. Strong buttresses hold up the remaining walls and prevent the edifice from collapsing into the ravine below. And within these walls a garden is being created; herbaceous borders glow that I have not planted.

On my doormat lands a letter bearing a foreign stamp.

Dear Uta,

Can I come and stay with you in your cottage? I want you to counsel me.

I know the writer. She is an experienced psychotherapist with a sought-after private practice in her own country. Why me? Can I really be trusted? The cottage is too small for both of us but in the village I find suitable accommodation for 'my client'. We work together for a fortnight, meeting on a daily basis. On the morning of the day on which she returns home happy and contented, I wake early. *Your exile is over. You may go home*, I hear Him say, and the following Sunday I am back in church.

"Nice to see you," smiles the parish administrator. "Have you had a nice holiday?"

Nicely – I reply, "It's not been a holiday. A lot of work was done."

"And above all," proscribe the Dutch therapists, "it needs genuine love from an older mature woman…"

I know that woman and I know the task. She is not to reparent the unaffirmed adult 'children' in the church nor is she to be a non-abusive substitute for abusive or neglectful mother figures. No, no more! She is to mother her *own* inner unattached Child whose Father is God the Creator himself. Mother-love and fatherly affirmation shall flow to the war child within, to the un-nurtured and socially deprived little girl. For that divinely-appointed task I have to 'die' to the longing to have my emotional needs met by another human being. And so: quietly in the cottage summer garden, in a blaze of roses and phlox and nasturtiums, I relinquish all my needs and rights. I 'die' without a struggle. It is a decision and it is a peaceful death. Now there is no way back into the abyss of dread. From here only the Creator Himself can fill the yawning void. Only the Man Christ Jesus, the fully Affirmed One, who himself tasted affliction, abandonment and death, can grow my stunted being as I trust him and commit myself to reality. I find my discovery confirmed in the writings of Frank Lake. The worst is over: I have crossed the 'doorstep' of "transmarginal stress". It is no longer either/or: neither the once familiar schizoid and detached stance, nor the hysterical clinging position that had been so frighteningly alien to me. I am free to relate to others without the excruciating need for their approval. My emotions are no longer my foes, but my faithful friends who tell me truth. But now that I have relinquished my need for a mother-substitute, I am finding myself floating in a cold universe, like an astronaut who has lost his attachment to his space capsule.

Christian healing conferences had come and gone; and many I attended had left me feeling more alone and abandoned, frightened or confused than before. Should I book a place for yet another? Leanne Payne's Pastoral Care Ministries are holding one in Hurlach, a German castle near Munich. I need to go to Munich where I have also arranged a rendezvous with a German-Jewish woman who has left her English husband to look for her roots in Germany.

In the castle a small band of musicians leads the worship.

"I have a picture in my mind and it makes no sense to me," announces one of the group, a Hawaiian woman. "I see someone chiselling mortar off old bricks and then piling them up into heaps."

Of course it makes sense! You are in Germany, lady, and there are several of us in this room who after the war have done just that! Bricks from the ruined houses, cleaned up to build new ones. The picture confirms that my decision to come was the right one. In the course of the conference I hear the call to those in the audience who feel themselves 'unaffirmed' to come forward to the dais to be prayed for. I am surprised to see quite a number of us. Several women from the leadership team step forward to hold those who are standing by the dais. I am held in the arms of a woman for a few minutes, firmly, not tightly who is praying for me. Back in my seat, I do not join in the ensuing song, but let music and worship wash over me – when a baby is laid at my breast, suckling from me! *I am the infant and I am the nurturer* – simultaneously. We are one. The splitting has been reversed. I am who I am.

From now on I will be attentive to this Child; will listen to her story; will follow her leading. I travel back with her in time, feel emotions that had been too strong for her, make connections with past and present, from her conception onwards, and I will make up for her deprivations as far as in me lies, believing that I will be given the resources.

And so the story of the War Child unfolds: in my memory; through a few black-and-white snapshots; through an informed imagination. Broken down is the Berlin Wall that had dammed behind it not only East Germans wanting to go west but had made inaccessible the worlds of my childhood. Maybe it will be possible to rediscover them. Maybe I can travel east one day, beyond Berlin, beyond Oder and Vistula, to the river that held for me mystery and melancholy: the Memel. Maybe...

15

Creativity

How irritated I had been with Bettina Eichin's tiny sculptures exhibited in the Swiss barracks, angry even at the artist's "audacity" to create such personal artefacts as diaries and "silly little mementos" for the public. "Such egocentric subjectivity!"

"Don't you think that an artist has the right to make art that has a personal meaning?" My companion had retorted.

"No, I don't think so. Artists are meant to depict things that have a universal meaning. I want access." I notice the vehemence of my feelings. But the Child within is wistful and sad. Will she never be allowed to share her memories other than in words?

Come on, creating art is reserved for artists; my German culture has taught me that. And artists live in a world apart and to that world I do not belong. Paintings and sculptures may be admired only in galleries. Music belongs to the concert hall and the orchestra pit. Creative writing is done by *Dichter*: poets and novelists. Yes, I feel strongly about this. We (I), the untalented, are barred from such inspired and inspiring echelons. Like pauper children, we stand outside the rich man's window, our feet frozen in the snow. We cannot take our eyes off the laden Christmas tree and all the presents wrapped in shiny paper. Out in the cold we can only sniff that faint delicious smell of freshly-baked biscuits. We have neither permission, nor the means nor any excuse to enter that magical room.

In the war years and the time that followed, a German child possessed no such treasures as plasticine, crayons, felt tips or watercolours. Paper was scarce, and even scarcer were incentive and encouragement to be creative when I was young. I was already ten years old before I was given a box camera, a wooden recorder and a neat white tin that contained a small brush and twelve tiny pots filled with watercolours. At school we were set the task of copying a wall paper pattern. Never had I been given anything so wonderful to do. Bent over the kitchen table, tongue between lips, I concentrated on getting it right. The good mark the teacher gave me was thrilling, so much so that I immediately began a second pattern. In my opinion the result was even more pleasing and I expected a 'very good', a straight One. She gave me a Three ('satisfactory') instead. I lost heart and interest in putting pen or brush to paper ever again. I even stopped what had given me so much pleasure: the tracing of line drawings in books, only just visible through the brown baking paper I begged from my mother.

When I was thirteen, it was she who took me to Amsterdam to visit the *Rijksmuseum*, my introduction to the visual arts. It was my mother who instilled in me a love for van Gogh's works and for good design in china, glass and furniture. Throughout my teenage years I became a frequent visitor to our Duisburg art gallery where some of the sculptures of its famous son Wilhelm Lehmbruck, once deemed politically undesirable, were again exhibited. Seldom did I miss a concert or any of the pre-concert lectures the city fathers laid on for us young people. In the rebuilt theatre *The Tales of Hoffmann*, my first experience of opera, opened the gateway to those by Verdi, Puccini and Mozart and all the Viennese operettas. I knew the librettos by heart. At the public library I exchanged books every week, and learning poetry was not a chore. But to write a poem or story myself – who has ever heard of such a thing? Art belongs to the artists, and only writers write. School essays, yes, I enjoyed writing them. And there were other outlets: I found my own recorder teacher and became an alto in the school choir. With my best friend we fashioned silhouettes by cutting along the contours of photographs we found in magazines and by projecting our pictures on a white wall with the aid of a torch, created our own 'film shows'. Her kitchen table became our stage on which we performed our own 'operas' or let the dolls act for us.

I had grown up considering myself wholly untalented and was generally encouraged in this belief! My chosen new life in England finally severed me from the last vestiges of my culture. Full immersion in religious education and parish life demanded that I strangle my love of literature and the theatre, of music and the visual arts. I lost my soul. And then, in the chapel in the mountains, when Pauline was wandering around in the fog, I had 'seen' it rise to life again.

I dare to pen a poem to Carole who is an artist. It is about the longing of my hands "to be creative". She hears the cry of my heart and one day arrives at the Vicarage with a plethora of art material. We squat on the floor and she spreads a huge sheet of white paper out in front of me! Here I am – surrounded by bottles of poster paint, jam jars and brushes of every size. This is scary.

"I think we'll start with a limited palette," says my teacher. "Which three colours would you like to work with?" I select black, white and red. She pours a generous amount of each into separate jars.

"Later you can add one more colour. Choose your brush." Gosh, which one?

A thick brush hovers above the red paint. Reluctantly I dunk it into the pot. Laden, I carefully bring it towards the white expanse in front of me... but the brush has a mind of its own...refuses to touch the paper...freezes in mid-air. And I am frozen inside. Patiently my friend waits…

"Try again," she says calmly. The brush remains suspended a few inches above the paper and heat burns behind my eyes.

"I can't do it!" I cry. Then the thaw sets in. Something begins to loosen inside: one red blob appears on the virgin-white paper. The spell is broken. Again and again I fill the brush and paint a red sky. Clean the brush. Paint white on white beneath that sky. I have to apply a thick layer to make it 'snow'. Black upright strokes at roughly the same distance suggest fence posts.

"A winter scene?"

"Yes." I say. "This is winter in the East."

I have not finished yet. Red must be dripped on to the white: drops of blood in the snow, and an ominous red sky hangs low. The fence posts add to the desolation.

"You may add some blue now if you like..."

Soon a rivulet flows in the snow and the thawed stream gives life and hope to the landscape. My heart is fluttering. "I think I know where this is..."

A copse on a hillside near home. Amongst hundreds of saplings, not yet in leaf, we find a flat rock. I am holding a pad of deliciously 'bubbly' paper.

"It's good quality watercolour paper," says my friend. "Look, here is some charcoal." In a tin lie small black sticks; some as thick as a thumb; others thin and fragile.

"Take one and draw what you see."

What I see! These thin stems all look identical and there are so many, standing so close together; some are straight, most of them crooked, a few leaning against each other, obscuring each other. I really don't know where to start.

"Why don't you just make a mark? Simply pull your charcoal across your paper."

Mess up this beautiful paper? A medium-sized stick strokes the precious surface – and the paper replies! This feels exquisite. I dare add more and yet more vertical lines, sometimes softly, sometimes exerting pressure. Always the paper responds in the same satisfying manner.

"Your first charcoal drawing. It's lovely," says Carole.

Having experienced the liberating power of making marks, I want to share this joy with the people in the church. We plan a creativity course for which Peter and I sign up but – surprisingly – very few others do. Every Thursday night a trestle table bends under the weight of art materials.

Tonight is our last session when anything and everything goes. Large sheets of lining paper cover the long tables. Does this mean that we all work on the same paper and that our creations will be connected?

"We use as our theme: Rest." I don't want to do this. I'd rather rest on a bench in the cottage garden all by myself. No, you are here. You asked for this course. Come on, start with a garden seat. Draw one. I can't. Find a photograph then. A pile of coloured magazines totters on the table. Frantically I turn the pages but find no picture of a garden seat. Try another magazine. Nothing. Pull yourself together, you are the

Vicar's wife. You will have to produce *something*. That silly wall clock. There is nothing, nothing on my large sheet. I pray for inspiration. And time is running out. I find an advert for cigarettes, a small image of a rock face from which water is cascading. What about that? Hastily I cut it out and stick it into the very centre of my white space – where it looks utterly lost. I feel Peter's energy, as he is working next to me. No, he is playing! I glance across. Skiers are racing down a slope. Everything shouts: fun, fun, fun. Holly opposite me has taken her shoes and socks off. Her paint-smeared feet dance on the table and she is shrieking with delight. My rock squats small and stark in white nothingness. Exposed, it is exposing me. I must shield it from sight. Large trees must shelter it. How do you make collage trees? The hands on the wall clock are moving so fast. The rock face stares at me, solitary and condemning. Admit it that you have not a shred of creativity in you. You see, you have no talent whatsoever.

On the resources table I spot a small roll of corrugated paper. Looks like tree bark, deeply furrowed. I paste several upright strips around the rock. Ridiculous. Foliage. How do you make foliage? There is no time to cut out leaves! I pour green poster paint into a shallow dish and dunk white tissue paper into it and pull out a soggy green mess. Smear PVA around the trunks. My hands up to my wrists are dripping with green gunge. Press the wet green stuff on to the slimy surface. Panicking, I manage to 'sculpt' the soggy paper into 'foliage'.

"Time to stop."

The worst, of course, is yet to come. Everyone will be walking around the tables, inspecting, admiring. There are meadows filled with flowers and pretty things and Peter's exuberant skiers and we laugh at the paint footmarks. My mess elicits knitted brows and 'hmms'...

"We'll let it all dry and tomorrow you can fetch your work."

Carole's words mark the end of the creativity course for which I had had such high expectations. Everyone leaves in high spirits; I prefer to start clearing up.

" That was hard for you?"

"Yes, it was. I panicked."

"Your collage has potential. Let's meet here tomorrow and talk about it."

"What's the point?"

The following day I am the only one who has returned to the hall to fetch my mess.

"What do you want to do with your picture?"

"Sever it from Peter's." We cut the rock with its sorry trees away from the skiers and it already feels better.

"We could take it to my studio where you can work on it whenever you have time and feel like it." When will that be?

But over several weeks, the collage takes shape: water gushes from the rock, forms a river that divides into arms to flow through undergrowth and sand. Wherever the river runs, red flowers and ferns spring up. I am learning how to create shadows in the foliage and on the tree trunks.

Finally the thin lining paper, heavy with collage, has to be carefully lifted on to a firm board and secured. We have saved it. I lacquer the whole scene with PVA and my picture gleams! I have bridged a chasm. The Child is excited and I am satisfied. I have found a medium in which the untalented, untaught me can express myself by making collage. Inexpensive, innovative, gratifying. There are so many 'found objects' the world has on offer: seeds and leaves; dried flowers and rough-textured bark; coffee grouts, lentils and sand; tissue paper, wrapping paper; images; even plastic nets which once held oranges and onions and kiwi fruit. I become an embarrassment, might even arouse suspicion, when I circle round and around the pot-pourri stand in *Boots*, surreptitiously picking out my shapes, colours and textures. Without mallet and chisel, I can be a sculptor. Without much paint I can be a picture maker. Without handling cold slimy clay, I can be a potter. My unskilled hands cut and paste and mould and give me joy. Even a sketchbook, bound in red hard covers, which my friend expects me to fill with pencil or ink drawings and small watercolours, is abused, has its spine broken by the three-dimensional collages bulging the covers. Yes, and it smells lovely, too!

Poems form in my mind – even if they sound 'archaic' – as do stories and fairytales. Perhaps I will write them down for the Child whose young life was filled with fairytales during dark and lonely years. And what richness I now recover in my mother tongue. I devour German literature and history. To a prayer journal I commit my thoughts, concerns and longings. A word processor becomes a treasured possession and in stilted and immature language I begin to write my own life story. I learn to appreciate the physiological kaleidoscope of emotions, allow myself to feel them, so that this "energy in motion" no longer breaks the dams. Billows reduce to ripples. Prophet and psalmist challenge and encourage me as my life rises from the ashes.

When Fiona perceived that I was no longer committed to fulfilling her needs, she turned against me. She had tried to instil in me the belief that I was "totally incapable of making relationships". Tentatively I now seek out old friendships with precious people, who had never exploited or manipulated me, who had done me nothing but good; friendships that need not be analysed; friendships that have stayed fresh over the years; friendships in which conversation flows easily, where thoughts, memories and experiences we have in common are freely shared. My friends inspire me. They say that I inspire them.

I leaf through family albums. The black-and-white photographs take on a new significance. Like searchlights they illuminate memories: a small grassy triangle...

In a dream-like vision I see myself sitting in dune sand. I appear to have been pulled from the sea after a shipwreck. In a small indentation next to me I sense the presence of my Rescuer. And though I foolishly remind Him that He has a whole world, indeed the entire universe to rule, He refuses to leave my side. Jesus is showing me that he never has and never will abandon me.

16

Exit

Chatter and laughter reverberate in the conference hall as people are filing into their seats. I slip into the back row. In a few minutes Leanne Payne will address the assembly. At the first chords from the grand piano the beehive hushes and the auditorium fills with song. Waves of worship break over me. With closed eyes I see a film rolling....

...a lofty sanctuary. A dazzling golden floor. Is this Solomon's temple? Sprawling on the shiny ground lies a human figure and a tall man, dressed in white, is standing close by. Slowly I make my way towards them and get a clearer view: the figure is a woman, clad in rags and bleeding from several wounds. She appears close to death. Who is she? Her face seems oddly familiar.

The tall man is bending down to her and helps her to stand. From somewhere booms a voice: "Murder in the cathedral!"

"Come," says the Man – and He is speaking to *me*! I get up and together we walk towards the high altar and straight through a huge stained glass window. Outside, a sunlit path hugs the building, but we do not take it. Opposite the cathedral looms a dark oak door through which we enter into a dimly lit vaulted space. It feels cool in here. My eyes acclimatise to the gloom and I notice on my right rows and rows of dark-stained pews. Above me – almost menacingly – arches a pipe organ. The place appears empty. For a long time I stand there, waiting, listening. No one comes to me. Cold and desolate I stand alone, until I feel a gentle tug at my sleeve. The Man takes my arm.

"Come," He says and leads me through a low door into the sunshine. A track wends alongside the church. Into freedom? I step on to the path but immediately in front of me appears a Gothic door and through it I cross the threshold into yet another dark, cold and empty church. Once again no one joins me as I stand in silence. I wait until the Man steps out from the darkness that had hidden Him. For a moment He stands by my side then He bids me, "Come."

We leave by a side door. Another footpath – bright and inviting. Again we ignore it and head toward a door made from light wood. The church furniture looks modern and functional, and though the interior is light, the loneliness is only too familiar. A sense of hopelessness settles on me as I stand there in my isolation. I no longer expect a human friend.

"Come!"

Can I bear it? Another tempting path which I now know we will not walk. The sun has sunk low and tinges the gravel with a golden hue. In front of us looms a neo-Gothic pile, its sandstone walls blackened by pollution. Dark oak doors open into a stone porch and the interior holds no surprises. Despair is choking me. Is there no way out? The Man is with me, watching.

"Come," He says and I follow lethargically. Come where? Only to repeat the pattern over and over? No. The Man is leading me into an open space: a lawned quadrangle, flanked by colonnades. In the centre I recognise a water hydrant of the kind I have often seen in Switzerland. *"He allured me out of distress into a broad place..."* There is still more. From the corner of my eye I notice a rocket ready for lift-off...

...the last chord from the grand piano is fading, the singing has stopped and I hear the final words: *I will blast you into the world.* I open my eyes and know: yes, we will leave parish ministry – it is just a matter of time.

"I need to go on a shopping trip, Nicky. Do you want to come with me?"

"Where?"

"On the Continent. I know of important teaching seminars in Holland and in Switzerland.

"What are they about?"

"The first in Amsterdam majors on child sexual abuse. The second is a conference convened for German-speaking Christian psychotherapists, psychiatrists and pastoral workers to which I have been invited. And at the third John and Paula Sandford from America are teaching on reparenting and related issues."

"How long would we be away?"

"Three weeks plus. My widowed mother will be moving soon and on the way I'd like to say 'good-bye' to the house on the Dutch-German border that has meant so much to us as a family."

We board the ferry and days later, aboard the *Rheingold-Express*, I 'sink my roots' back into my homeland, from which I had severed myself thirty years earlier while flying across the Channel into the British dawn where my new home was being prepared for me.

Nicky and I return laden with information to be sifted and assimilated. The mental stimulation, objectivity and new relationships have filled my empty spaces and converted question-marks into full-stops. But I am running ahead. Something extraordinary happens to me in Amsterdam.

It is peaceful sitting here by the *gracht*. It is nine in the morning and already the May day feels warm and pleasant. This canal, this city, the myriad of bicycles, they bring back delightful memories of family holidays in Holland in the 1950s. I tell Nicky about the cheese market, the dunes and *stroop*-filled waffles, about the smooth safe cycle paths and the kindness and hospitality of the Dutch people towards us. As I am describing my childhood memories I am overcome by a growing unease; something sinister appears to be creeping up at me from behind; a heavy blanket is going to suffocate me. Furtively I look behind me. We are alone and only a warm breeze is cosseting us. Nicky does not share my sense of foreboding. And yet. The whole city, this entire country is pressing down on me, condemning and dangerous.

"Let's go back to the house!" I say, hoping that I will feel safe there.

The lecture is already in progress. The speaker acknowledges our late arrival with a friendly nod and continues, "I felt the gun against my forehead. 'Where is your father?' they asked…"

We take the two free chairs right at the back.

"…one of our Australian students drove a Beetle with a German number plate through Amsterdam on Liberation Day and he was terrified of being lynched…"

Is today Liberation Day? Is that why I had those sensations at the canal just now?

At break time Téo van der Weele, our Dutch lecturer, comes across to welcome the English visitors. Picking up on the sentence I heard when we entered the room, immediately I say to him, "I am so sorry, for what my people did to you!"

He pulls a chair up to join us. "Now listen," he says to me, his face close to mine, "my father was a Nazi."

I hear the words but they mean nothing. I see him looking at me. His eyes are fixing on mine.

"Listen very carefully. *My* father was a Nazi." But I still I do not comprehend.

Nicky is nudging me.

"Listen to what he is saying."

Téo repeats the sentence and I stare at him in disbelief. My brain is somersaulting. I sense him holding my hands and right in front of me bobs a mop of white hair.

"Watch my lips," he says. "Listen. Hear me." And once more, very slowly, making sure that I perceive the emphasis, "*My* father was a Nazi. It was *one of our own* soldiers who pointed a pistol at my head. They wanted me, the seven-year old, to reveal where my father was hiding."

Inside me – fast and furiously – a coil is unwinding. I lose my orientation but Téo has got through to me. I finally understand: *Dutch* soldiers had threatened the little Dutch boy at gunpoint! Not *Germans*! My numbness thaws. I tell him of my subjective experience at the canal earlier this morning. And *he* understands.

Back in England, I leave Leanne Payne's Pastoral Care conference a day early. I have had enough. Yet the next morning I know that I must go back. Why? *Formulate your question.*

The final session is just concluding with rousing song. *Find Leanne.* I do not have to search for her. There she is, standing by the door – alone.

"How can a *German* find her true self?" is all I ask her.

"Are you German?" I nod.

After a moment of silence she declares, "Your Father will give you your Fatherland." And somehow her words grant me *permission to search for my own roots.*

Twenty eight years we have been in parish life. Although a Sabbatical is due every seven years, Peter had never been offered one nor asked for one. The time is right to apply for such a time for refreshment and reflection. He asks for four months out of the parish and is granted the leave as long as he forgoes his salary for the fourth. How do we spend such a precious time? Where do we go? How do we fund it? Since the vision of a therapeutic community has not dimmed, the Sabbatical could give us a chance to explore how existing communities function. We know of several healing communities in Britain, Germany and Switzerland, some of which are involved in the rehabilitation of drug addicts, others seek to stabilize young people who struggle with mental or psychological problems, some see their calling to provide a secure base for people who were deprived of love in childhood. We want to discover the criteria to create a safe place for wounded people.

Before we embark on our long journey Peter goes into solitary retreat in a Swiss chalet in the mountains of the Bernese Oberland which he has been lent free of charge. It is February and in April I will join him. The weeks by himself in the Alps allow him time for reflection on his life and our future. He fills many notebooks. He writes

I wonder how the kids I hung around with fared. None of their Dads was there for them. We were a generation of fatherless children whose mothers coped amazingly well, considering that hardly a day passed without fear. Apart from one clear memory of him between 1936 and 1945 Dad was a bar of orange-cream filled-chocolate hidden beyond my reach on top of his compactum (part of his Service rations sent from wherever he was stationed). When I was about six or seven I fell off a chair, trying to reach him! He was a treat to be enjoyed sparingly.

My toy cupboard was filled with model farms and loads of wooden domestic animals, mostly made in my grandfather's factory. I wanted to

be a farmer then, I think, a dream that took off as I grew up post-war on Dad's farm – with all the space in the world and the knowledge that I could do anything and go anywhere. In later years, studying the laws of tort and property, I discovered that there was no mileage in the script 'trespassers will be prosecuted'. They cannot. And I enjoyed that liberty to the full well before I knew it to be true. The only ministry that made sense to me was the Ministry of Agriculture and Fisheries. The ministry of the Church of England never entered my thinking.

Everything was challenged in due course. My adult commitment to the Christian Way turned my life around. And even after I had trained as an Anglican priest I kept the door open to missionary work as an agriculturalist. Why should all the earlier study and experience be wasted?

The Church of England is a strange animal and I sat uncomfortably with its disciplines and legal formularies. Routine was no issue for me; the seasonal calendar imposes routine on every son of the land. It was wonderfully creative to work with spring, summer, autumn and winter. The rewards of labour follow naturally despite the hiccoughs of climate and national recessions. But conforming to fruitless dictates and imposed programmes was a lifeless retroactive experience. I was bored until Pentecost happened to me and even then my wings were clipped and flying was frowned upon. But the impact of the charismatic renewal bringing to life my earlier sacred commitment to Jesus turned everything up-side-down. The stale air became fresh. I could breathe. I could trespass. I was free.

Two things are unassailable in my life: first the Lordship of Jesus Christ, second my marriage. I will allow nothing and no one to come between these. Jesus is for ever; marriage is for my life time. That is where I stand. All else is for a season, be it short or long.

Before I arrived here, I already knew where the Sabbatical would take me: out of parish ministry. My time here is confirming it. With a new field of service before us, all I have to do is to 'tidy the house': leave the church more or less as I found it, pack my bags and move on.

Just before Easter, Peter meets me at Geneva Airport, bearing a single red rose.

On our way to his chalet in Därligen we bump into Kim who works in Châtel and share a pierrade with our son. What a lovely beginning to our travelling time all over Europe. We will visit therapeutic community after community, observing, learning, applying. One morning we wake in a hotel in Leysin. From the balcony the Dents Du Midi are clearly visible. When Peter goes to settle the bill, it has already been paid. Grace is overflowing. On our way to eastern Switzerland we are halted by a herd of cattle, each cow wreathed with spring flowers, bells ringing. They are lolling along the road on their way to the high meadows where they will spend the summer. Their calves are kicking up their skinny back legs, skipping from their winter byre. Why are we both in tears? We remember the promise given to us a long time ago, *"You will skip for joy like calves when they are led out into the meadows."* We, too, will be taken into a broad place. It is just a matter of time. And when later, in Germany, in a leafy bower we look down on the weir of the river Lech, both of us know that we will create a safe place for people from many nations. It is just a matter of time.

There is something else this Sabbatical will enable us to do: to follow the urging of my Inner Child who wants to take us beyond the torn Iron Curtain, east, east, east, into the Russian Kaliningrad Oblast and the independent republic of Lithuania, where she had to leave her world behind. And together we will find it.

After months of such an enriching time, how difficult it is for me to return to the parish where I am still the Vicar's wife.

"What are you actually expecting from me?" I ask the parish administrator.

"We would like to see you in the Parent and Toddler Group to give a hand with the little ones and pour their orange juice." She really means it. Does she notice that I am close to tears?

"Is that part of being a healing community?" I ask.

"This church is *not* a healing community!"

That has to be the final verdict. So, there is little more for us to do here. Peter's account of his Sabbatical is described by the Diocesan Officer as "thin and lacking much reflective depth". "Raw" is the word he uses.

"Perhaps," Peter muses, "I did not make it sufficiently clear that the 'rawness' indicates that it was too precious to describe – in an official report to the Diocese – the unspeakable riches I discovered. I had not expected that Jesus would introduce me to His Father and mine; that the deprivation of earlier years would be restored in a miraculous way; that I entered into an indescribable measure of love and acceptance. But they were early days and the new relationship much too private to tell about."

In the spring, Peter announces his resignation. In the summer we start counsellor training. In the autumn, after exactly fourteen years in the parishes, and thirty years since ordination, we leave the security of Vicarage and payroll. Having shared Holy Communion in the main church, Peter and I remain on the chancel steps. The congregation with warm words, hugs and tears, come forward and bid us farewell. We ourselves have no tears. Not now. As a family we walk down the aisle and out through the dark oak doors into the warmth and light of a September day. Lunch marks the end of three decades of family life.

Three days before that final Sunday Peter's mother had died unexpectedly. A small cavalcade drives to the hospital. In the chapel of rest we all take our leave from Mum and Grandma and in the car park the family disperses. A new life begins for each one of us. Now the tears flow.

For a few more days we stay on in the Vicarage. All is very still. No phone rings. No one visits. No one sees us off. During the last years in parish life I have carefully extracted the rootlets of 'the clump of violets in the lawn', as the dream image had instructed me to do. I have found myself, my roots. The pastures of the wilderness have turned green.

When we bought our miner's cottage the ground surrounding it was being choked by undergrowth and dehydrated by self-sown trees. It took Peter years to clear it of bramble, fell trees, restore walls and create terraces so I could plant a garden. In the same way the Lord of Life had patiently cleared my life of choking weeds and desperate needs and made a garden where flowers of creativity could bloom and a harvest could be gathered. Still, sometimes incessant rain would breach one or the other of the old dry-stone walls and send rocks crashing. One day an inexperienced feller had not been able to stop a tree huge falling and destroying much of what had been created. But Peter patiently rebuilt the walls and cleared up the devastation wrought by falling trunk and branches. I can see now that

Jesus had rebuilt my boundaries and made a way through the chaos. And in the same way that the cottage and its garden became our refuge during turbulent parish times, God had raised 'small islands' in the surging ocean of war-torn Europe on which my family could survive.

An old boat had been rotting by a canal wharf for years and we had watched its gradual silent decay. Today we are standing by its black skeleton, a ribcage of mouldering timbers. We have burnt our boats.

I had made renunciations that have been costly...Nobody understood why I was doing this...The shell of my professional routine had been broken but the seed inside was to be slow to germinate.

Paul Tournier

Book II

Islands in turbulent seas

1938 – 1947

1

Under a birch tree

Before she was ten she was deprived; before she was twenty she was bewitched; before she was thirty she was a mother; before she was forty she was betrayed. Next year my mother will be one hundred years old. Today her world is in the here and the only time is the now, though she glides contentedly from one day into the next and has no conception of where she lives. The charity *Caritas* provides her home and seeks to stimulate worn minds and bodies. Her carers praise her openness, her willingness to take part in all that is on offer and her accuracy in answering questions. I watch her sing from a score sheet; she knows the lyrics of the communal songs by heart. However, when I ask her about her past, our past, my past, the answer is always, "I have forgotten", though her memory is crystal-clear as to names and life events prior to the age of six.

In her late teens she was drawn into a cult. She, a war child, assailed by the insecurity and meaningless of the 1920s and '30s, fell for the artificially induced sense of sublimity and solemnity National Socialism claimed to offer. A great river of words, inflated with emotionality, swept her from her moorings. The emotionally deprived girl easily succumbed to the pathos of "the Fatherland" and "the Great Mother Germany" and did not discern the hollowness of the dramatic utterances that promised her secure parenting, safety and a hope. My mother was self-effacing, enthusiastic, romantic, sacrificial and open-hearted; it was easy for the poison river to flow into her soul. It flooded the child-like trust that was ever looking upwards for something great and wonderful. She was being deceived. And suffered the consequences

I inherited a number of her traits which – in a different religious context – left me vulnerable. Maternal deprivation was also passed down to me. My pathway to healing from the traumas of insufficient attachment, uprootedness and the terror of war has not run in a straight line, has been convoluted but purposeful.

My mother should have conceived me where the Rhine flows wide; where he wills his waters to strain towards the Dutch border; where the Ruhr joins him, who, having left her idyllic youth behind becomes an abused and polluted river, forced to serve factories and mines. Both my parents hail from Duisburg at the confluence of these two rivers. But I might equally well have been brought into being close to the black waters of the Wupper, above which hangs suspended the unique *Schwebebahn*, the hanging railway. My parents had chosen Wuppertal for their marital home but for their brief honeymoon my mother knew where *she* wanted to go. Following a simple wedding ceremony in a registry office, Hein and Ello had wasted no time on a reception but travelled a thousand kilometres east to seal their marriage; to the furthest north-eastern corner of the German Reich where, dividing the Baltic Sea from a freshwater Lagoon, lies a very narrow sandy land strip: the *Kurische Nehrung*, the Curonian Spit.

Before her wedding, Ello had enthusiastically served one year of her youth as a domestic and agricultural worker in the fishing hamlet of Gilge on the eastern shores of the Curonian Lagoon. *Arbeitsdienst* was a State requirement for young women. When on sunny days she lifted her eyes from her zinc tub and washboard and let them wander across the waters teeming with fishing boats and steamers, she could trace the golden outline of the Spit, the mighty wandering dunes lit by the sun. Over there the quaint fishing villages and alluring landscape had become a highly sought-after retreat for artists, nature lovers and the romantic at heart. My mother, too, held the long narrow land strip in idealized affection. A one-day excursion in an open boat across the lagoon had confirmed her dreamy notion, and so it *had* to be on the *Nehrung* where she would spend her honeymoon. The couple boarded a train in the Ruhr Region and travelled far beyond Berlin, beyond Königsberg and finally crossed the lagoon by steamer to Rossitten, a village famous for its bird ringing station, gliding school and Curonian hospitality to the city dwellers that flocked from the industrial west. Wild geese, gulls and a multitude of sea birds soar above the Baltic and the lagoon, alongside the silent wings of the gliders. On stormy days the fragile land spit is assaulted from both sides: the high salt breakers from the west and angry freshwater waves from the east. When the wind ceases both waters caress the shores, gently lapping against them.

Maybe something else urged my mother to travel to that Spit in far-away East Prussia. In the land north of the river Memel lay her mother's roots.

Memel. The name itself for me held a mystique, and as a child it had always seemed to me that the grown-ups had uttered the two syllables with affection and awe and a tinge of melancholy. The thousand kilometre long river rises in Belarus, flows through southern Lithuania and finally gives its name to Memelland, the crescent-shaped land strip that hugs its northern banks and stretches even further north east. That the Memel is also called Njemen, Neman and Nemunas, I never knew, nor had I ever considered that the river might also be loved by other nations, nor was it known until the year when the Berlin Wall fell, that the centre of Europe lies in the vicinity of that river. When finally the Memel reaches the *Kurische Haff*, it extends to the lagoon a hand with long wet fingers and the lagoon receives the delta and preserves its fresh water. The *Nehrung*, like a dam, prevents the sea waters from robbing it of its origin and identity.

The *Nehrung*, a near-hundred kilometres of dune land, was home to many tribes and peoples: to Narva and Prussians; Sambians and Curonians; Vikings and Germans; Lithuanians and Russians. In this same dune land began my life.

The sandspit had long served as a thoroughfare for travellers in war and peace: stage coach route and bridge between Russia and the West. But in the early part of the twentieth century it was discovered to have more to offer than a means of convenient transport: it is achingly beautiful. Writers flocked to it, extolling it in poetry and prose; artists arrived to capture its glory in painting and photograph. Suddenly the *Kurische Nehrung* was known all over Germany. Like my parents thousands arrived by train and steamer and found hospitality in fishermen's huts and newly-built hotels.

My story of my beginnings has no witnesses to confirm it. It has sprung from my own impressions and calculations, snatches of conversation, photographs and informed imagination. I paint pictures of my genesis which can no longer be verified, but which carry the lingering scent I smelt in the years that followed.

At the summer solstice, when all the day and most of the night belong to the Midsummer Sun, not a grain of sand moves. The dune lies still under the brooding heat. The wind has gone to sleep and the clouds have sailed north, leaving the sky deep and clean. Pale gold touches deep cobalt blue. Land and sea kiss; and their union reflects in the calm waters. A young birch has found a foothold on the edge of the dune; she stretches towards the sun, so graceful in her slim white skirt, flecked with black. On this June day, her heart-shaped leaves hang limp from slender limbs; the heat has made her lethargic, robbed her of the desire to sway to her own rustling music. She needs the wind to partner her in the dance. The afternoon sun's rays pierce the silent foliage and leave black-and-white patterns on the tufts of sparse dune-grass, where the man spreads his jacket and the woman lowers herself on to it. They lean against each other and talk and kiss – when suddenly from among the white stems of the birch copse emerges a dark hulk slouching towards them. Unmistakable are the lowered palm-leaf-shaped antlers, and the elk rolls forward, like an advancing tank. The man and the woman stare at the giant, too scared to speak or move. Its nostrils quiver. He stands head held high. Then, as suddenly and silently as he had appeared, with a nod and a deep bow, he turns and lumbers back into the shelter of the trees.

They find each other's hands and sigh as they slide into the indentation their bodies have made in the sandy ground. He holds her tight and a little too vehemently unbuttons her floral dress. She allows him, as she knows she must. A few years ago she had given her yes to becoming a mother as she knew she must. For the honour that awaits her, for the approval she will receive, she lets the man do what he must. It does not hurt much. Throughout the short embrace she does not look at her handsome husband. Her eyes stay closed but another image intrudes: a black-and-white photo, framed in ebony. Silently she breathes "for you", and her husband is oblivious to this inner dedication. There is a little blood on the lining of his uniform jacket. A blood sacrifice, expected of her as of millions. Shyly they adjust their clothes and he holds out his hand to help her up. Side by side they walk, sinking into the deep sand waves the wind has created. They do not speak until they reach their room in the fisherfolk's homestead which they have rented for a few days.

Their hostess carries a large ewer of hot water to their room and fills the small zinc bath. While the young bride washes, her husband stands by the low door, inhaling from his cigarette. He does not watch her. Instinctively he knows that she would not like it. Evening is slow to settle on the *Nehrung* and brings with it a strange melancholy. Glow-worms dance and bats swoop. The man by the door feels the uniform enclosing him. This furlough is short: a special dispensation for their wedding. He stares up into the pines. How long and how harsh will be his training? Is war inevitable? Where will they send him? He knows he should feel brave and proud but tears burn behind his grey-blue eyes and a clammy fear crawls all over him, settling on his heart. An owl hoots close by, menacingly.

My father inhales deeply, leaves his tears unshed and stoops under the door frame. My mother has dried herself and is dressed again. Their Curonian hostess serves them a simple supper and then together they slip beneath the snowy duvet mountain. Shyly she tells him that she wants to bear many children. He will supply the seeds.

Inside the cottage they listen to the wind waking and brushing the birch branches against the wooden walls. Across the roof dances smoke from the tiled stove in the fisherwoman's living room, fragrant almost. The breeze from the Baltic is sculpting the malleable sands into the shapes of its choosing…

…and I have begun.

I read out the crossword clues and my mother's answers fly out, even French and English words. We are one in this joint task. I admire her intelligence and swift responses. I also admire her resoluteness and the way she makes choices. But she does no longer understand that I am her daughter, and when I have travelled back from Germany to England, she will not know that I have been with her – but I have come to love her.

2

The godmother who wasn't a Godmother

Is it possible to relinquish that deeply buried and unconsciously nurtured hope that one day the perfect parent, the all-fulfilling mother, will be *there* just for me? When all my unsatisfied needs which smoulder like peat fire beneath the surface will be fully met? When a sweet peace and enduring contentment will supplant all restlessness? When the black abyss of emptiness is finally filled and no longer threatens to engulf?

Certainly the Great War had stolen sufficient maternal nurture from the woman who was bearing me. During the years of separation from her husband and the hyperinflation that followed, my grandmother had neither time nor energy to be a continuous loving presence to her little daughter. She had to secure a livelihood for her family. Long before daybreak, pulling a handcart, she delivered milk to her customers and a neighbour's face bent over her child's cot, lifted the little girl and dressed her. On a stool in the kitchen corner the child quietly, patiently waited for her breakfast. At the end of the day my grandmother ferried the day's earnings to the bank in a suitcase. And she buried gold.

In my mother's ageing mind a picture rises and replays itself; a brief scenario that she shares with me. In it she sees her mother crouching on the floor and herself as a little girl wriggling on to her lap. Although my mother has trained herself to forget many things, this brief film she has not deleted. Her fading memory has preserved this vital encounter. It was a moment when her mother had been present and accessible to her. If the births and deaths of her tiny brothers had affected, wounded, her she has never spoken about it. One thing is quite certain: this five-year old child had lost her mother to pain and grief and fear. The malaise of that war-child's maternal deprivation was passed down to me and it will deepen throughout my own childhood, which is also to span a World War. How would my mother be able to give to me something she had never adequately received herself? Had not her heart yearned for a powerful parent, someone to fill the void, someone unaffected by personal loss, someone to enflame her soul? She had longed for a homecoming.

By the end of the summer the white-golden dunes, cobalt sky, birch tree and fisherman's cottage have become like a fleeting dream. Ello's time with Hein in paradise had been so very short and feels unrelated to the grim prospects facing the pregnant woman. Now she is alone in her small sunny flat, stroking her new furniture of moulded golden elm, waiting for her baby, waiting for news broadcasts. Had my father been allowed to write to his wife? Had he found time in the training camp? Did he have permission to visit her? Did they ever share with each other the memories of the time under the birch tree? Did they recall the days between sand and sky? Did he share in the pregnancy at all? Before his death my father told me how vicious and humiliating his training schedule had been, how incessant had been the indoctrination. Compelled to take the solemn oath, his life and loyalty were bound to the Führer personally. And to the Fatherland. Rhetoric. In uniform he married my mother and God had certainly not been invoked to bless their union. The couple's calling was a 'higher' one: a walk-on part in an epoch-making drama, in a tragedy which the whole world was to watch with horror but in which it would also fully participate.

Ello is lonely. The newly-wed woman is afraid. She must go back 'home' to her parents. She packs a little case, locks the door to the flat in Wuppertal and walks to the station. In Duisburg her father meets her off the train. He is glad that she has come. They are fond of each other. Amongst the familiar dark oak furniture she tells her parents that she is expecting a baby. The china figurines smile behind the glass of the high sideboard. Everything feels solid and comfortable here. Her mother listens, her hands folded on the black leather-bound Bible.

"Does Hein know?"

"Yes."

"How will you manage?"

"I'll be fine. Women must relinquish their husbands; that is what he… our Führer asks of us."

There is silence. Her mother looks grave and grips the Bible on the table in front of her as if to cling to some security. A small child without a father! Yet again!

"I want to see Leni tomorrow." Ello changes the subject.

"I saw her in the market the other day and she asked after you," says her mother, "I found her so…so effusive. Over-enthusiastic, I would say. Hardly recognized the Leni I thought I knew."

"The party is all-important to her," says her father and Ello detects the slight tremor in his voice. And dismisses it.

"It is to me, too, Vater." She turns away, fearing her parents' looks of disapproval, concern and sadness.

Leni lives with her parents in a detached two-storey house with a beautiful garden. When she opens the door and sees her friend standing there, she throws up her hands in a wild gesture of delight.

"It's you, Ello! I had absolutely no idea you were in town. It is utterly wonderful to see you!" she gushes. "You do look magnificent. And you come at this so very, very happy time. How very much we have to talk about! Do come in, do come in. Oh Ello, how wonderful, wonderful to see you."

Leni is still unmarried. Not the status the Führer approves of. The two friends talk politics, enthuse about low unemployment figures and about a better standard of living. Leni's words flow like torrents. She swims in superlatives and her enthusiasm knows no bounds.

"He has been leading us from success to success, hasn't he? He will give us back everything we have ever lost. All we have been robbed of, our lands, our honour. He won't ever let us see defeat again." Her voice sings with the drama of an opera alto. Her friend – quieter – bathes in Leni's cascade of adulation; it is contagious, feeds her need for romanticism, sentimentality, myth. This afternoon her own niggling doubts and fears which she had found so difficult to fight on her own, are being quenched. The sun slanting into the grey room catches Leni's Aryan hair. It is gathered into a bun at the nape of her neck. On the radio plays the ubiquitous brass band. The two women tap their feet to the marches. The music stops abruptly and a broadcast is announced. Leni turns up the volume and their eager faces almost creep into the radio. The bakelite box crackles but they catch the words. He has a way with words: each phrase inspired and inspiring! They feel their spines tingle; they take leave of their own prickling skin; follow his words, transfixed and transformed. They know that he will fulfil all he promises. The evidence is there for all to see. How much joy he gives them! He has made them a part of a great people and an even greater future. The speech finishes, the cheering finally subsides.

Leni says, "I'll make coffee," her voice still trembles with excitement as she fills the kettle and places it on the coal-heated cooker in the corner of the room. She reaches for the blue and white box of *Linde's Kaffee-Ersatz*. Real coffee has not been available for a long time. Ello is watching her. She knows that she needs to tell Leni. But how? When is the right moment? The familiar anxiety returns.

"Do you think there will be war?" she asks Leni's back. Her friend spins round, raises her arms in a defensive gesture.

"War?"

"Yes, somehow I feel it ominously near."

"I ask you! How do you come to such an absurd idea? He is the man who wants peace and prosperity for his people. Would he plunge us into war?"

"Hein is training for something. I think they are making ready for war."

"He is being taught discipline. That's what a German man needs. Discipline!"

"I am expecting a baby." There, now she has said it. Silence. The sun has moved westwards and taken gold and glory from the room.

"When?"

"Next spring. That's why I am frightened that we may be heading for war."

Silence. What is Leni thinking? Have I lost her as my friend?

140

"Have you got a name?"

Relieved, Ello says, "If it's a boy, Hein will choose the name."

"And if it's a girl?"

"Uta."

"That's a wonderful name!" Leni's effervescence has returned. "She shall become a *real* Uta." And the two women exchange meaningful glances.

Almost everyone in Germany knew that name and the black-and-white photographs of her face and figure that were being disseminated throughout the Reich. Only the photographer knew how through clever lighting he had 'loosened' the early gothic sculpture from its niche high in the west choir of the cathedral of Naumburg and manipulated it in such a way that the viewer forgot that the figure was made of *stone*; he imbued it with life and personality. Little is known about the Countess Uta, one of twelve *Stifterfiguren* (founders) carved by an unknown medieval master, and little attention was paid to her and her stony companions until the first decades of the twentieth century. Progressively, "Frau Uta" became a national icon. In this godless era 'pilgrims' flocked to the cathedral to adore the stone figure that had been elevated as an archetype of mythical womanhood, exalting and venerating her like a Madonna. The heroine was celebrated in novels, films and on the stage. She was hailed as *the shining example of German* art. The romantic picture enriched the heart but also deceived it. In years to come, I, too, will travel to the *Naumburger Dom* to meet the twelve figures myself – and step out from intentional myth into reality.

"Will you be her godmother, Leni?" Ello asks shyly.

Leni's hands go up in that dramatic gesture that now seems part of her.

"Her godmother? You are not going to have her *baptized*, are you?"

"Of course not. But I thought you could be a special person to her, *like* a godmother, a sponsor she can look up to."

Leni is thinking… Finally, she agrees to play that role in my life.

Ello turns in the door as she leaves. "You know that I am having this child for him, our Führer, don't you?"

"Natürlich, Ello, naturally!" Leni's voice and hands are raised towards the ceiling, "and you will bear many, many children for him, won't you?"

This conversation may or may not have taken place at the time when my mother returned to her parents' home for solace before I was born. I have constructed it from later conversations I witnessed, from impressions, from gestures and attitudes. The National Socialist Uta-euphoria was a politically created myth that affected thousands of men and women, and in a peculiar way, bearers of this forename. Maybe it burdened me with an unconscious obligation. The black terracotta replica face of the *Uta von Naumburg* which since our wedding had hung in our English living room I later smashed into many pieces, declaring myself free from its hold.

My grandparents-to-be are watching their daughter with apprehension as she sits transfixed in the plush armchair, stroking the long silk of her dog, a toy spitz. Her thoughtful father cautions her not to let herself be seduced by "this Hitler". Her mother blames Hein for addling their daughter's mind and arousing her enthusiasm for Nazi ideology. And now a child is on the way...

Yet here, in her parents' home, Ello can sleep without anxiety. The day when her courage and sacrifice are required is still a long way ahead. Will Hein be granted leave when the time comes for her to give birth? She returns to their flat in Wuppertal, happy to know that her mother will come and look after her – and the baby. It is also good to know that Leni will be the child's godmother. In the meantime she must prepare for her ordeal. To give birth is *her* task, *her* contribution to her Führer.

3

The Clinic

S nowy voiles screen the high windows and the March breeze wafts them like bridal veils into a clean and chilly space. Icy-white tiles are reaching up to a lime-washed ceiling and reflect the light of a hazy sun. White metal furnishings provide surfaces for weigh-scales, a rubber-protected mattress and, covered by a bleached sheet, surgical instruments that lie arranged in neat rows: scissors, forceps, clamps, surgical thread and needles. Under the windows waits a wicker bassinet on a wooden stand. A small white duvet bulges over its rim and the sides of the cot are hung with diaphanous material. On bare floorboards stands a small zinc bath beside a metal hand basin. Beneath a bright light bulb protruding from a white enamel shade a white metal-frame bed faces a black-and-white portrait in an ebony frame.

A young woman is shielding her eyes against the glare; writhing; groaning. Pain and the odour of the antiseptic make her nauseous. She struggles not to fall into a black hole of nothingness; takes deep breaths. Her eyes meet his. They demand courage from the German mother; total commitment to him and to her task of bearing children.

"For you," she whispers as the vice of pain grips her.

Along the white-tiled corridor a uniform is marching up and down. Giving birth is woman's domain and he is not allowed to see his wife. He lights a cigarette. Does she know that he is outside the room, pacing,

pacing? Has somebody told her that he is not far away? Her eyes cling to the black-and-white image on the wall. This is her hour of sacrifice for *him* and for the Fatherland. The man in the corridor lights another cigarette.

Something wet and warm is flowing down her legs. Her eyes leave the picture and watch the sheet turn crimson. The stain grows larger and her terror mounts. She listens to her own scream and the man in the corridor hears it, too. The white door opens. A young doctor, his starched coat flapping, his blond head held high, strides towards the woman's bed. Steely blue eyes fix on her. Two starched caps and aprons have followed in his wake. The groaning stops: the woman has finally succumbed to the faint against which she has been battling.

Hurriedly they drag out the child. When the woman regains consciousness her anguish gives way to exhausted indifference. A blond nurse wraps the child into a stiff cotton sheet and lays it aside. Voices and brisk movements bring the sterile room to life. It takes time to staunch the haemorrhage. From the ebony frame the dark eyes look on.

When she is no longer needed to attend to the mother, one nurse picks up the child, holds it against her starched cold apron, unwraps it, scrutinizes it and places it into the weigh-scales, then lowers the small slippery, blooded body into the zinc bath and cleans it as efficiently as she has been trained to do; holds it correctly; places it on a small rubber-covered mattress; grabs the layette so lovingly chosen over the past months. Tiny arms are thrust into the sleeves of the minute white cotton vest, then into a cotton jacket. The newborn is turned on to its face and both garments are fastened with cotton ties at the nape of the floppy head. Turned again a triangular gauze nappy is deftly applied; and finally the baby is swaddled in flannelette. Watery blue eyes are searching for human eyes. The nurse neither smiles nor speaks to the child as she performs her tasks. She scans the little face a second time and places the infant into the bassinet while the doctor is still attending to the mother. The child lies alone.

"You can show her the child now," comes the doctor's clipped order. The nurse strips away the duvet, picks up the little bundle, holds it away from her starched apron and lowers it into the arms of the exhausted woman.

"It's a girl. She weighs three point eight kilograms. She appears healthy and racially pure." A girl! The words she had read with ardour, the Führer's words, rush through her mind:

Not in the respectable bourgeois or in the virtuous spinster does the nation see its human ideal, but in the defiant embodiment of masculine power and in females who are again able to bring men into the world.

She has failed him. She has borne him a girl. But the young mother is pleased with the perfection with which her little daughter has been dressed. The voile curtains that had bulged like sails in a storm now hang limp.

The man in the corridor finds his cigarette packet empty. At last my father is allowed to see us. I think he likes me.

"The Memelland has just come home into the Reich," my father announces. "Hitler was received in Memel three days ago. A lot of song and dance!" From his ebony frame the moustached one stares down on our little family.

"We will have many more children," my mother says as if to comfort my father, "if there is no war!" One day a row of little boys will be sitting on her new corner bench. One day she might wear the blue ribbon, that coveted medal, inscribed *The Child Ennobles the Mother*. This child has cost her blood and strength. Her future sons will ennoble her. My father has been ushered out of the room; the infant finds the nipple and suckles, and her mother is strangely nourished.

Regulations demand that each neonate be checked out with regard to its racial features. Confidently my mother takes me to the doctor. The female practitioner does not hide her consternation.

'We have here more than a mere *hint* of Mongolian influence,' she pronounces icily. "Your child exhibits marked eye folds; she therefore cannot be considered a pure Aryan."

My mother is distraught. Her child contaminated by an inferior race!? How had this unwelcome genetic trait invaded her family? She reads all the entries in the obligatory *Ahnenpass* and is relieved to find that it documents *four generations'* racial purity. And yet, she anxiously scrutinizes my face.

"The epicanthic fold, the skin of the upper eyelid," explained the ophthalmologist to me years later, "may be seen in young children of any race. This trait is found before the bridge of the nose begins to elevate, usually before or during the first well-baby examination."

There will be war. Its flames can hardly wait to be set free to lick at all that has been accomplished. Its imminent onset can be felt, smelt, tasted. Confidence, national pride and dread mingle. Of their private fears no one dares to speak. Must not speak. Oma, having looked after us well, has returned home, leaving my mother and me alone together. I am six weeks old when my mother takes me to Duisburg on the train, back to her parents and introduces me to my other grandmother, Helene Fischdick. We never meet again.

Adolf Hitler decrees the total destruction of Warsaw.

4

A thousand kilometres east

Into my adult mind float the earliest disconnected memories of a two-three year old child. She does not understand about cinemas, bombing raids and air raid shelters, eating difficulties and grown-ups' fears.

...a large sandpit...children playing...I carry sand on a small twig... suddenly Mami drags me away...we are running...

...a dark hall...real fairytale figures flickering in a bluish glow... moving... talking... a wailing noise...Mami pulls me outside...running...

...at a kitchen table. Spinach is spooned into my mouth. Mami tells me about Little Red Riding Hood, Hansel and Gretel, Snow White... chewing...retching...a small blue chaise-longue...a big woolly black toy terrier and a shiny pink dog made from waxed cloth called *Cheri*... I am being sick again...

...*Bimberlein*, my small teddy, and a handkerchief have to come to bed with me every night....

...deep, deep snow...riding high on a man's shoulders...and the way to the clinic...at home with Mami and a new baby brother...Oma's yellow blouse feels soft... I play with the yellow buttons...Tante Leni is here...by Mami's chair I watch the baby eat her breast...

The German Army has laid siege to Leningrad. Thousands of people are dying of starvation and cold.

Black-and-white photographs tell stories I do not remember:

Mami bending into a white wicker pram...

Papi in uniform in a park, smiling down at a little girl in dress and bonnet...

A serious girl standing on a leather chair, a large bow in her hair. She is holding a teddy bear. It is not her own. The photographer cannot coax a smile from her...

In Oma's yard. A girl in her nightdress, so sleepy....

A little girl is dancing with other children. Bulky knickers showing from under her dress.

A narrow corridor has been created across the frozen Lake Ladoga. Supplies are brought into the stricken city of Leningrad. The 'Road of Life' is alleviating some hunger but the cold prevails and thousands are still dying.

Plans are laid by Britain to bomb flammable German city centres "to render the German industrial population homeless, spiritless and as far as possible dead".

On a balmy moonlit May night in 1942 Cologne is bombed. It is not the first time; it has already happened one hundred and eight times before. But tonight the city will undergo its "ordeal by fire". Leonard Cheshire described it as "the most monstrous sight in all the history of bombing". (So far.) Six hundred acres are a solid blaze. The glare of the burning city outshines even the sun. My grandparents in Duisburg, a few miles further down the Rhine, watch the crimson glow with horror and in Wuppertal my mother, my tiny baby brother in her arms, stands by the bedroom window, terrified. A pillar of smoke rises five kilometres into the atmosphere.

The flight of the panic-stricken traumatised homeless, pouring out of the devastated Cologne, acts like a shot from a starting pistol, triggering wave upon wave of evacuees packing trains to the East. Children must leave industrial cities, like Duisburg and Wuppertal, to escape their meticulous destruction. So my grandmother, mother, baby Gert-Dieter and me, also board an east-bound train that takes us a thousand kilometres to a land where not *sirens* but *stork nests* crown the roofs; where no bombers darken the sky but larks trill above the fields. In Memelland we will sleep safely through the night. With us travel the proverbial "thirty three pieces of luggage". My grandfather in Duisburg, my father in France, no man accompanies us. In our family, as in millions of others all over the world, our fathers will not see us children during our formative years. Women must fend for us and for themselves.

Memory fragments of the last kilometre of the journey: Uzballen... Mami's summer dress is strewn with large flowers... she wears a scarf wrapped around her head like a turban so you cannot see her black hair parted in the centre...two brown horses are trotting...an open carriage decorated with green birch twigs that rustle in the wind...it is Whitsun... Elly Wolff is clicking her tongue...leather reins run through her fists... Clop, clop, clop...cart wheels rattle and rut a sandy path...I sway from side to side...a warm wind is blowing my plaits...

Oma will stay in the little farmhouse where she was born and which now belongs to her eldest brother Georg and his wife Emma. Mami and Gert-Dieter will live there too. And I? There is no room for me. See the big pink-brick house over there? That's Elly Wolff's farm. That's where *I* shall live, with Tante Elly. But Mami and Oma and Gert-Dieter are not so far away. I only have to walk past the old barn with the storks' nest.

5

Summer paradise

G reen blades are shooting from the sand. In the course of the summer the young rye will turn into a cloth of white gold, and amongst its dense stalks poppies will glow like rubies and cornflowers like sapphires. In the dry sparse meadow grass wildflowers abound. A palisade of spruce shelters field, meadow and a few scattered farmsteads. Like a great army the dark trees encircle the undulating land; tall soldiers stand shoulder to shoulder, dressed in black-green tunics, their long wide sleeves sweeping the forest floor. Who knows of this hamlet's existence? A sandy path veers off the main road, easily missed by the traveller on the ancient trade route which we call the *Chaussee*; for some it is the Castle Road.

Running parallel with the sluggish waters of the river Memel, it intersects the vital thoroughfare from Königsberg via Tilsit, across the river to Tauroggen and on to Riga and Leningrad and also linking Lithuania Major with the Baltic. Uszballen: tiny and unimportant, unengaged in the terrible dramas that are currently running in the theatres of war to its west, its east, its north, its south, not interfering in its quiet way of life. It is true that over centuries European tragedies had also been staged in its vicinity, but I doubt whether this hamlet has ever held any place of importance in the world of trade and politics. In the summer of 1942 it offers idyllic peace. No harm will come here.

At Wischwill railway station Elly Wolff meets our family off the 'toy train', the *Bimmelbahn* (because it rings its bell as it goes: bim, bim, bim) and takes me into paradise. Behind a weathered fence, silvered in old age, several black-and-white cows graze without looking up, but the geese by a half-timbered barn stretch out their necks menacingly and hiss their protest as we drive by. On the roof of the barn, on one long red leg, rests a stork. Mami has come back to her idealized world: East Prussia, of which Memelland is a part again. Forty years ago my Oma had left the Uszballen smallholding in search of work and found her new life in Germany's industrial west. Today she is back in her birthplace – for the first time. In less than six years her homeland will be irretrievably lost, but during this brief period my childhood becomes woven into the landscape; its beauty and tranquillity become part of my fabric. I become a *country girl*, no matter how many years I will later spend in cities.

Oma is pointing out the little school where she had learnt to read and write and understand numbers, the rudiments of her shrewd business sense. It is not for me to know how she feels being back in her birth home, amongst rye and forest, with her brother and the storks. The Child knows neither past nor future, has no sense of context, makes no enquiry into the circumstances that caused her forebears to settle and to farm in this borderland between many cultures. She is here – making her internal home in a fairytale world. Whether her ancestors had been part of the re-colonization of the land from which the Teutonic Knights had driven the Slavs in the Middle Ages; whether they had survived the plague which in the course of two years had savaged the peoples at the beginning of the eighteenth century; whether they had been part of the re-population of the near-empty wasteland by the Prussian king who showed himself tolerant to Europe's persecuted minorities; whether they had come with the new settlers from Salzburg or the Netherlands, or Swabia, Franconia or the Swiss Alps; or whether my great-great-grandfather had crossed the border from Lithuania to farm his own soil: by whichever route this family arrived in Uszballen to find liberty and safety, it is of no concern to the Child who herself finds security here and the freedom to roam. In the post-war upheaval many documents were lost, but the Child has locked and preserved in her heart the wonder of this peaceful island in the turbulent seas of a World War. Frontiers moved and languages changed and she, in early childhood, is given a heart open to the nations.

Oma went west at the same age her granddaughter would do so. Her journey had taken her to the Rhine, where mine would begin. She would have boarded the narrow-gauge steam train at Wischwill and crossed the Memel over the *Luisenbrücke* into Tilsit, then westwards into the Ruhr Region. Had she been homesick? There in the grimy steel city, running her shop alongside her husband, had her thoughts wandered to the dark forests? Had she painted for my grandfather a picture of her beautiful home that he had never seen? Why would I care about such grown-up matters? I am three years old and know nothing of the thousands of panic-stricken Germans fleeing from the infernos and rubble of their cities, nor of the cattle wagons filled with children and their families being taken to their deaths. Here in Uszballen the sky stays blue without menacing droning black birds laying devastating 'eggs'; here the nights are not broken by the whining of sirens and the terrified rush into cellars or air raid shelters. Here is *Lebensraum*, my living space. Tante Elly's red-brick farmhouse is spacious, and in the yard, the byres and the stables, something interesting is going on all the while. At bedtime Tante Elly reads me fairy stories while I watch the last of the sun's rays make the golden bed-knobs sparkle. I become, no, I *am* the youngest *Geißlein,* the Little Goat who helps her mother rescue her brothers and sisters from the Wicked Wolf. The seeds are sown: I shall become a rescuer. My life's *Leitmotif* will be rescuing others, with all its unforeseen and unhappy consequences.

A few days after our arrival, the main transport of Königsberg Jews leaves in the direction of Minsk.

Even if the horrors of war do not reach us here, the Child is not entirely sheltered from suffering. The little brooch Tante Elly buys for her is sold for "*die Winterhilfe*", to send warm clothes to "our soldiers in Russia" so they do not suffer in the cold and snow. The farmyard itself is witness to unimagined cruelty. With mounting horror the Child watches her beloved Tante grab a goose by its neck, clamp it between her knees and push into its unwilling beak long 'sausages' of dough! The goose squirms but has to endure. The Child's cries of, "Please, let the goose go," are not heeded.

"Its liver will grow nice and big," is the explanation for this terrible thing.

Good things also happen in the farmyard. Especially in the byre; when Tante Elly squirts warm foamy milk straight from the cow's teat into the lovely cup she has given me. It has golden words written on it which she reads to me every time.

Ein Kind …
A child that is as good as you
shall have her milk
and a lump of gold, too.

I drink while she makes the cow splish splosh milk into her bucket. Slowly a lump of gold appears at the bottom of my cup. I am a good girl!

Only women people the Child's world. Oma's brother, Onkel Georg is not here, Tante Elly's husband is "at the front", Opa is in Duisburg and Papi is "in the war". But there is Ronni. He is a man. He works for Tante Elly. Ronni likes me. He smiles at me. He speaks different words from me. His trousers are baggy and hang loosely on broad suspenders; his shirt sleeves are rolled up; and from his wooden clogs peek his toes. Rain or shine, his felt hat (it looks like a little upside-down boat) is cocked to one side. Ronni mows the meadow with a long-handled scythe and when the blade is too blunt he props the scythe up on one knee, "whets" it, dunks a rag into some liquid in a tin next to him and taps and scrapes the blade until his thumb running along it tells him that it is sharp enough. It's fun to copy him. She finds two sticks and from behind a pile of birch logs drags an old wooden sledge and sets it next to her friend. Just like he, she 'sharpens her scythe' and does not forget to dip a rag into the tin filled with water. Ronni laughs.

Did the little girl remind *René*, this Frenchman who had been forced into agricultural labour far away from his own country, of his own little daughter in Lyon or Anvers or Paris? And did he make it home safely through a war-lacerated landscape in 1945? And did *his* fatherless child recognize him when he stood on the doorstep? Did she bond with him then?

The little house where Oma grew up and now lives feels dark and cramped, especially when the oil lamps cast strange shadows on the bare walls in the evenings. But in the daytime it is lovely because it has a real garden – with an apple tree that spreads its branches across grass, flower bed and a deep well. Tante Emma lifts the Child to see over the rim of the round brick wall. It is scary to look down into the gloom, where dark water hides. From a shaven tree trunk hangs a bucket on a long rusty chain. Tante Emma levers the bucket over the side of the well. The chain creaks; the bucket clanks against the bricks. The Child eagerly anticipates the splash! When the full dripping bucket reaches the top again, she looks to see if a frog has taken a free ride up. In the shade of the apple tree the summer wind rocks the old family cradle. Flickering shadows dance on baby brother's face and white restless clouds sail towards Russia.

Only once during that summer do I meet other children, in the schoolhouse where Oma had sat at the same desks fifty years ago, and where I soon will learn to write and read letters and numbers, now that Uszballen is our home. From behind her grandmother's skirt the Child shyly watches boys and girls write on slates. Some of the older children are bending over the little heads of the younger, helping them. Oma is talking with the teacher while slate pen screeches on slate and some of the children are secretly watching me. Quietly I slide out of the door into the heat of noon.

The path feels soft under my shoes. Insects hum and buzz and drone and whirr. Poppy petals flip-flap gently in the breeze. Just look at the cornflowers! As blue as the sky. And the marguerites: white with a butter middle. The rye is now taller than I.

"Come and pick us. Come and pick us," sing the flowers. I must not go into the rye, because deep inside lives the *Roggenmuhme*. It is she who sows the flowers to lure children into the field. I am not really going in, no, just far enough to pick this poppy and that cornflower over there. The Child climbs across a shallow ditch. The poppies have hairy stems. Cornflowers and marguerites lure her deeper and deeper into the corn which rustles above her head. The long beards tickle her face. The flowers are so beautiful and are calling, "Come. Come." The air is alive with the music of crickets and bees and it smells of straw and warm sand. Somewhere up there in the never-ending blue sings a lark, full of joy but the Child's heart is climbing into her throat.

"Oma! Oma!"

Lark and crickets are still making music but the beards scratch her hot face. Flies buzz around her menacingly. Are the stalks not rustling wildly in there? Oh no! The *Roggenmuhme* has seen her. She drops the bunch of red and white and blue she has gathered; it is no longer a treasure. She is crying, trampling corn and flowers... Someone is calling her name. *The Roggenmuhme!* She looks up - into two concerned faces: Oma's and the teacher's.

My grandmother takes my hand and pulls me out of the field. Are there children watching and laughing at me? No matter. I have been found. But I still love to wander when the grown-ups are too busy to notice.

They say that Opa is coming on the train to live with us. He has sold his shop in Duisburg. Will I know him? On Oma's photograph he has a very shiny head. When I was really little we would play a game. He would carry me to the lamp post, put me down, make me walk to the next, pick me up, carry me to the next, put me down – all the way to the end of the street.

And now he is here. He looks tired, having travelled for many days and nights. I watch when he covers his face each morning with white foam. In neat little strokes he scrapes it off again with a savage-looking knife. And then his face feels soft, like mine. He and Oma move into a fairytale cottage in the forest. They have bought chairs with hearts carved in the back - just like those that belonged to Little Red Riding Hood's grandmother. The little house has wooden shutters and a bench beneath the window. Opa must work on Elly Wolff's farm because he is too old to be a soldier. Exhausted from many broken nights and constant fear in the Ruhr city, my grandfather is finding peace amongst fields and forests.

The landscape is brooding in the mid-summer heat. Everyone is asleep like the people in Sleeping Beauty's castle. No one sees me sidle out of the back door. I set out to the fairytale cottage. The sun is baking the sand on the path and the soles of my feet burn through the sandals. Insects move drowsily. A blue cloth stretches from tree top to tree top; from forest to forest. Today no white woolly lambs are chasing each other across that sky; they have gone to sleep, too. Today the blood-red poppies cannot lure me but the forest opens its doors to me. I have never walked so far by myself. The sun has kept watch over me, but has left me now. The spruces tower like giants. Sometimes they allow a few rays to reach the forest floor where the bilberries are turning blue. There is the cottage! The shutters are folded back against the log walls. I knock. I am Snow White; I am Little Red Riding Hood; I am Gretel... No one stirs inside. The door handle is too high to reach.

"Oma, Opa, are you there?" I climb on to the bench and peer through the window. The heart-chairs are arranged around a bare pine table on which rests a glass filled with marguerites and grasses. I will sit out here and wait for them. They won't be long..I am tired...I want to lie down...

"Oh there you are! I have looked for you everywhere." Tante Elly lifts sleepy me on to the luggage rack of her bicycle. "Hold on tight," she says. The sun has already sunk behind the dark forest as she peddles towards the red-brick house.

Ronni has scythed the meadows and the sun has dried the grass. I have helped to stack the hay on the wagon. My baby brother can sit up in his pushchair. The baby stork has learnt to fly. The geese can scarcely totter around the barn, so heavy are their chests. The rye is ready for harvest. My sandals fill with warm sand as I saunter along the path. The sun, a fiery ball, is preparing to go to bed, pulling its crimson curtains around. I sing my own song, my very own song:

Die Sonne geht ins Himmelbett
hinter roten Gardinen…

Air and sand are cooling. White veils rise from the meadows like ghosts and the forest forms a dense dark wall. From behind the spruce palisade rolls up a huge yellow moon... I shiver and do not know why tonight everything feels so scary, as if the very air is loaded with sadness. "Mami!"

Behind the farm gate, *Wölfchen*, Tante Emma's guard dog, is tearing at his long rusty chain. It clanks in the darkness. *Wölfchen* can reach me! He has always let me stroke him but now – he bites my leg! I scream out of pain and fear. Tante Emma comes running and orders *Wölfchen* back into his kennel. Mami is just behind her, picks me up and carries me into the house. The wound is not deep and will heal but my heart hurts: *Wölfchen* is no longer my friend. I cannot trust him after this.

Leningrad is being shelled mercilessly and many children, their mothers and grandparents are still dying of starvation. Nobody here talks of the tanks that had waited camouflaged in the forest a year ago before breaking cover and rushing to assault not only that city but countless other towns and villages in Lithuania, Belarus, Ukraine, and in Russia's heartland. No one mentions Jews who had been neighbours.

Here in Uszballen – throughout all that wonderful summer no tanks leave track marks in the soft sand; only the hoofs of Tante Elly's horses and the tyres of her bicycle and the soles of my sandals.

Here in Uszballen – the sky is filled with clouds and birds and insects and no bombers unload their lethal cargo.

Here in Uszballen – we do not hear menacing sounds of engines and detonations. Here bees buzz and storks clack and cows moo and geese hiss and my baby brother gurgles and *Wölfchen* barks and wags his tail and Ronni laughs and owls hoot and frogs give evening concerts.

Here in Uszballen – grown-ups talk in whispers.

The German Army has reached the Volga and is fighting desperately over Stalin's city on the river's banks.

The storks have abandoned their wagon wheel on the barn roof and are on their way to Africa. The golden rye field now is stubble. The farm cart is stacked high with crates and cases. Elly Wolff's horses veer off the sandy path and turn on to the *Chaussee*: Mami with her two children are on the way. To where?

For summer bliss, for safety and freedom to roam, I will have to wait.

6

Green grassy triangle

Tante Elly says "brrrr", the two brown horses obey and her farm cart comes to a halt by a grey wall. I am glad when Mami lifts me off our crates and cases where I have perched uncomfortably as the horses clop-clopped down the sandy path from Uszballen on to the main road. But where are we now? Mami carries Gert-Dieter through a low gate into a yard stacked with birch trunks and I trip behind her, clutching Klaus, my boy doll. Over there: that looks like a cowshed, but much shabbier than Tante Elly's. The stone steps leading into a grey house are steep for me and we still have further to climb: up squeaky wooden stairs, their brown paint chipped, into an attic, a dingy open space where the floor boards are dark and on which the sun, slanting through tiny windows, paints small squares of light. Above the staircase tattered wallpaper hangs loose. It feels sad up here. There are several doors. Mami unlocks the first one and the room that opens before us is bright, full of light from two windows. Two huge brown beds with high wooden headboards are set against the wall. They have no shiny golden knobs. Who has bought all this furniture? Wardrobe – table – chairs? Where can my dolls sleep? Oh yes, over there in the corner by the big green-tiled stove. Mami and Tante Elly are dragging our cases and crates up the stairs. I run to one of the windows. "Look, Klaus, look! See that tiny meadow? See the daisies on the green grassy triangle?"

"This is our home now." Mami's voice sounds tired and sad and from the window, both clutching our babies, we watch Tante Elly's horses and her farm cart disappear under trees with brown and golden leaves. We have left all behind in Uszballen: Oma and Opa, *Wölfchen*, the cows and the geese. And Ronni. And my cup with the lump of gold. And Tante Emma and her well and apple tree. And now Tante Elly has gone, too! How it hurts. What is there to explore up here? There is just this dark loft. I watch Mami unpack. I also notice that her eyes are all red. We are back in *Wischwill*, where Tante Elly had met us off the *Bimmelbahn*.

"To save electricity", we "go to bed with the chickens". It is not long before ice flowers grow on the window panes. When I huff at them, they change; I can make new patterns and bore little holes through which the stars twinkle. Mami wants me to learn this song – for Christmas.

> *Hohe Nacht der klaren Sterne,*
> *die wie weite Brücken sind.*
> *Heut' soll sich die Welt erneuern*
> *wie ein neugebor'nes Kind.*

> High night of the clear stars,
> spanning like wide bridges.
> Today the world will renew itself
> like a new-born child.

How brittle, how cold the words sound. Like icicles. Not like Oma's song. That makes me feel all warm inside. I remember the velvety sky in Uszballen filled with twinkling jewels when she sang it to me:

> *Weisst du, wieviel Sternlein stehen*
> *an dem blauen Himmelszelt?*
> *Weisst du, wieviel Wolken gehen*
> *weit hinüber alle Welt?*

> *Gott der Herr hat sie gezählet,*
> *daß ihm auch nicht eines fehlet*
> *an der ganzen großen Schar.*

Do you know how many stars there are
under the blue sky's tent?
Do you know how many clouds
sail across the whole world?

God the Lord has counted them all
so that he should not lose even one
from this great host.

...The stars become the Child's friends. From afar they bring their light into her tiny world. Sometimes she gets out of the big bed at night, peeps underneath the black-out blind and watches them until she feels numb with cold, and hears the mouse squeak and scurry along the skirting board. Quick, get back under the duvet...

In the daytime the green-tiled stove roars happily because Mami feeds it with birch logs. She opens its little black door to push them inside and the flames lick at them greedily. Outside, just like in the fairy tale, *Frau Holle*, keeps shaking her duvet and the feathers turn to snow, piling up higher and higher on the trees and the houses, the street and the grassy triangle. It is not often that we leave the attic, but when we do, Mami pulls us on a sled and I wear my white soft fur coat and hat and muff.

The butchery in Stalingrad is over. The Red Army begins to move westwards.

When the snow has melted, I sneak down into the yard. The woman living downstairs does not like me, shoos me back up the stairs and has forbidden her little girl to play with me. That girl eats raw potatoes! I saw it! The grey wall of the house has a few windows; one looks different from all the rest. The grey wall is my playground. It throws my ball back to me and sometimes I can catch it. Mami's washing line makes a good skipping rope. A very old wooden fence guards our house. Rough boards are nailed to uneven stakes. And who lives in those wooden houses across the road?

"*Da wohnen die Litauer.*" If the Lithuanians live there, I'd better not cross the road and go near those houses.

In our room, by the window, we have a machine on which Mami sews things. The golden letters on the black iron frame say that it is a SINGER, but sing it never does, it only rattles and whirrs. There is also a photograph in a frame. Mami looks younger and is wearing a hat and a white coat. With her is a man in a smart uniform, wearing a shako. The man is called *Papi*. The two are smiling because they have just got married. I feel a bit funny when I look at the picture.

The man called *Papi* comes to visit. It is Christmas and the *Weihnachtsmann*, Father Christmas, has climbed up to our loft. He asks me whether I have been a good girl and I say 'yes' because I am frightened of him. Then the *Weihnachtsmann* takes my hand and leads me into our living room. A fir tree has grown between the windows! It is full of small flames on the top of white candles and they have made our room magical. Then the *Weihnachtsmann* lays into my arms the loveliest doll in the world. Her dress and bonnet are of pink silk and her cornflower-blue eyes look at me, while four small white teeth show between her red lips and I can see a pink tongue move. The *Weihnachtsmann* shows me that if I tilt her backwards, she closes her eyes and her long black eyelashes hang like curtains.

"If you press her tummy, she cries *Maman*," he says. Yes, she does. "She has come all the way from France," he tells me and I see tears above the long white beard. When the *Weihnachtsmann* has gone, the man called *Papi* comes into our room. I show him my new doll and tell him that I will call her *Friedel*. While Papi is with us I have to sleep in a dingy little chamber under low beams. I don't like it there but *Papi* does not stay long. I promise myself never to take Friedel out of the house. At night I dream of dropping her, or pushing her eyes in and I am so scared that I wake up.

January is bitterly cold and the stove is very hungry. Mami has to carry many birch logs up the sqeaky stairs to feed it. In February Gert-Dieter is one year old and I am four in March. In my red wooden birthday-ring burn four small white candles and I am wearing my special hair-band, made of velvet primroses. Oma and Opa come to celebrate and take photos of us by the grey wall. And now another scary dream wakes me: we are all sitting around the table, my candles are burning in the birthday-ring, and I reach over to touch my Opa. But my arm catches fire and I burn to death.

No one reads me fairytales, but I know them by heart and tell them to the dolls. When I am thirsty I drink the water Mami has boiled and left to cool. When I am hungry I eat *dicke Milch*, milk left to sour in small bowls on the window sill. The snow has finally left the grassy triangle and it is dry enough to take the dolls out to where daisies crowd around us with upturned white and pink little faces and the same woolly lambs that had sailed above Uszballen, play in this sky, too. In the enclosure across the road frolics a horse, happy that it's springtime. I miss the rye field and *Ronni*, but this is *my* little meadow. In armfuls I carry my dolls over to my small paradise: Klaus is wearing an orange-and-white crocheted dress; Erica is much smaller than Klaus and has wiry yellow hair; Dieter, smaller still, is a real *Schildkrötenpuppe*; on the nape of his neck you can clearly see the marque of the tortoise; Marianne by far the oldest, with a leather body and Oma's *real* auburn hair, was once Mami's doll. On my grassy triangle we eat red radishes and talk and when we feel tired, we lie down among the daisies and I sing a lullaby for them.

> *Gänseblümchen, mein Engelchen,*
> *fall nicht von deinem Stengelchen.*
> *Geh zu Bett, mein Kind.*

> Little daisy, my little angel,
> don't fall off your stalk.
> Go to bed, my child.

And when the sun slides behind the grey house and the air begins to cool and the daisies hide their faces, I carry my dolls to their corner by the stove and kiss them good-night.

Now that I am four I am old enough to walk by myself to the Day Centre. From the window in the grey gable wall Mami is watching me stride under the greening lime trees towards the big white house, but when I think that she can no longer see me, I dawdle, pick dandelions and buttercups, always careful not to let the stinging nettles catch my legs. I like my Kindergarten very much; especially Tante Hildegard who is the older one and Tante Gabi who has long blond hair; both laugh a lot. Only when Tante Hildegard waggles a raw ox tongue to make *us* laugh, I feel scared. In the mornings we sit at long tables, play and make things. We sometimes sing and before we have lunch, Tante Gabi says, *"Händchen falten, Köpfchen senken; immer an Adolf Hitler denken."* Fold your hands, bow your heads; always think of Adolf Hitler.

After we have eaten we sleep on little mattresses on the floor upstairs, with the curtains closed. Then I dawdle back home. I can see the grey wall. I make no friends and take nobody to our upstairs room.

The nursery teachers are very excited because soon we will celebrate a *Special Day*, a birthday. I know that it cannot be mine because I have just had it. Whose then? We learn new songs and practice marching and waving a small red flag which has a black wheel painted on it. In the morning of the *Special Day* we pick violets, because "they are the Führer's favourite flowers". On a small table, draped in white, has been set a large photograph in a black frame. It shows the stern face of a man; and I don't want to look at his eyes. One by one, we come forward and lay our little blue bunches down before the man's picture, then we sing to him because "we are happy that he is our Führer". Tante Hildegard makes a speech and we all stretch out our right arms as far in front of us as we can and greet the picture: "Heil Hitler". Tante Gabi hands us our flags and we line up to walk under the lime trees. Our flags flutter in the wind and then I see big flags like ours everywhere, hanging from windows and high poles. "Heil Hitler. Heil Hitler" we greet everyone and I add, "It's the Führer's birthday today, you know."

In the summer we go to the river, the Memel, and play on its muddy bank. And there we stumble on a small grey bundle that smells bad and is covered in white wiggly worms. What is that?

"It's a drowned cat," explains Tante Hildegard, "and the maggots are eating it." Sometimes I think about that body by the river.

The day centres in the East were particularly well run by the National Socialist People's Welfare, the NSV *(Volkswohlfahrt)*, to indoctrinate the children and create an ideological stronghold.

Clouds are racing along the blue that spans my grassy triangle, spans the whole wide world. Suddenly they are torn, tattered – then disappear altogether. A big brown beetle unfolds its large wings – and is off. A May bug. I sing:

Maikäfer flieg.
Dein Vater ist im Krieg.
Deine Mutter ist im Pommernland.
Pommernland ist abgebrannt.
Maikäfer flieg.

Fly, May bug, fly.
Your father is in the war,
Your mother in Pomerania.
Pomerania is burnt down.
Fly, May bug, fly.

Isn't Papi in the *war* – somewhere? I remember a parcel with "peaches" arriving which Papi had sent from the *war*. But they had blue furry skins and we could not eat them.

A sweet scent wafts across the yard: it is the lilac in blossom and butterflies and bees jostle for places. Under the eaves hang swallows' nests, like dark round cups, that keep the chirping baby birds safe. And when I stand on tiptoes and bend my head right back I can see their orange throats. Their parents fly low, sail back and forth, back and forth, and the wind tugs at my rye-blond plaits. A long farm cart is unloading birch trunks which are piled high in the yard. The snowy stems look beautiful. If I climbed them I could touch the sky…

…I have reached the top trunk. My arms and legs feel so warm because I am closer to the sun. I am a queen on her throne.

"*Mami, kuck mal wo ich bin!*" I wave to her, wanting her to see how high I have climbed. Her face turns white. I feel something moving…Mami is screaming…the woodpile has come alive…I am slipping…rolling… Mami catches me by the arm and just in time pulls me off the rolling trunks before they can bury me. Seconds later they lie strewn across the yard. Mami's ruby ring has rolled somewhere beneath them…

In Wuppertal people are getting stuck in melting asphalt; the air is filled with the stench of gas and fire and earth; flames are racing through the narrow valley of the Wupper. More than a quarter of a million bombs have rained on the city of my birth.

In Duisburg the dazed residents are leaving the air raid shelters after the two hundred and seventy second bombing attack on their stricken city.

The July evening is light and balmy. There has been an accident in Uszballen. All night the naked light bulb glows and each time I wake up, Mami is sitting at the table...waiting... her voice trembles as she tells me,

"Opa was helping to bring in the cows for milking, when he stumbled over a ditch. They have taken him to hospital in Tilsit and Oma has gone with him".

Tonight there is a full moon and somewhere a dog is howling. I am scared. Morning comes: *Opa is dead.*

Oma arrives in Wischwill. She and Mami have to catch an early train "to buy a coffin". Someone in the village is looking after my brother but I am a big girl and must stay by myself until they return.

"There is the potty under the bed, and at lunchtime the woman downstairs will bring you something to eat." The door closes behind them; the stairs squeak; the front door clicks shut.

I rush to the window. Their backs are already hidden under the lime trees, getting smaller...smaller. I clatter down the wooden stairs. Neither the front door nor the gate are locked. No one stops me. I am running, running, past the Kindergarten. In the station yard a pile of birch trunks hides me as I watch the train puffing and whistling into the station. Its doors fling open; I see Mami and Oma climbing into the carriage. Now I stumble towards the train, howling, screaming, flailing my arms. Just as the train is about to pull out, they see me – and jump off. Upset and angry, they march me back to the house, drag me up the stairs, push me back into the room – and turn the key. Rattling the door handle is fruitless. I race from door to window; from the window to the door, crying, pumping the handle again and again. But no one comes. Exhausted, I curl up on the floor at the foot of the door and fall asleep. At midday a key turns and a bowl of strawberries is pushed towards me. Then the door is locked. I don't want the strawberries but cry myself to sleep again... It is dark outside when Mami and Oma are back – and they are entirely dressed in black.

Black also is the sombre knot of grown-ups towering above me. Words drone. Soil thuds on wood. Sobbing. They are burying my Opa.

Without her husband there is nothing to hold Oma in Uszballen and from her fairytale cottage she comes to live with us in the dismal crate-like chamber under the rafters. Uszballen is pushed away like an empty plate after a meal.

What is a hernia? You die from it. At least the Nazi-run *Kreiskrankenhaus* in Tilsit, the regional hospital, had more important tasks than wasting time on an elderly civilian who cannot hold the Eastern front like a good German soldier. They let him die – in pain.

Though the summer is hot and lush, a dark winter has entered our loft. Oma's black clothes hang loose on her sunken body and her cheeks are hollow. Mami takes a photograph of her and me leaning against a big metal drum.

Something akin to a grey army blanket has also spread over our playroom in the Kindergarten. Gone are frivolity and fun; we have become sombre children.

...On the grassy triangle the Child dreams and makes up stories, far removed from the sadness and worry in the attic rooms where tears flow, voices are hushed, odd glances exchanged...

The air itself seems to be filled with fear as people expect the Red Army.

"*Die Russen kommen.*" It is just a matter of time.

When I cannot sleep I slip up to the window and lift the black-out. The sky is red and orange and far away rumbles a thunderstorm.

"*Die Russen kommen.*"

Like a dark shadow Oma is moving amongst us. She is no longer there for me. Nor is Mami. Blackness.

...The Child immerses herself in arranging the houses and trees of her wooden village on the table in the centre of the room and in the corner by the big stove she cares for her dolls. Her mother recites sad ballads. But the Child shuts out what she does not want to hear or see. Nightmares of burning to death and of Friedel losing her eyes wake her...

Because Papi is in the war I must from now on pray for him every night. I must ask *God* "to bring him back safely" and learn songs with many verses until I know them by heart. One is about the blood of Jesus, and angels who are required to sing in order to stop Satan from gulping me down. I dread bedtime. I squirm but must not show it. Mami, too, is feeling uncomfortable about all this. I can tell. But it must be done. Why does she not read me fairytales instead?

Every child is to be immunised. The medical officer is rough and hurts me very badly. Mami calls him "a butcher". The two big blisters on my upper arm will accompany me through life. Against measles there is no immunisation. Our room is now also blacked-out in daytime so that Gert-Dieter and I "will not go blind". A lady doctor (in trousers and riding a bicycle) visits us and pushes a cold thermometer into my bottom, pulls it out and tells Mami a number. Soon the measles have gone.

Christmas. Without Papi and Opa. Oma and Mami are crying by a bare little fir tree. The *Weihnachtsmann* has obviously forgotten our attic: this time there are no presents, no biscuits, no apples. Mami has sewn a bag for each of us, from old sheeting, and has embroidered our names on them with thick blue cotton. The bags are empty.

My grassy triangle has pushed off the snow and my fifth birthday is forgotten. Mami has no candles for my wooden ring. Next year I start school. I can now skip without tripping up and I catch my rubber ball as it bounces off the grey wall. The sand on our road feels warm as it squiggles between my toes. The rumbling thunder is coming closer each day and at night the sky flares red.

"*Die Russen kommen.*"

The lilac is wilting and the woodpile has shrunk down to a few trunks; the swallow fledglings have learnt to fly and I dawdle back from Kindergarten. Why have they sent me home before I had my nap? Our window in the grey wall is open and someone is standing by it, looking out for me, and it's not Mami. It's a man! My heart is beating fast. I feel strange, and when the man calls to me, I pretend not to hear. I sneak round the corner of the house, out of his sight. I don't want to but I must go upstairs. Slowly I press the handle of the door into our living room. A man in uniform and boots, a man with sandy hair, bends down to me. It's *Papi*. He wants to kiss me but I squirm out of his reach. And then I see the half-packed crates and cases all over the room. What is happening?

Papi has come from the *war*, for a just few hours, to help us leave Wischwill. From the road, below our windows, a loudspeaker blares. "All evacuees must leave by six o'clock tomorrow morning! All evacuees must…"

Evacuees. That's us. The dim light bulb burns all night. I doze and wake and doze again while the grown-ups are frantically stripping, wrapping, folding, packing. My last night in Wischwill. I have not said *Auf Wiedersehn* to Tante Hildegard and Tante Gabi. What have they done with my dolls? They are no longer in the corner by the cold stove. Who will play on my grassy triangle and make daisy-chains?

Our "thirty three pieces of luggage" are standing ready at the top of the stairs. Our furniture has to stay behind. For the last time I look around the room and see saucepan handles and a frying pan poking out from under my bed. Then I pull the door shut and run into the yard. The lilac's umbels droop limp and brown. Few birch stems are left. The family is waiting by a farm cart. The sun peeps over the roof tops and greets the grey wall. Dew glistens on the grassy triangle. I want to stand among the daisies – just once more. There is no time. We must go now! The grey house disappears behind the lime trees. No children's voices sound from the Kindergarten. The horses are straining forward. The evacuees stuff their belongings on to the impatient train. A whistle shrills. Black smoke shrouds the meadows. Where are we going? West. I listen to the rhythm of wheel on rail. No one weeps. We cross the bridge over the Memel into Tilsit, but I do not remember...

We got out of the territory *north* of the river in the first of three evacuation waves. I understand the order to clear the Memelland of civilians to have come from Hitler himself. Had we lived *south* of the Memel, we would have been forbidden to leave and would only have fled when it was all too late; when the tanks of the Red Army were already sweeping everything before them; when cold and hunger would surely have killed the two lone women and their young children; or my mother and grandmother gang-raped in our view; or I might have been left a wandering orphan, a *Wolfskind*, a feral child, to die of exposure and hunger in the East Prussian forest.

7

Village of refuge

How far, how long have we travelled? Days and nights. Were we pushed into sidings to let some all-important trains roll east? I remember nothing, except that it is late afternoon when we, two women and two young children, stand huddled together in a small village square; our luggage surrounding us like a wall. Many other refugees are also waiting for accommodation. Above us a big metal mushroom grows on the roof of a high building. Oma's name is called, and she is led away. A little later a farm cart, pulled by two horses, takes Mami, Gert-Dieter, me and our cases along a straight street into a wide gateway. A farmyard! Right in the centre a rooster crows from the top of a dung heap. Hens flutter away nervously as the cart rattles to the front door. Loud squeals and grunts sound from a dirty brick building. Two high gates open into a threshing barn. The farmhouse is one storey higher than our house in Wischwill and also has grey walls. Mami is heaving our cases up curving linoleum covered stairs. The banister feels smooth as I let my hand glide along it.

A *yellow-tiled* stove, a tatty plush sofa, a table, chairs, a sink and, on a high shelf, a radio: this is where we are going to live. The window does not look out on a grassy triangle but across a low roof into the farmyard beyond. In a tiny adjacent room two single beds touch each other under the window and there is just space for a wardrobe. Where can the dolls live? Where can we play?

I do think Oma's new home is nicer. A garden path, lined with blue iris as tall as me, leads into an orchard where apples and plums hang in clusters above a meadow of high grass. The farmer's wife says kind things to me and loves my brother's long dark eyelashes. No one has ever talked to me like this. She sends cakes and plums and freshly boiled *Apfelkraut*. (apple molasses). Her house welcomes me when I visit Oma.

In daytime huge dark birds drone above us and scare me. At night, wide arcs of light sweep the sky and the "siren" (the metal mushroom I had noticed) whines and howls. We are always waiting for that alarm. At its first sound Mami hurriedly wraps us in scratchy grey blankets. Bent low, carrying Gert-Dieter in her arms, she rushes across the yard to the air raid shelter and I run behind them. Some nights we are too late and have to crouch on the bottom step by the front door. Outside, thunder upon thunder, and even the black-out in front of the window cannot keep out the bright white flashes that turn the stairwell into a horrifying ghostly place. Mami is pressing her head against my brother's face. I sit beside them, wrapped and upright. Dangerous things called "bombs" may hit us at any moment. When the siren sounds again, the stars burst from a dark-blue sky. And we are alive!

We are in Saxony, the very heart of Germany, and Glesien is the name of the village. It has no Kindergarten. My playground is the busy farmyard where no one watches or even notices me. The great barn swallows whole carts loaded high with corn. The threshing machine pounds all day. Pink fat creatures squeal for food and bury their snorting snouts into the steaming swill. I count the new piglets as they greedily push into the tummy of the big sow with the small blue eyes and fair eyelashes. A man is chopping fodder beet. The big blade falls: chop, chop, chop. They have a Frenchman here, too, but it is not Ronni.

In the farthest corner of the yard I discover a gate; the latch is easy to lift. A deep damp ditch bars me from a meadow – full of flowers! I scramble down and up out of the ditch and then the grasses reach up to my neck. Where to start picking? Blue harebells. Marguerites. Pink clover balls. Golden buttercups. I stuff my mouth with sorrel, love its sour taste. Here in the meadow the insects go about their own business and do not mind me. Back in the house it is different: flies invade everything, and fleas and bedbugs make nights a misery. Here in the meadow I can escape the dark feelings that float all around me, feelings I do not understand. Mami and Oma still wear black clothes. All colourful dresses were dyed after Opa's death. But the meadow is bursting with colour and its smells and sounds are sweet. Here in the meadow I am never sad and always free. No one knows where I am.

Right under our window the pigs are being slaughtered. People shouting; frightened squeals; silence. I have no appetite for the steaming broth the farmer's wife sends up. Sausages follow a few days later. They taste good and make a welcome change from the slimy oat gruel, grey pearl barley and black bread (sometimes spread with a little margarine but mostly without). Oma brings a large slab of plum cake from her farm. Gert-Dieter has learnt to say "the biggest" and gets the largest slice. When Mami wheels him down the Hitlerstraße in his pushchair, people stop and admire his dark lashes and deep brown eyes. I tell them that black bread, coffee and plum molasses have turned them that colour.

The siren now howls all the time. The brown radio plays marches. It feels as if all the air is filled with fear.

"*Die Russen kommen!*"

There is no grassy triangle for the dolls; only a small dirty patch outside the pigsty. One night I forget to bring my Dieter-doll home and in the morning shreds of celluloid and the rags that had been his trousers are strewn around! I did not know that pigs eat dolls.

In this house I am allowed into one of the downstairs rooms to watch an old lady pedal her sewing machine. She is patching bed linen and the farmer's shirts, deftly turning the material this way and that. The needle rushes up and down; up and down. A scream: blood spurting like a fountain. The needle has run right through her finger. I don't want to go downstairs any more.

In Duisburg and Wuppertal explosives tear the roofs off houses and uproot trees. Fire eats children and mothers and grandmothers alive. Many are gassed by the stored coal in the cellars of their houses. Falling debris shreds human flesh and blood spills.

I come home from my meadow and I see a man lying on our sofa. Papi has found us, but he is in shock and very sick. I listen to his laboured breathing and watch his fevered face. He brings the terrible news that his mother (the grandmother I never got to know), was killed in an air raid shelter and my eight-year old cousin Kriemhild who had been staying with her, died with her.

Mami takes me on the train to the *Lazarett*, the military hospital in Leipzig. There is no Leipzig left; just high mounds of rubble and cratered streets. It is difficult for me to walk across the debris to reach the field hospital. I learn that Papi's sickness is called "double pneumonia". And though he recovers I do not see him again. He is ordered "to the front" but has left for me a bright red scooter and for Gert-Dieter a wooden tank and a metal lorry with a real tarpaulin. We now also have a wooden handcart with iron-clad wooden wheels and a long handle. Papi's comrades had made all these things for him.

In a munitions factory near Leipzig a young girl and her sisters are put to work for gruelling twelve-hour shifts. They have been sent there from Auschwitz and have no protection from the bombs.

The Red Army has broken through into Memelland, into East Prussia, and the *Wehrmacht* is in retreat. Stories of atrocities are circulating. Germans are fleeing in great panic and many die on the way. Churchill called for a "clean sweep" of all ethnic Germans from Eastern Europe.

In Glesien I hear the frightened whispers:

"*Die Russen kommen!*"

The winter is harsh and keeps us indoors for days. I long for the meadow. The big puddles in the farmyard are frozen over. I slide back and forth – and fall, hitting my head on the ice. The buildings around me begin to spin and then a black curtain falls. Mami has to carry me into the house.

In Yalta on the Black Sea: Roosevelt, Churchill and Stalin meet to consider the final thrashing of Germany and the future of devastated Europe.

With the glory of the spring days comes more terror. My sixth birthday is also forgotten. I could go to school now but there is no school as there are no teachers. All the children stay hidden inside their houses. But the skies have become quiet. Mami has had a birthday: she is thirty three. Most of the day she buries her face in the brown Bakelite box. She wants news. Solemn music is interrupted by a grave voice:

"*Der Führer ist gefallen.*"

Has the Führer fallen over? Has he fallen as a soldier? Mami's face is ashen. She is weeping whilst she is feeding the tiled stove with books. The room becomes unbearably hot. I cannot breathe here. I run from the house, past the pigsties, through the gate, down the ditch, up into my meadow. That feels better. Against a cloudless sky I watch the larks rise and fall. They are jubilant. May has come. Children have always longed for May:

> *Komm, lieber Mai und mache*
> *die Bäume wieder grün...*
>
> Come, dear May,
> turn the trees green again.

Here in the meadow there is now a profusion of wildflowers. Butterflies love them and I do, too. The wind blows warm like Mami's hairdryer. And...hmm...such delicious smells. Is the ground moving? Is a big insect droning close by? The meadow is shaking! I raise myself on tiptoes above the tops of the grasses but I can see nothing. The noise! Rattling, clanking, humming, droning. The ground no longer feels safe; it is trembling, shuddering. Shivers run down my back. I drop the flowers. Someone is calling my name. I run towards the ditch. Mami is waving and shouting on the other side. She reaches out her hand and pulls me up the side of the ditch and through the gate into the farmyard. By the little gate she stops, panting, staring out of wide-open eyes. Her face – it is as white as chalk! Next to her stands the Frenchman, in torn uniform and a kepi like Ronni's. No, he is not standing. He is jumping and throwing his kepi high into the air! He has gone wild with joy. Excitedly he points to the farm gate. I see a star painted on to olive green. Is that a tank? There are soldiers with round helmets and guns and a man with a black face! The Russians must have come!

Ducking low, running, Mami pulls me across the yard. Yes, it is a huge tank and it is blocking the main gateway. The star painted on its side – is white!

Back in the house, the living room is still stifling hot as the stove continues to eat Mami's books. She locks the door and orders us children into the bedroom. I somehow do not want to play myself but I watch my brother roll his wooden tank to and fro across the floorboards. Broooom... brooom...

Something wild and frightening is happening in the house; heavy boots on the stairs; a sharp rap on our door.

"Open up!" The voice is loud, commanding something I do not understand. But Mami does and she unlocks the door. I hear a man's voice speaking in a foreign language and now a huge soldier fills our door frame, looking down on Gert-Dieter and me from a great height – and leaving without another word.

Mami is holding us tight. "*Amerikaner!*" she whispers.

We hear screaming and swearing and shouting and thumping. The farmer is being dragged from the house. His wife shrieks and wails and pleads. And then suddenly all is still. I climb on to the bed and from behind the net curtain peep down into the street. It is filled with tanks, all crammed with soldiers. Humming and clanking the column moves away.

The Child stops her ears to shut out the terrible wails rising up the stairs from behind a locked door. The May sun takes no notice of all that is happening and is stealing into our living room.

"Sh. Sh." Mami's head has almost disappeared into the material-covered hole of the brown box. We creep around her. She comes away from the radio. I have never seen her look like this. In a flat voice she says,

"*Es ist alles vorbei.*" And I wonder what it is that is all over. "*Kapitulation*" must be a terrible thing.

Today is Mothers' Day in Germany and the war is over. The footpath leading to the edge of the village is carpeted with camomile, a fragrant soft rug. The larks are still spiralling and singing their little hearts out. I want flowers for Mami. To bring her joy. Everything is so terrible. White 'snowballs' are bulging over a garden fence. I can just reach some and pick an armful. I also notice that the name of our street has changed. The Gothic blue letters on the white enamelled sign that read *Adolf-Hitler-Straße* have disappeared and a make-shift wooden board has 'Rooseveld St' painted on it. In snatches of conversation I pick up that the farmer, a party leader, has fallen off the tank. The farmer's wife stays indoors and the farmyard is quiet.

I discover that my red scooter, Gert-Dieter's tank and lorry and other things have disappeared. I am told that they have been buried. My dolls are missing, too.

"You haven't buried Friedel and Klaus and Erika and Marianne, have you?" I cry with alarm.

"No, they are already packed."

"Are we leaving again?"

"Die Russen kommen."

The Allies are discussing the future of Germany. Is this defeated nation to be an industrialized country once more or become a land for peasants and swineherds?

8

The Ruhr Region: ruins and rubble

Silent and empty lies the farmyard every day and even the animals have hidden themselves. The happy Frenchman has disappeared. Maybe the Americans have taken him, too. We are all shut up in our room. Nothing happens. I stare into an empty yard and long for my meadow. We have to talk in whispers, because "walls have ears."

A light rain is falling as I walk down an empty 'Rooseveld St'. I feel strange and turn back. From the main gate I watch Mami as she is hastily pulling her laundry from the line in the farmyard. I run after her into the house. Upstairs she is stuffing the damp clothes into the orange crate I know well from last autumn's journeys. Our beds have been stripped. I have so many questions but she is too harassed to answer.

"*Die Russen kommen!*" Everyone knows that.

The next day a farm cart is waiting in the street on to which our luggage is being stowed. Behind us – stacked high with belongings and faceless people – a convoy of carts is slowly moving down the street. Goodbye, Glesien, you have not been much of a home. Goodbye, my beautiful meadow. Where are we going?

"West. We are going home." A railway station. A huge locomotive. Reeking black smoke. Compartments bulging with women, children, old people, luggage…

Days later. How many days later? A loudspeaker announces 'Hannoversch-Münden'. Since the main station at Kassel is destroyed, we are spewed from the train here, without food or water. Will trains run to the Ruhr Region? How long will we have to stay on this station? Oma and Mami are going on a search for something to eat and drink and they are taking my brother with them. And what will happen to me?

"You must stay here and look after the luggage." With a piece of rope they tie me to the largest trunk. The day drags on, hot without shelter from the sun. I am hungry. I need to do a wee. Will they come back for me? Don't cry. You must watch the cases. Don't go to sleep. I scan strangers' faces. So many turbans! All the women wear them because they cannot wash their hair and hope to deter the lice. How the gleaming rails dazzle! Metal strands – all entwined. The air flickers into the hazy distance. No trains. I look around: other children have been left like me. The rails glisten. I am asleep.

"Uta!" They are back! And then there are *Butterkeks* (petit beurre) and a sip of water from a tin mug. They untie me and help me change my pants.

Rumours. We live by rumours. No train will be leaving from this station tonight. Maybe tomorrow? Perhaps next week? Oma and Mami have arranged for us to spend the night at the Red Cross hostel. People are sleeping there standing up, their arms hanging over stretched ropes, their heads drooping. Many are snoring. We are given a straw-filled mattress to share. As soon as my matted plaits touch the palliasse I am asleep, dreaming of trains pulling out of a station and leaving me behind. We are up very early and back on the platform. Our luggage has been to and from the hostel. We must not miss any train that might be heading west.

New rumours stir the crowd. Rumours raise hopes; rumours dash them. Around noon, when the sun is beating down on the rails, a goods train is spotted arriving at the farthest end of the station.

"It's going west!" I help to load the *Bollerwagen*, our little handcart which Papi had left for us, and I am again tied to the trunk. From the platform I watch Mami bump the cart across the rails. Oma is carrying my brother and when she reaches the goods wagons, she stays there to guard the baggage. Mami is back with the empty cart. Again she piles it high and manoeuvres it over the rails. The rope keeps me from following her. Back and forth bumps and clatters the *Bollerwagen* until everything has been stacked by the train. Now comes my turn to clamber across the track. My legs are short and I have to step on the high hot rails. I feel them burning through my thin soles and the high sun is beating down on my face. At last we are all together. I look up; the sides of the wagons are so high and above them tower mountains of black shiny stones. It is coal. I have never seen it before.

People are helping each other, hauling up cases, crates, children and grannies. We have left behind a platform teeming with refugees who are trying to go to the south or north of Germany. The east is being closed off. Nestled in the coal I feel safe. The sun is setting and I have not been left behind. The engine sends a long black cloud to the back of the train, whistles and puffs. We are moving. Ra-tat-ta. Ra-tat-ta. No one knows where we shall end up; everyone hopes it will be in the Ruhr Region. Mami's face is black! And Oma's, too!

"*Sie schiessen*! Duck low, someone is shooting at us!" The engine driver does not stop.

"West we go. West we go," sing the wheels throughout the night. "Going home. Going home." A glittering tarpaulin stretches high above us. My friends, the stars. 'God, the Lord has counted them so that not one should be missing in this great multitude...' Buried in the coal I am happy that we are all together. The wheels of the open freight train sing me to sleep.

Dawn unveils a grizzly picture: a sea of ruins; burned-out skeletons of buildings; tottering walls; yawning hollows; hills, mountains, mountains of debris as far as the eye can see. I hear names that will one day be familiar: Dortmund, Bochum, Essen, Mülheim, Oberhausen. Amongst the ruins and the rubble wade matchstick women in head-scarves, children and old men pulling handcarts, pushing battered prams loaded with furniture and wood. The grown-ups stare in silence. White streaks run down my mother's cheeks and Oma wipes her reddened eyes. Dandelions blaze in neglected fields where no cattle graze. Burnt farms; scorched trees. Rubble, rubble, rubble. Sometimes our train stops and a knot of 'passengers' clambers over the sides on to potholed station platforms. Everyone is black! They have come home – or at least where home had once been. And we roll on...

"…*Alle aussteigen!*" Everyone has to get off. The train has come to a halt in… nothingness. Like moles we, the refugees, dig ourselves from under our black mounds and help each other into stinging nettle, dock and dandelion. Shivering, I watch our luggage being thrown to the ground. Be careful: my dolls are in there! A fiery sun reflects in brown water and turns it to blood. An iron skeleton lies half-submerged in the canal: the blown-up rail bridge. Abandoned we stand on a high bank. Where are we?

"*Rhein-Herne Kanal*", someone says.

"Then we are not far from home," Oma sighs with relief.

"At nine o'clock is curfew. We can't stay here in the open."

Something is moving in the crimson water: the silhouette of a man in a rowing boat. Mami slips and slides down the grassy slope. Oma's hands hold ours. Now Mami has reached the water's edge and is talking to the boatman. She beckons to us and we slither down the embankment. The sun's glow is beautiful: fire on water. The oarsman and we children are gently rocking while the grown-ups are frantically loading the cart, steadying it, and lowering it down to the boat. Racing against time. The sun is sinking behind ruins; shining unhindered through empty windows and we are crossing the canal. I am hungry and tired. Where will we sleep tonight?

As if by magic, a horse-drawn cart is waiting for us. Oma thinks she knows of distant relatives that used to live close to the canal. She asks the driver and at nine o'clock his cart stops outside their house. It has been spared by the bombs and the family welcomes us with food and a real bed. Of course, they had never expected us!

When I wake, Oma and Mami and Gert-Dieter are gone!

"They are looking for your Oma's house to see if it is still standing," says the mother of my cousins. "The children will show you their playhouse."

In the yard, my cousins have turned a rusty car (I had never seen a car before) into a real room! I watch them play, laugh and squabble. Anxiously I am listening – for familiar voices I know. Will Oma and Mami find their way back? Will they forget about me? Perhaps I have to stay here in this strange house for ever!

They are back and the smiles on their faces tell me that everything is all right. Yes, the house is standing! One of the few in the street that has not been destroyed. They found it badly damaged and crammed full of people. A thin and tired horse pulls us and our belongings through streets that are no longer recognizable. The cart has to avoid massive water-filled craters in the torn-up asphalt.

We arrive in a shabby grey yard. A rat slinks along the wall. Oma's plum tree is bearing a mass of small green balls. She has the key to the back door: the patterned tiles in the entrance hall are grubby and cracked. The stairway reeks – of toilet and animals and boiled kale. On the first landing by the lavatory we meet rabbits in a primitive cage, chickens and pigeons. I am retching. Doors remain closed but behind them a hubbub of agitated voices. Oma knocks on one door. A sliver of light.

"Frau Nehles!"

Johann Heinen, the tenant, weeps when he sees her. He invites her in, leaving us to wait outside the door on the little landing. They have much to talk about but when Oma eventually emerges, she is waving another key. Two rooms have been kept for our arrival and my grandparents' furniture is stored here. All is undamaged except for the huge oak sideboard. A deep burn scar runs down its side. Gingerly I touch the injured furniture, all blistered and flaking. The grown-ups say that an 'incendiary bomb' had sliced through the entire house but that the tenants had acted quickly and bravely and put out the fire in the cellar. Otherwise Oma's house would have burnt down. Her crockery and china figurines have survived unbroken. In a drawer I find her button box and remnants of Mami's dolls' house. At the big oak table in the middle of our new 'home' I play with the tiny china set and place buttons on the heads of the people in Mami's old picture book. At last all my dolls are released from the crate where they have slept throughout the whole long journey and *they* were not blackened by the coal.

Here in Duisburg-Meiderich there are no meadows and no forests and no farm animals; just a mountainous landscape of rubble and skeletal houses. Very few rise intact out of the devastation and one of them is 'ours'. It is dark; stuffed full with strangers; echoes with loud angry voices and cursing; is pervaded by stench of every kind; paint is peeling everywhere. And this they call home? Who can bear such ugliness?

Our flight from Saxony has made us all ill. We are covered in eczema. Worms eat our insides and lice our skins. We suffer from dysentery and there is no doctor to call and no medicine to take. But we sleep in comfortable clean beds, covered in the linen that has travelled with us to the Russian border and back. Soda crystals, dissolved in hot water, kill the 'nits' and leave our little scalps sore. We spend much time in bed – and get better.

Oma and Mami look so haggard and grey and worn. How do they secure food for us so we do not go hungry?

Ruins are a dangerous playground. Anything can collapse at any moment; everything can be a trap. But who can resist such an exciting treasure land? As I ferret in the dirty debris I discover charred books, twisted metal objects, patterned shards, roof tiles, molten glass and things I do not recognize, like this small yellowing rectangular 'brick', smooth to the touch on three sides.

"What is this?"

"A piano key. We had a piano once and I learnt to play it when I was young," Mami sighs.

"And this?" I wave fragments of charred paper with dots and lines on them.

"Sheet music, look these are different notes..." I wonder what 'sheet music' is used for.

Prayer times begin again, those dreaded embarrassing minutes before I am allowed to go to sleep. We need to pray that Papi will come home safely. Do I want this man, this stranger, to come home? Despite my squirming and insincerity our prayers are answered.

It is very early and I am slowly waking when I sense someone bending over my bed: a thin man with a bristly face. I quickly shut my eyes again and pretend to be asleep. I can feel him standing there; I can sense him crying. Sooner or later I must 'wake up' and greet this worn man in uniform trousers and a crumpled shirt. Papi has a long story to tell of how he searched for us all over Germany and found us here. He does not stay long but sets off for Glesien to retrieve our buried goods. Soon I will have my red scooter again. Prayer times start afresh.

Within days he is back. There is no red scooter – nor anything else. The Russians are already across the Elbe and have overrun Glesien and prayer times come to an end. So does the peace in our household. Life with three warring grown-ups is suffocating and there is nowhere where I can be by myself: no warm sand to kick up by the barn with the stork nest; no grassy triangle; no meadow. The ruins are the only escape from this over-crowded house.

Tante Leni has also survived the war. We find her and her parents in the cellar of their bombed house. There are no windows to allow sunlight in. Tante Leni has become quieter and sighs a lot.

"*Tja, wat sol ma da make.*" She speaks in Meiderich dialect and this is her favourite phrase, "Well, what can one do?" There is resignation in voice and gesture.

In the garden that had once produced a good crop of vegetables and been ablaze with summer flowers, her father has erected a cage. He catches sparrows to provide meat for the little family, making up "calories".

The concentration camp at Bergen-Belsen has been discovered; burnt down to the ground.

The leaders of the United States, Britain and Soviet Russia are meeting in Potsdam, not far from Berlin, to decide on the administration of a Germany in purgatory. Many problems stay unresolved. Unease and suspicion mark the conference.

And then the cases and crates appear in the living room. Mami is packing again.

9

My world is the street

The short pockmarked platform is yellow with dandelions. Through every crack in the bombed asphalt they push and shout: life! A high mound of twisted metal, charred timbers and bricks is all that remains of the railway station at Wuppertal-Wichlinghausen. I blink against the light, watch the silver rails follow the train as it becomes smaller and smaller and smaller. I sniff the air. This smells a good place.

My parents have already set off with the suitcases; they are pulling my brother along on to an iron bridge. On my back bounces the faded little khaki rucksack I have carried on all our journeys. Through the rusty metal bars of the footbridge that spans the rails, I spy something I have never seen before: a rock face, a high wall of grey shiny stone. I press my face against the iron railings. Fine grasses wave and harebells nod out from small fissures in the rock. The landscapes I had known were flat and sandy. This is different. I want to touch the silver stone and get closer to the delicate flowers.

"Come on!" shouts Papi and I run to catch up with them.

"We are nearly home. This is our street." My parents have put their cases down on the pavement, puffing. Their faces show me that they are happy. Perhaps for the first time. Home. Is *this* really my home? Here, high above the smashed-up, burned-out city there are *no* ruined houses. Smoothed cobbles glisten and are *not* torn up. Our street has *not* been cratered. Large solid and sombre houses throw their shadows halfway across the street while the tall bright houses on the opposite side are bathed in sunshine. They rise from grassy banks and I count the shining windows. Wrought-iron railings surround each entrance. It is beautiful here. So this is where I lived when I was very little. Mami and Papi have climbed up a flight of white steps; they wait for me before Papi turns the key in the front door. Light falls into a main hallway and it feels cool and smells clean. A few more steps and we are standing at a glass door, the entrance to "our flat". The small corridor is dark because all the doors leading off it are shut. I sense that this is a strange moment for my parents. How long ago is it, since they had made this their home in which to have children and to be happy? Mami unlocks the door to her kitchen. It is just how she had left it when the bombing raids drove us east. I see her tears and understand for the first time that you can cry for joy. The afternoon sun is streaming through two tall windows and shows up the thick layer of dust on everything. Papi has already opened the bedroom door. All the furniture is blond: the bed ends, the three-door wardrobe and the chest of drawers with its huge mirror...Is that me?! I have blond plaits...my coat is too short...my dress is showing.... What a strange face!

Through a wide window we look down on two squares of grass – without marguerites and clover and daisies! By the high factory wall I count eight vegetable beds; they look like graves. In one grows deep-green curly kale. The factory lies silent, but its name – in large metal letters – is silhouetted against the sky. I have a warm feeling in my tummy. Now we shall never have to move again. We will all be happy together. I have really come *home.*

I need the toilet. Opposite the bedroom is a real bathroom with a huge bath, a toilet and a basin, all in white. An enamelled cylinder overhangs the end of the bath, a *Badeofen,* to provide hot water. I climb on to the toilet seat. Small squares of newspaper hang threaded on to a piece of rough string. I sit enthroned. Those two toothbrushes in the smeared glass...whose are they?

One door leading from the corridor remains closed.

"Can we see that room?"

"No. *Herr und Frau Hellen* live there."

"Why do they live in our flat?"

"Because they are bombed out."

My brother is not yet too big for the cot; I sleep on a mattress at the foot of my parents' bed. My bottom itches. It itches badly.

"Don't scratch, we'll look in the morning."

…Shiny rails…harebells stuck into rocks…a factory wall and grass without flowers…two toothbrushes… and then I am asleep. I have worms.

I have not yet seen the couple in "our" living room though light sometimes escapes from under their door. I think *Frau Hellen* is a witch and I know that *Herr Hellen* makes 'stinkies' in the bathroom. Though Mami is in her own home again, she tells me how much she misses her elm furniture behind the closed door.

"I used to stroke it when first I was married," she tells me wistfully.

In the corner under the kitchen window I am making a nice home for the dolls and Papi is out looking for work. One day his lorry is parked outside our flat. Behind the cab is a boiler from which escape roaring flames and smoke. Wood makes the lorry go because there is no petrol. I am not comfortable with Papi. His voice is rough and loud and when Mami reminds him that "walls have ears" his face turns red and he shouts. He likes to rub his scratchy stubble against our faces to make us laugh, but it does hurt: only, we don't tell him to stop. When he comes home, it is our job to pull off his heavy boots, his "devil's shoes". He threads huge leaves on a piece of string and suspends them above the cooker to dry; they turn from green to brown, begin to crackle and smell good. But when Papi crushes them and rolls them into cigarettes and lights up, they make a fog in the kitchen and a horrible smell. While Papi drives the lorry, Mami follows rumours as to which shop *has* something to sell. She is gone for hours to queue for bread or fish. Often we are alone in the flat. I think frying fish is worse than cigarettes. The kitchen fills with black acrid smoke that makes us cough and my little brother wails "no more fish!" But it is really the rape oil in which Mami cooks. Yet worse than the smells of cigarettes and fish and even the stinkies in the bathroom is the atmosphere in our kitchen when my parents row. The Child sits quietly beneath a barrage of angry words and tears and tries to concentrate hard on chopping fodder beet for her dolls' dinner. She longs to run out of the door but cannot. Papi earns Reichsmark which buys coal for the cooker and briquettes to heat our bath water; milk, kale, potatoes, fodder beet and horrid maize bread. When he is out in his lorry, home feels a better place.

Germany has been divided into four parts, ruled by four different armies. We live in the British Zone.

When our parents are not rowing, they talk in whispers and I catch small fragments of their conversation. I am becoming a good listener. They are planning a 'hamster trip'. On a 'black' market they buy bales of material, braid and elastic, all manufactured again in Wuppertal. These useful things they want to exchange for fresh fruit and vegetables from the country. For that they have to travel from farm to farm. When they are away, sometimes for days, Oma comes to look after us. In the grey of the morning, before we are up, my parents leave with rucksack and suitcase. And Oma makes us pray again. When they return, sausages and potatoes, ham and apples are spread out on the kitchen table and best of all, black-red cherries that look like plump little hearts. Now we can feast.

There is a song everyone knows:

> *...und wir sammeln Kalorien,*
> *tauschen ein für Gummiband...*
> *...und die Bauernsäcke*
> *geben kein' Kartoffel her*
> *...und so ziehn wir durch die Lande*
> *mit dem Rucksack immer leer...*

It's about collecting calories, bartering elastic, slagging off the farmers for not giving up their potatoes and condemning the poor 'hamsters' to roam the countryside with an empty rucksack!

On their next trip they take me with them. Before dawn we travel by train to Cologne. The platforms are teeming: a sea of grey and haggard, angry and hard faces. Among them British soldiers with guns parade up and down watching men on crutches; men with empty sleeves; men with a black patch over one eye; women in shabby shapeless clothes; quiet, anxious, skinny children; rucksacks and suitcases held together with string; cardboard boxes and bags.

The cathedral's two black spires stare into Cologne's roofless station. We change trains. When the engine, belching black smoke, stops, everyone surges forward, pushes with hands and elbows and no one cares about children. Papi fights himself into a compartment, Mami lifts me through the window and climbs in after me. Our train leaves the wounded city behind and puffs into a landscape of fields and orchards. In Troisdorf, my parents hand me out of the window. Rucksack and suitcase follow and we start off on a long walk on a straight road stretching endlessly before us. In the kitchen of the first farmhouse we reach, my parents open up their treasures and the farmer's wife rubs the material between thumb and forefinger. She buys a few metres. Ham, eggs and a handful of potatoes disappear into the rucksack and we trudge on to the next farm. I limp in my ill-fitting shoes, my heels are blistered, and I am crying with pain.

On our way back to the station a star-crowded sky stretches above us. On *Köln Hauptbahnhof* the tension is palpable. Will our hard-won loot be confiscated? Apparently the military police tonight have better things to do. Our train to Wuppertal pulls in and once more I am suspended in mid-air until someone hauls me into the compartment. Sighs of relief. We arrive home at midnight, tired to the bone. My heels are bleeding. This was my first *Hamstertour* – and my last.

Despite our prayers the day comes when my exhausted and deflated parents walk into the flat without rucksack and without suitcase. In Bavaria they had been caught by an American patrol and held in custody for a day. All their bartered treasures had been confiscated. We go back on to a diet of kale and fodder beet.

All over Germany, and particularly in Berlin, people are living in shock and abject poverty. Thousands are dying from starvation and the rats populate the streets. People are too weak to work. Work at what?

In November trials are beginning in Nuremberg to hear evidence of Nazi atrocities. The defeated people are further shocked by the revolting crimes committed in their name.

Curled up on the window sill, surrounded by the dolls, I watch children in the street: small and tall children; boys and girls. They call to each other:

"Fischer, wie hoch ist das Wasser?" (Fisherman, how high is the water?)

"Three metres!"

"How do we get across?"

"Hop on one leg!"

And all the children jump across the cobbles on one leg: one – two – three. A boy is riding a scooter; two girls play with a coloured ball; one is pushing a real dolls' pram! Activity. Energy. I would so like to join them but feel too shy to take my blue wicker dolls' pram into the street.

Things change when I meet Christa in the hallway. She lives right under the roof, she says, and would I like to come and see where she plays? Eagerly I follow her up many stairs. The room where her toys are kept is tiny; it also holds the toilet. And there we play. Imagination is contagious. I have a friend! She is already eight years old and tells me that she is Catholic. On Sunday afternoons I enviously watch her walk to *Kindermesse.*

"Can I come with you?"

"Ask your mother."

Mami says, we are *evangelisch*, but my Protestant parents do not go to a church at all. They don't actually belong to one because they were *ausgeschieden* some years ago which means that they had chosen not to be church members any more. That is why I am not *baptised* like Christa. From her I learn about christenings, the mass, weddings and funerals. She teaches her baptism song to the dolls.

> *Fest soll mein Taufbund ewig stehen,*
> *ich will die Kirche hören…*

> For ever shall stand the covenant of my baptism;
> I will listen to the Church and obey…

Christa's church is really a pile of rubble. But the hall has not been bombed and has been made into a beautiful place. You become very quiet when you go in, dip thumb and two fingers into an enamelled basin fixed to the wall, and with this 'holy water' you touch your forehead, both sleeves of your dress and your tummy button. Before you can sit down in one of the special benches – they call them pews – you have to make a curtsy and again touch your forehead, your sleeves and your tummy button. Then you kneel on a wooden board that hurts your knees, and do all that touching again. You put your hands together as if you were making a wigwam; and when you have knelt like that for a moment, with your eyes shut, you do the touching all over again and sit. I copy Christa because you have to get it right. Sometimes I cheat and squint through my fingers to see what is happening at the front. There are candles and drapes, and out from nowhere appears a man in a long red dress. Two little boys help him to put a shorter lace dress over the top. The boys also wear dresses. The man begins to sing on one note and all the children answer him "*Ex-kum spit-it-to-to*". It is all so exciting, so solemn.

"Who's that man?" I whisper.

"Our priest," she whispers back.

The priest-man tells stories – not fairytales – but true stories of children who loved Jesus so much that they had died for him! I learn new words like "martyr" and "saint" and "genuflect" and I teach the dolls all I know.

Corpus Christi is a very special day. There will be a *Prozession* in our street. Many houses are decorated and special tables have been set up here and there, draped in white-and-gold embroidered cloths. "Altars" they are called. I am standing at the edge of the pavement, my heart is beating so hard and I crane my neck to see her. Christa is "making her first communion". Music. Trumpets. Drums. Closer and closer. Grown-up men in dresses. Some wear special hats. Four are holding up a tent above something shining like gold. Little boys in black suits with brushed hair. And then: little girls, dressed all in white, except for their black patent leather shoes. Look, their hair hangs down in corkscrew ringlets! And they wear a little white wreath on their locks. Cradled in a lace hanky, boys and girls carry a tall white candle in one hand and a small white book in the other. Look, here she comes! An angel! My friend Christa. I cannot take my eyes off her. How solemnly she walks and how beautiful she looks.

We know something no one knows, Christa and I. We are about to tell our secret to the older girls who live in the Sombre Houses. They are crowding around us on the stone steps. They wear navy-blue knee socks and skirts that spread like flat plates when they twirl!

"We are princesses!" There, the secret is out.

What happens now is shocking. All the girls are screeching with laughter, doubling over, holding their tummies. "You – princesses?"

On girl points her finger at Christa. "*Your* father is a factory worker! And *yours*," the same finger prods me, "*yours* is a lorry driver!"

Years later a fragment of this memory will rise up unbidden, out of context and without me grasping its meaning. It acts as a signpost to my past.

And there are other important truths to learn: *better* people live in upstairs flats (except those whose flat is under the roof) and the *best* people have big Sombre Houses. From now on we no longer take our world into the street but keep it safely behind our house, on the sun-warmed slabs and in the recess of the cellar window. There is one game we *do* play in the street: *Refugees*. It is my idea. I show Christa how to pile all the toys on to our dolls' prams. For effect I add Mami's footstool. Then we push our belongings on long treks through streets we do not know, right to the outskirts of town. No one watches us, no one misses us. Somehow we always find our way home.

On the first floor lives a boy whose father does something really lovely. I watch him squeeze beautiful colours from tubes and brush them on to some stretched material.

"What are you doing?"

"I am painting."

Mami said he was an *artist*.

October 1945. I should have started school at Easter, but they had not finished the war then and we still lived in Glesien. But now the time I have been longing for has come. In my papier-mâché satchel bounces a wooden-framed slate; against it rattles a slate pencil. At half past seven it is still dark, the brown leaves slippery and the school a long way from home. After a few days the dawn-walks finish because still there are not enough teachers. Too many men are still held in prison or 'missing' or have 'fallen'.

November. The children are talking of *Sankt Martin* and the lanterns they are making. There is to be a children's procession soon after darkness falls and this time I am going to be part of it. My parents help me make my lantern out of cardboard and baking paper; Papi fixes it to a long stick for me to carry very carefully so that the candle inside does not blow out in the wind. Walking down our street we sing about a nobleman who with his sword had divided his cloak and given one part to a shivering beggar. Afterwards we ring doorbells and ask for goodies; and at the end – with rosy cheeks – I display my St. Martin's treasures on our kitchen table. Mami tells me, that *before the war* children were given *chocolate* and *sweeties* and *oranges*.

December. *Sankt Nikolaus* brings gifts in a different way. He comes at night when all are asleep. We leave one slipper outside the bedroom door and listen...and fall asleep...and wake up to find a biscuit and a shiny red apple in it.

Mami and Papi have become very secretive. We can tell by the way they smile at each other and talk in whispers. Why do they send us to bed so early, far too early to go to sleep? We listen to what is going on in the kitchen. Sawing and hammering; the sewing machine rattles and what is that strong smell? In the morning you would not know that anything unusual had gone on the night before. Christmas has woken from its long wartime-sleep. Christmas is coming again.

Tonight Gert-Dieter and I are locked in the bedroom in the dark. In the kitchen there is scurrying, swishing, rustling, clattering, whispering. A bell tinkles. Papi unlocks the door. His eyes are running over. He is reunited with his family! Warmth streams from our kitchen. No, this is not our kitchen. It is a room transformed by magic. Candles on a Christmas tree, hung with glass baubles. Our parents are standing side by side under the tree and singing

Stille Nacht, heilige Nacht...

I cry with them and don't know why. Tonight is Christmas Eve, peacetime Christmas Eve. Tonight we have reason to be happy. A white sheet covers the kitchen table. Now my parents lift it off: I have eyes only for one thing: a *Puppenstube*, not an entire dolls' house as I had seen in the Sombre Houses, but two dolls' rooms, set out with shiny blue furniture, painted with small red and yellow flowers. Four little chairs have hearts carved into their backs like those in Oma and Opa's house in the forest in Uszballen; they are arranged around a square table. There is also a corner bench and a shelf fixed above it. The bedroom is separated by a curtained-off doorway and contains two beds with duvets, a wardrobe, bedside tables and even a cradle! Two wooden dolls, *Sigismund* and *Tusnelda* (they have funny names because they look funny) and also their baby, live in all this loveliness. To think that the *Weihnachtsmann* has brought me all this!

Will winter never end? The washing is drying above the cooker and cannot be laid on the grass in the garden to bleach and dry. Christa and I cannot hang upside down from the iron bar our mothers use to whack out the dust from the rugs with a carpet beater. Held captive in the kitchen, the only place of warmth, I play with my *Puppenstube* on the window sill and with my dolls in the corner. Through the upper window pane the sky changes from slate-grey to lead-grey and then to pale blue and finally the spring sun climbs across the Sombre Houses and the shadows shorten. I am seven now. The school at the end of our street has been opened to pupils. From my satchel hangs a small crocheted white square that serves two purposes: to wipe my slate and to tell the world that I am an "*i-Dötzken*", a beginner, which evokes a mocking chant from the older children. My school, a large stately building, has escaped serious bomb damage and, though grey with age, looks friendly because of its high windows. Mami plaits my long blond hair into a crown and I am wearing an apron with a big pocket on the front, which Tante Else, Mami's cousin, has sewn from an old flag. While she is staying with us, she sleeps in the kitchen and makes us dresses and coats from Opa's clothes; even Gert-Dieter's flannelette nappies she turns into warm petticoats for me. From my crocheted bodice hang long suspenders, holding up stockings that are knitted from a grey yarn that itches unbearably. The girls from the Sombre Houses take every opportunity to point out my unfashionable attire. Where did they get their navy knee socks and wide skirts? I push my stockings behind the wardrobe where no one can find them. "Now the seriousness of life begins," are Mami's words as I leave for school. I think she really means it.

Under high old trees in the school yard we line up in twos; then file into our classrooms. Each pair shares a wooden desk with an inkwell that is encrusted with some flaky blue stuff. A huge blackboard fills the entire front wall. There are many of us in this light room; fifty or more; thin; in plaits; dressed in an assortment of patched and darned clothes. I think we are all happy to have made it to school at last, we, the seven-year-olds, witnesses to another age. Frau Kerk, our tall teacher shows us a *Fiebel*, a Primer, full of pictures and neat letters and with a warm encouraging smile tells us that by next Easter we will all be able to read and write. Imagine it! I like Frau Kerk. At the end of the lessons, a photographer arranges each of us in front of the old oak entrance door and gives us a large cone to hold. (In the old days each child would have had their own, filled with sweets and chocolate and apples.) This one is empty and I pass it on to the next girl to have her photo taken. I like walking home with Frau Kerk. She holds my hand and when I let it go to cross the street to our flat, she calls "Good-bye", which she says is English for *Auf Wiedersehn*. During the night someone has painted big white letters on our wall: TOMMY GO HOME. That is English, too.

I have taken to lying. It gets you what you want. So I lie about almost everything. Mami has warned me that "lies have short legs," but mine have really long ones...until one day one of my lies is so huge and my story so improbable that I have to be punished: I have to learn a long poem by heart, line by line.

Du deutsches Kind, sei tapfer, treu und wahr...

You German child, be brave, faithful and true,
Let never lie defile your mouth.
From ancient times t'was honourable
In German lands to be loyal and true.
Now you are young, now it is not so hard,
But a boy grows into a man;
The sapling bends

But not the tree.
Say yes and no; do not pervert the truth,
Let what you say be short and plain.
Your word is holy
So do not waste it.

Awake and fight, an enemy is ready:
The lie within you threatens danger.
Child, Germans have ever bravely fought.
You German child, be brave, faithful and true.

I can recite the poem but it does not stop me lying. I get better and better at it. There is a boy in my class whom I like, or for whom perhaps I feel sorry. Adolf's shabby clothes are never mended. He is called an *Asozialer* because he lives in the *slums*. For *Sankt Nikolas* he had not put out his slipper. He has no slippers. So he has gone without even a biscuit. I have made up my mind. Mami is washing the floor as I push Adolf into the kitchen.

"Adolf here is a refugee from East Prussia," I say, because I know that is what Mami will like to hear. He leaves confused, clutching a handful of spicy biscuits. See, lying works!

At school, when lunchtime comes, we all line up by a huge tub. Into our empty cans (Papi has fixed a wire to mine, so I can carry it like a little bucket) they ladle thin grey soup. We are not allowed to go home until we have drunk it. It tastes horrible. So secretly most of us tip the 'English washing-up water' underneath the school fence. How is that for gratitude to our conquerors! It was said to be the sixth boiling of mutton bones.

It is break time but the rain keeps us in the school building. We cram into the corridors and line the stone staircase. What to do with all these children?

"If anyone wants to sing a song or recite a poem, raise your hand!" Several hands shoot up; and so does mine. At the top of the staircase I, the youngest, deliver the poem I know: *Du deutsches Kind....*

When I have finished I am ushered into a classroom and nervously told, never to recite that again! Why not, I am not told. From Mami I keep the whole incident a secret.

The street and the back garden, the cellar and the railway station ruins are the stages on which imagination and creativity are acted out. Agonisingly I learn the difference between winning and losing. Another child has won all my beautiful glass marbles which Mami had kept from her childhood. There is so much to learn about showing off and jealousy; about stealing and lying; and sex play in cellars.

At school we have no books, no paper, no crayons, no watercolours and no plasticine. But Frau Kerk's husband is an artist and he has coloured chalks. Magically he creates wonderful pictures on the blackboard: of a farmyard and an autumn scene in which children are flying kites and potatoes roast in open fires. We learn the sound of letters and today we have tried to write the first one ourselves...

"Look, Mami, I can *write*. " I yank my slate from the satchel. "See how many '*i*'s I've done!"

"Mm," Mami scrutinizes my slate, "You've gone over the lines. Look, here and here."

"For tomorrow I have to finish the *whole row*."

"You'd better fill the whole slate."

"The *whole slate*?"

Mami clears the table for me. The sun pours over the roofs of the Sombre Houses.

I crouch over my slate. A whole slate! How long will that take? The slate pencil scrapes, the slate squeaks. Up down up dot. Up down up dot. I spill over the line!

"Rub that one out," Mami says. The doorbell rings.

"Can Uta come out to play?" I know that voice…that accent – it's Dirk.

"She has to do her homework first."

The glass door clicks, the front door thuds. Up down up dot. Up down up dot. Up down up dot. Slowly the second row fills. Smudges. The doorbell rings and I get up to answer it, but Mami orders me to sit down.

"Can she come and play *now*?"

"She is still doing her homework?"

"How long will she be?"

"Until she has finished." Click. Thud. The sun is hiding behind the roofs of the Sombre Houses. I have filled five rows. I am tired. Up down up dot. A tear drop smudges the last two letters.

"Can I go out *now*? I have done so many rows."

"Finish the slate." I wipe my eyes on my sleeve. Up down… Dirk's voice. Click. Thud.

"I've told him not to ring again."

Shadows are creeping across the street. I've finished! I race outside. Dirk is grinning, happy to see me.

"You've been crying!"

I grab hold of him, push him against the wall and thump my little Dutch friend, pummel him as hard as I can. Now he is crying. I never see him again. I am told that his family has moved away.

Next door lives Waltraud. Her Mamma sells yeast and always looks harassed and angry. Waltraud's father "is left in Stalingrad". Her Mamma never lets her do anything exciting. I think she is becoming a dull girl. What she needs is some adventure! On the way home from school I take her on long detours, and she gets into trouble.

"When your Mamma is out, can I come to your flat?"

"I'm not allowed to let anyone in."

"Oh go on, she won't know, will she."

In their living room above the old settee hangs a big picture, not a picture really, just big gold letters in a gold frame:

Ich bin der Weg und die Wahrheit und das Leben

I am the way and the truth and the life? Who is this "I"? *Who* is way, truth and life all rolled into one? In the bedroom we spray ourselves from Mamma's scent bottle – mmh, gorgeous! In the kitchen I open all the cupboards and mix egg powder, milk powder, rolled oats and a few precious grams of sugar in two cups. Yummy, yummy. Waltraud is not enjoying this. A key turns in the front door.

"Quick, where can I hide?" It is too late. Mamma is very cross and sends me home, "never to play with Waltraud again". Where is her sense of fun? Her poor daughter.

And then war breaks out. An ugly war between Number ten and Number twelve. Missiles are being hurled over the garden fence, aimed to hit: stones, toys, any object; and many angry hurtful words. Ouch! I've been hit by something. I run my hand over my eyebrow; blood is dripping from it. I see the rusty buckle lying by my feet and scream. Waltraud disappears. On the slabs, all through the cellar and up the steps I leave a trail of blood. I keep screaming, partly out of shock and partly for effect. Mami sticks a huge plaster over the gaping wound; the buckle has missed my eye by a centimetre.

The plaster is impressive and Waltraud needs to see it. When the bleeding stops and shock and pain subside, I parade under Waltraud's window and I hope her Mamma can see what her daughter has done.

Until evening I march, back and forth. I have triumphed. (Had the wound been stitched, I would not still bear the distinctive scar where an eyebrow should be.) The deadly feud ends our relationship. And its aftermath? Waltraud is not allowed to play with *anyone*.

One million tons of food is imported into the British Zone between summer 1945 and spring 1946. People are living on fifteen hundred calories a day.

Rumours spread that a shop down the road in town is selling *ice-cream*. Mami weighs out ten grams of sugar and I carry it on a saucer to the shop. I recognize it by the long queue in front of it. I join it, carefully guarding the tiny heap of sugar. We shuffle towards the shop. And then I can see it – for the first time in my life: vanilla ice cream. I hand over my sugar and a whole tablespoon of the magical stuff is tipped on to my saucer. Careful not to spill my treasure, I carry it home: a saucer of lukewarm vanilla sauce.

The girls in the Sombre Houses have 'a rich uncle in America' who sends them CARE packages. Sometimes they share a little from their treasures and I get my first taste of chocolate and of chewing gum.

Fairytales – my old friends – are acted out by the older children in the garage drive and by grown-ups in a small theatre in the factory hall. I am enchanted. How I wish I could have a role. I am too young, they say. Perhaps next year…

Snow falls thickly on the Wuppertal hills and there it stays for weeks. Papi pulls us on a sledge to the park teeming with rosy-faced children. Shrieking, they come whizzing down the hill, haul up their toboggans and do it all again. A watery sun watches sadly through the branches of a snow-laden tree. I cling tightly to the sledge sitting in front of Papi and hope we will not turn over or crash into someone. The wind stings my face and makes my eyes water. Before we reach home it snows again and I catch the fluffy flakes. They tingle and melt on my tongue.

Herr and Frau Templer are *better* people because their flat is on the *second* floor. They have no children but they like *me* and take me to horse racing and street cycle tournaments and they always make sure that I get a good view from the front row. Once on our way home, on an overcrowded platform in the *Schwebebahn* station, I am in danger of being pushed over and trampled on.

"Please, watch out," shouts Herr Templer, "here is a young child."

"Take your child to the devil!" The Templers are outraged and shield me as best they can from the surging crowd. I adore them.

Our bathroom is a private place. I lock the door and am all by myself. On the toilet I 'read' the bits of newspaper hanging from the string, looking for the letters I can already write myself. Finished. I run back into the street to play. The bathroom window flies open. Papi's face appears.

"Come inside! Immediately!"

My knees wobble. He meets me in the hallway and pushes me into the kitchen. Throws the door shut. On the table lies the dreaded bamboo stick. What have I done? In Papi's hand is a scrap of newspaper. He thrusts it into my face.

"You wrote this?" he roars. I see the naughty word.

"I didn't write it!" I wail.

"You did, you dirty girl." He picks up the cane.

"No, no, I didn't write that. I've never seen it before. Herr Hellen must have…" The cane comes down hard on my bottom.

"I didn't write it!" I scream.

But the bamboo rains down blows. When my father has finished, he sends me to the bedroom where I sob until I have no tears left. It's not fair! Where is Mami? I creep to the bathroom, splash my face with cold water and run back into the street. My bottom burns, but no one knows that I have been beaten.

We see this strange figure walking down our street. Is it a man or a woman? Trousers. Basque beret. A shopping bag. Is that full of tins? Every day this person appears and then disappears towards the station. We watch from the safe side of the road.

"A mass murderer!" We are quite sure. "…kills little children and has them tinned!"

Under our breath we sing

Warte, warte nur ein Weilchen...

Wait, wait a little while,
soon Hermann will also come to you
with his little axe
and make tinned meat out of you.

Today we play in front of our house and I have not seen the stranger come. Suddenly the man-woman is there, hugging my little brother! I scream and try to tear him away.

"Let go of him! Let go!"

The arms release Gert-Dieter and the person hurries off. My little brother is safe. On the kerb I sit and cry with tiredness and relief: I have rescued my little brother!

I live in a world of secrets, become secretive and learn to barricade myself within my inner fortress. The adults around me also move in a world to which I have no entrance. They tell me little and do not draw me into any of their plans or purposes. I am sent on errands to other parts of the city. I have to walk long distances or ride on the *Schwebebahn* above the ruins of Wuppertal. I deliver mysterious packages and am given others to take home. I deliver messages I do not understand to people whom I do not know in streets I have never visited before. I am entrusted with secrets without knowing what these secrets are.

Wuppertal is my home. I have let my young tender roots grow down into its soil. Here I belong. The school, the street, the children, the theatre: they all belong to me.

Coming home from school today, I have a queasy feeling in my tummy and do not feel like making a detour. I walk straight into our kitchen – and stand rooted on the spot: Oma and Mami are packing cups and plates into a laundry basket. Cupboard doors and drawers are wide open. My window sill is bare and the dolls' corner empty! My legs tremble but no one can see. My tears stay in my head. We are moving! This is the end of my childhood!

"Tomorrow, we are going back to Duisburg." The Child hears the words, yet does not. She does not know the word 'betrayal' yet but feels its impact. They had told me that this would be our home for good! There is not even time to say 'good-bye' to Frau Kerk or to Christa or the Templers or to any of the children in the street.

I run outside. Shadows are lengthening across the cobbles. Here are the hopscotch squares chalked on the pavement and over there our marble holes. And here the lamppost from which we had swung around on ropes, like on a carousel. Tonight no theatre curtains span the driveway. The play is over. I feel a pang of guilt when I remember Dirk...and Waltraud... and the crack in the iron door of the factory from where I had furtively prised a handful of coal to take home in triumph. Home? Tomorrow this won't be home any more.

I am eight years old. Tonight I am running my last errand in Wuppertal. The house I am to visit lies in a street I do not know. It is dark and cold and lonely up here amongst house skeletons and mounds of debris – and a little scary. Tomorrow night I will sleep in Duisburg again, in that ugly grimy city and from my window will only see a field of ruins. Will there be other children? Where will we play? In the cellars of the smashed-up houses? Why are the grown-ups doing this? I am hurting. Feel abandoned. Of course, I do not yet know that as an adult I will find it almost impossible to abandon anyone whom I perceive as suffering; that I will stay with them long after it is appropriate to do so and in the process I will injure myself.

A low-hung moon – huge and red – tints the bomb sites with an eerie light.

The moon is bleeding.

Ruhr Road

Grey is the road:
Like a steel girder,
It carries
Germany's post-war economy
Into a miracle.

Walls grey with grime
Rise high, forbid
Access
To the peaked heaps of rusty ore
And flaring Bessemers.

Furnace and crane
Defy boundary walls;
Proudly
Ascend to a sky laden with billows
Of multi-coloured belchings.

Trees grey, stunted,
Metal-dust-stricken
Lungs
In this asphyxiating world,
Pulse with seasons' rhythms;

Time-worn survivors:

Audience at grim
Dramas of street-fights
By youth.
Then rumbling tanks.
Markers for dreary steps:

Oil-smeared red-eyed
Steel workers cough;
Poisoned
By dust and gas.
A child is counting her paces
To the swimming baths.

Book III

I have a rendezvous with Life

1993, 2007, 2008

1

Nostalgia Tourists

Hanover sleeps. At the bus station a man is pacing up and down, another shifting his weight from foot to foot. From time to time each glances at the large clock. The long hand has jumped. 8.55. It is Sunday, the ninth of May. Below the platform, in the ladies' toilet, a police search is underway and Peter is discussing something or other with our German hosts. I am too nervous to chip in. My mind is elsewhere, anyway. Memories and fears fight for attention in my brain. Yesterday, forty eight years ago, a grave voice had droned from the brown Bakelite box: *Deutschland hat kapituliert.* Then the war was over and my mother's ashen face had mirrored the profundity, the shock, the relief and the fear of the hour...

Each time that minute hand jerks, I feel my gut churn. The coach may not turn up. Or maybe the driver has forgotten to pick up his only English passengers. Dieter and Vicki are kindly garaging our car for a week: to take it where *we* are going would not be safe. Our suitcase holds sweets and crayons and pamphlets in Cyrillic writing, and, buried in underwear, a drum containing a thousand Paracetemol. This whole thing feels so unreal. It is ten past nine. Right then, a black coach with darkened windows and the name of the travel company emblazoned in white capitals all along its side, turns into the bus station.

"See you in a week's time." We hug each other. Our driver heaves himself out of his double seat and stows away our case. On the coach we find the seats assigned to us for a week. Hubert starts the engine. This is for real! The coach threads its way through empty streets towards the Autobahn and we are on our way to Russia. A small new Russia, to be sure, wedged between Poland and Lithuania: the Kaliningrad Oblast, the lost *Ostpreußen*, East Prussia.

It had all begun on the day when fists and hammers and bulldozers demolished the concrete graffiti-daubed Wall that had sliced Berlin into two, a vivid sign that the Iron Curtain also lay shredded. When the Baltic States regained their independence an idea – though I had immediately dismissed it – nevertheless kept intruding into my thoughts: now that the way is open to travel into East Germany, could it be remotely possible to venture further east? Maybe beyond Berlin and Poland and Königsberg to the river Memel? After all, the former Memelland is now part of free Lithuania. The Child held her breath as I read the following article in *The Times*:

> *Kaunas lies on the Nemunas, Lithuania's largest river. The A228 "Castle Road" follows its wide, willow-lined valley westwards to Kursio lagoon and the sea at the port of Klaipėda, 134 miles away…From Klaipėda, ferries cross the lagoon to the Neringa Spit, a 30 mile peninsula of dunes that stretches down towards Russian Kaliningrad…Fishing villages are spun out along the side of the lagoon…On the sea side, the Soviet army has not long departed, leaving nothing. It is hard to imagine that these beaches like the rest of the pristine sands of this Baltic coast will remain empty for long…*

Despite the unfamiliar names, I seemed to know that Castle Road. The Child had long treasured the black-and-white photos in Mami's album… I now pored over my dusty school atlas, scrutinizing the former north-eastern part of Germany. Towns and rivers bore Russian or Lithuanian names. *Viešvilė*! 'That is *Wischwill*', the Child assured me, 'that's where my grassy triangle is'. I bought a modern map of the area and sent a photocopy to my mother, asking her, who would surely remember, to put the German names against the Russian and Lithuanian ones. I sensed her hesitation. Peter had put out his feelers in another direction.

"David, do you have any pre-war maps of Germany and the Baltic States?" he had asked our local bookseller.

"I believe I have. A while ago a German sold me some Luftwaffe bombing maps. They must be in the loft somewhere. When I go looking for the Christmas decorations…" and days later, "…I've found the maps you are looking for. Come to the shop."

In a quiet upper room we had compared his maps with ours. I read out the German names which Peter then wrote against the foreign ones. And as I spoke them out loud, it was my grandmother's, Oma's voice I heard: her East Prussian accent and intonation unmistakable. 'I want to go home', whispered the Child.

Unexpectedly I came across four black-and-white photographs of the small town, (including a picture of the Magistrate's Court hidden behind leafy trees) and a grey post-card-sized immunisation certificate, dated 1943, signed in Wischwill. 'Wischwill exists, see', triumphed the Child. She wants to stand again on her tiny daisy-meadow, her grassy triangle, the one she had shown me on the night when I had first felt her terror.

A triangle? The whole of East Prussia is triangular and, strangely, so is also the Curonian Lagoon that lies embedded in it. But the one I need to find is very small indeed. How much would such a journey cost, even if it were possible to undertake? In a waking dream I see the sum needed 'written' in front of me and I know it will be affordable. A few days later a wad of Swiss francs arrives in the post, accompanied by a brief letter:

Beloved Peter and Uta,
why do you not go to Russia…?
Love,
Yours, Claire

To Russia? Our Swiss friend had no idea of what was being quietly hatched here in England; none at all. Another world is breaking into our life of which no one in the parishes has any inkling. Prospectuses drop through the Vicarage letter box, depicting places whose names I now know; offering possibilities I could not have imagined. The other world is my lost world, the world of the Child. We could fly via Moscow. Decidedly not. Cross the Baltic by boat. Too expensive. In the end we booked seats on this German tourist bus which promises to take us to

Kaliningrad (the old Königsberg) and other East Prussian towns, and also on to the Curonian Spit. The most exciting prospect of all is the opportunity of a taxi ride across the Memel into Lithuania. The company warns its travellers of a possible "depressing encounter" in the Kaliningrad Oblast and comforts them that in Lithuania they will find "properties reasonably cared for".

Christmas slipped by. In January our local newspaper carried a picture of a man operating a spinning wheel. Anthony was the first person we had heard of who had returned to his roots: to the Lithuanian village where he had grown up and where he remembered his grandmother spinning wool. We invited ourselves to his home. At first he was reticent to speak about himself but gradually warmed to his story. As a teenager, along with thousands of Baltic and German refugees, he had joined the panicked flight from the advancing Red Army, crossing the frozen lagoon. Still moved, he recalled how a loaded wagon right in front of him had been hit by a Russian shell and sunk under the ice. Having safely arrived in Germany he had been put to forced labour in a factory and endured gruelling hardship and brutality. The end of the war found him a homeless and stateless person. He made his way to Britain and married an English girl. (He smiled warmly at the woman sitting by him.) In our plans he showed no interest, but it was good to have met this quiet man.

After the war the Allies divided the German regions of West Prussia and East Prussia, ceding the West to Poland; the East came under the rule of the Soviet Union who renamed it the Kaliningrad Oblast. Memelland, further east, was ceded to Lithuania again, when the Baltic States became independent. The Oblast is an enclave, a land island, separated from Russia. Those German civilians who had been trapped by their own leadership and prevented from being evacuated *before* the Red Army broke through their border, experienced a terrible treatment and were further traumatized by an act of ethnic cleansing. Their war-torn region was left to newcomers, peoples from all over the Soviet Union. The Oblast became a kind of orphanage, filled with 'children' devoid of roots, history, culture and relevant skills. Mother Russia, having attained a coveted place at the Baltic, had to repopulate an empty and devastated land. She had many mouths to feed.

And now we are rolling eastwards towards that land. We have crossed the border into the former East Germany, impoverished and long separated and estranged from her sister, prosperous West Germany. They are holding hands again. We pass deserted factories and the landscape looks dismal. I count twenty four fellow travellers on the coach: all Germans, obviously; mostly middle-aged or elderly. In Frankfurt-an-der-Oder we pick up two beautiful blond sisters in whom the tall grey-haired twin brothers at the front take an immediate interest. In the course of this week the blondes will spurn the single red rose and break hopeful hearts. But before this sad demise of love, each one of us will have been affected deeply and uniquely by our journey.

Geese, pigs, churches and signposts with unreadable and unpronounceable names float by. This is Poland. An empty factory yard serves as a less than romantic picnic spot: and throughout the afternoon the flat landscape lulls us into a stupor. One old gentleman, who was born in Tilsit, has spread out a pre-war map on his knees and momentarily jolts us awake when he shouts out names of towns some of us recognize from school geography lessons. Our hotel in Pila (*Schneidemühl*) exudes quiet luxury but at dinner the waiters' deference saddens me, especially so, when some of our fellow travellers exploit this servile posing. Before breakfast – dawn promises a warm day – Peter and I take a short walk through empty streets. I cannot help feeling uneasy.

Safe and invisible behind smoked glass, we speed towards the newly-opened frontier between Poland and the Oblast. It sounds as if we might be the first German coach to use this crossing and it is by no means certain that the border controls will allow us through. They may well send us on a far longer route by which we would enter the Russian province via Lithuania rather than Poland.

A toilet break in the Polish forest. Big Hubert knows of wooden huts in a clearing. There is a rush! And a rush back with handkerchiefs pressed against nose and mouth. "Disgusting!" Boys to the right – girls to the left – into the undergrowth.

From our elevated position we anxiously watch our courier's negotiations with the Polish border guards. Bundles of Deutschmark change hands and finally a sigh of relief: the barrier lifts – and we are in East Prussia! No. Correction. We are in Russia.

Kaliningrad Oblast: the name sounds cold and impersonal and finds no resonance in me. The once arable land lies eerily empty. Unkempt meadow, yellow with dandelion, devoid of cattle, stretches into nothingness. We are keen to glimpse houses, farmsteads, just anything. Silence has fallen on the coach, except for an occasional gasp or sigh. We travellers share a deep knowledge: this soil is fertilized with human blood. Suddenly someone jumps up and points eagerly at a circular structure on a telegraph pole. Big Hubert stops.

"*Ein Storch!*" And there it stands on its nest, resting on one long red leg as you would expect: our first East Prussian stork. Once every barn roof here had welcomed the black-and white travellers from Africa; now only a few ramshackle buildings bear a wagon wheel. We are happy to see that the Russian population also values these once deeply loved birds.

As evening falls, we reach the outskirts of the city. Kaliningrad. We circumnavigate the grey sea of high-rise buildings; pass a multitude of tiny allotments; a small airport; abandoned building sites; a cemetery. Each grave is marked with a large Orthodox cross, has a primitive bench and is surrounded by a white metal fence. Private gardens of remembrance. Had such 'private ownership' been granted to the Kaliningraders in Communist times, I wonder? Big Hubert is keen to reach our destination: the shores of the Baltic.

The Baltic had always held a kind of spell over me. When I was twenty I took a holiday in Travemünde, where I met up with Elke from Lübeck with whom I had become friends convalescing in the Eifel Mountains. I had not realised how close the Baltic resort lay to the East German border. At night, with the bright lights from restaurants and nightclubs behind me, I had peered behind the Iron Curtain into a dark void. Four years later, on our honeymoon, we crossed the Baltic from one Scandinavian country to another but when in Finland Peter suggested we drive to the *Russian* frontier, I begged him not to. I felt scared.

Tonight I am looking across the 'East Sea' as the Germans call it and this time I am actually standing on Russian soil! In Zelenogradsk the last rays of the May sun tint our Soviet-built hostel as well as the old German villas, with the same rosy glow. Gone is the elegant clientèle who at one time whiled away their leisure hours in luxurious hotels, ballrooms and chic restaurants; sauntered along the elevated timber promenade; watched the carefree sun-worshippers and playful bathers on the beach where the golden amber hides; charmed by the white sand meeting the blue waters of the Baltic and the cloudless azure of an untrammelled north-eastern sky. This was the German resort of Cranz, and its opulent facilities created after the First World War also suited the Nazi elite. The Soviets had let its glory slip into dereliction. Today the handsome buildings are vacuous shells. In a doorless ballroom water runs from a broken tap. Along a grey concrete walk-way shuffle former Red Army officers; their eyes vodka-glazed; medals dangling from shabby uniforms. They make war – against myriads of mosquitoes. They whack the air with birch twigs and ignore our smiles and greetings. "Sick souls": these words uttered by a young Russian ring in my ear. Do these robotic soldiers even *see* the evening glory, the glow that is transforming sea and sand?

We scramble down on to the empty beach. Is this wise? From nowhere appears a man who must have been watching us. He tries forceful persuasion to make us buy small pieces of amber. When politely but firmly we decline he presses a rouble into Peter's hand. That's strange! We have already found such a coin on a shelf in our wardrobe and wondered why it had been placed there so obviously. Blessing or curse? Who knows?

We have to sleep in separate rooms and I find my bed most uncomfortable. Armchairs are only on the landing and the drains from the shower room reek. Dinner, our first Russian meal, evokes childhood memories of chives and soured milk. Our coach rests floodlit behind a safety fence. Hubert sleeps in his double seat. Without wipers and wheels we would be going no further. In the morning he drives us into the city.

Here our companions' eyes search for anything German, even the slightest indication that there had ever been a Königsberg before Bomber Command and the Red Army blew it out of existence. The old city, world-renowned for its university, had been home to merchants and craftsmen, scientists and artists, philosophers and poets. Its medieval *Schloß* had witnessed the coronation of two Prussian kings. Today we bump along on absurdly wide traffic-free streets. Horror-struck by its unspeakable ugliness, we can only shake our heads in disbelief when our Russian guide shows off "our beautiful city Kaliningrad". Natasha's auburn hair reflects the sun as she addresses us in fluent German. How can such a beautiful butterfly have emerged from so hideous a chrysalis?

To the people of Kaliningrad (named after one of Stalin's political henchmen, who had never stepped foot in the city) our blacked-out conveyance must look like a sinister alien from another planet. But perhaps they are already getting used to the ostentatious tourist buses rolling in from Germany. The street economy is certainly well geared up. Trestle tables line the tourist routes.

We glide on to a huge open square and come to a halt at its very centre. Our black fortress oozes superiority – and fear. Gingerly we climb down on to the tarmac. Immediately children descend on us like swarming bees, unfold concertinas of post cards or open their grubby little fists to display tiny splinters of amber which they are unlikely to have found on the beach themselves. The now ageing former 'children' of the city, the Königsbergers, distribute sweets and crayons as they have been instructed to. The young Kaliningraders' hard little faces do not hide their disappointment. Sweets and crayons? They clamour for Deutschmark.

The bulk of the coach almost blocks out the grey colonnaded neo-classical façade, the former North Station, built in the thirties, one of the few German buildings left intact. We walk around the columns. Is this the station where our little family would have changed trains to Tilsit? No, from here the trains went to the coast.

We move as a group. Natasha leads us towards the former Prussian Stock Exchange, a marker of that era when Königsberg had been a well-to-do centre of Baltic shipping and trade. Double-winged – the imposing building's façade is painted in white and pale-blue – it survived the two extensive RAF raids and years of Soviet wanton destruction. This survivor, a lifeless relic, stands alone in an alien land. In the large stone containers, placed to enhance the entrance, grow dandelions in grey dust.

Hawkers behind their tables urge us to buy postcards, babushkas and amber necklaces, bracelets and rings; we smile politely and hurry on towards the ruin of the Brick-Gothic cathedral, the Dom. Reconstruction is clearly in progress but the builders have taken a holiday until more German funds flood in. Nothing guards the safety of visitors. With trepidation I watch Peter climb higher and higher up into primitive scaffolding, crumbling debris and charred beams – just to take photos of the cityscape below. When the Dom is finally rebuilt, it will not ring with Lutheran liturgy but with Russian Orthodox chants and the strains of classical music. Be that as it may, the real 'god' of Kaliningrad is Emanuel Kant, focus of adoration; the city's celebrity. At the philosopher's tomb in the lee of the cathedral wall, a young couple are posing for their wedding photograph.

If cathedral, stock exchange, railway station and a few red-brick gates, remnants of former fortifications, are the relics, the bones of a dead city, what is the flesh of Kaliningrad? Concrete boxes pollute the May sky. Rumour has it that they were purposely erected on German cemeteries and that today they are 'unfit for human habitation'. But they *are* inhabited – by uprooted Soviet citizens from every corner of its vast territory.

For lunch we meet at Kaliningrad's biggest hotel. The dining room is gloomy, the food nondescript. I wade ankle-deep in ill-smelling dark water, relieved to reach the elevated island on which the ladies' toilet is mounted. Around the hotel entrance dealers lie in wait for us, dark characters who seem to rule over a horde of youngsters. As the afternoon approaches, I feel saturated with "our beautiful city" and not even the sparsely-planted 'park' can alleviate my sense of oppression. A faint smell of sewage hangs in the air and it is difficult to shake off the suspicion of an underground 'sewage' system of a different kind beneath the bleak poverty and neglect on the surface. Avoiding large puddles in which a red-brick building reflects, we enter the Amber Museum. We are too spoilt to be impressed.

The climax of our visit: *The House of the Soviets*. This huge grey concrete building stands isolated and exposed in all its ugliness. Were the architectural plans drawn up by primary school children, sticking together shoe boxes and cereal cartons? Covered walkways connect two towers – many storeys high and standing on a kind of plinth. The edifice seems to scream horror into the cloudless sky. Uninhabitable and uninhabited (is there really nobody looking out from one of so many windows?). Outrage by our group is accentuated by the knowledge that this grey monstrosity had been erected on the foundations of the royal *Schloß*, the ancient castle, with its coronation hall and splendid interior. Leonid Breshnev had given orders to dynamite it, to remove all traces of "fascist militarism". The irony is that this lone bunker-like colossus poses the real danger: its foundations are hollow. The royal castle's underground tunnels were never filled in. What treasures might they hold? One day they will surely have to demolish this horror. And rebuild the castle? I long for the Baltic breeze. The Child wants this sun-lit ugliness to end. A small grassy triangle is luring...The day after tomorrow...

We are all relieved to be safely and comfortably back on board. Dilapidated houses hide behind mercifully dense leafage, and as we leave the city, only a tiny stall, set up in a doorway, selling a few bunches of bananas, a dozen apples in a bowl and something green – is it a lettuce or a cabbage? – captures our attention.

2

Jewel Peninsula

Our mobile fortress will surely shield us from all danger as we cross the border between the Russian Oblast and Lithuania. This frontier slices in half the slender peninsula: the Curonian Spit. Our destination is Klaipėda (once Memel), Lithuania's third biggest city, but for me the journey is the destination. Hubert will drive us the entire length of the Spit: ninety kilometres. To the Child the *Kurische Nehrung* spells magic and excitement as she has been well fed on romantic ideas about this extraordinary land tongue.

Russia and Lithuania are equally concerned about the conservation of the fragile land strip and have designated it as a nature reserve. We pay our toll and immediately enter a tunnel of dense forest which crowds the thoroughfare. I know there is water on both sides of the Spit. The Baltic and the Curonian Lagoon can only be a stone's throw away, yet it is impossible to catch a glimpse of either. I expected the vista to open out before us as soon as our wheels rolled on to the peninsula but where is that landscape, eulogized by poets and writers, the "European Sahara", the "Italian look"? The black-and-white photographs Mami kept had stirred the Child's imagination. I crane my neck to catch the first sight of the famous dunes or espy an elk amongst the birch stems. But thick dark-green foliage occludes everything. I feel irritated. I have come all this way to touch *the reality of the dune-land where my life began*, not to drive mile after mile through this unrelenting forest. I can make no connection between this monotonous leafy subway and the romantic notions I had imbibed and once written about:

...Seven thousand years ago, rising out of the Baltic Sea, the great dune was born and when the wind saw it, it began to play with the white grains of the new creation, shaping and reshaping patterns on its virgin surface. The dune grew in height and curled and slunk like a big cat. It gave rise to the legend of Neringa, the giantess who had made her home on the eastern half of the peninsula and had a lover on the shore of the Haff, the sweet-water lagoon. When the God of the Sea threatened to destroy her fisherman by his great storms, Neringa carried aprons full of sand and built a dam against the open sea. The sandy dyke so protected the Haff from the wind that her lover could take out his little boat in safety.

Families from the East came to settle in the shelter of the dune. A forest of mighty oak and pine, of birch and willow, rooted and held the sands in check. The lagoon provided the people with an amazing variety of fish, and the forest with meat from elk, deer and wild boar. Then came men who were neither fishers nor hunters but whose ambition and foolishness knew no bounds. They turned the dam the giantess had built as a blessing – into a curse. First the Teutonic Knights used the forest's timber for their castles. Later soldiers from Russia and far-away France felled a great number of the ancient trees to build ships and ramparts. The dunes were deforested, stripped of their protective clothing and disaster followed. War destroys all that is good and beautiful and cares nothing for landscape or human life, and Neringa's slim land knew it.

The people who had come to this land had wandered in from Latvia and were called Curonians. The language they spoke they never wrote down. The tribe adapted itself to life on the land tongue and over centuries built picturesque villages, planted gardens and made their living by fishing in teams. A hand-knitted net trawled between two heavy flat-bottomed boats. Unique in the world are these *Keitelkähne, Kurenkähne, kurenas*. Muscled brown arms hauled the catch ashore. Then women's hands threaded the fish on lines to dry in the sun or above pits from which blue smoke rose. Even during the harsh winters, when the lagoon lay under a thick crust of ice, the fishermen ventured on to the shimmering sheet with sledges and snow shoes tied to their clogs and to the feet of their horses. With specially forged long-bladed axes the men would cut a hole into the ice, lift the 'lid' by means of iron tongs and slide a wooden plank into the water beneath. At the edge of the hole one man drummed a wooden mallet on to a hollowed-out piece of timber to make a clapping sound. This made the fish curious – but they knew nothing of the net stretched out beneath them. The lagoon was the tribe's treasure chest from which a small silver lid could be lifted at whim to extract a portion of the hoard that richly replenished itself.

For generations the people had danced to a simple rhythm, a slow dance in a universe of sea and sand and sky, so beautiful that they had lost their hearts to it. But the dune had the power to strike a subtle but deadly chord. With the removal of the trees it lost all discipline. It could wander where it pleased. Driven by the sea-wind, it shifted its vast hulk relentlessly and regarded the long curved land that threads itself between sea and lagoon as its own domain. Only to the wind, its master, did it submit its rule. Neringa had lost her power.

The dune, when in the throes of passion with the wind, raced heedlessly and covered all in its way, without mercy smothering, choking, burying all that had been built and tended. Fourteen villages it devoured; ate its way into the huts and gardens that had once trustingly huddled beneath pine and birch. The fishermen and their families warily watched the dune and entrusted themselves to their Creator God, who had set them into this world, both so lovely and so harsh. They built new villages and started life afresh.

Yet whatever might befall them, their boats (the dark heavy hulks built from oak and pine and thickly covered in tar) sailed out on to the Haff. Each mast bore its own rigid pennant, carved like filigree: outlines of houses, churches, lighthouses, trees, storks, elks, gulls and open gates stood silhouetted against the sky. During the day the masts lay folded back, and from trees and fences hung the nets to dry. Each night a flotilla glided out into a red glow or on to a silver path. Diaphanous rectangles flashed a last signal to the women on the shore.

After the bustle and bellowing that accompanied the men's departure, a deep silence fell. Their women, rooted into the sand, their aprons billowing like sails, braced the gusts, defying their force like the whirling and shrieking gulls above. The fisher wives' sun-dried faces, furrowed like the sand and shrouded by heavy head scarves, remained turned toward the greying lagoon, their eyes shaded against the slanting rays until the darkness had swallowed up the last sail. Only then did the women return to their low-slung wooden cottages, whose pastel blue was no longer distinct amongst the dark pines. By the light of their swinging lanterns they hustled back to spinning-wheel, loom and cradle and fed the last birch logs of the day into the tiled stove.

When the waters grew angry and turned the Haff into a cauldron, many a fisherman lost his life. Suffering and hardship were woven into the Curonians' lives, etched into their faces, and death was never far away. Each man carved his own "grave board" which, like a headstone, would one day mark his and his family's burial plot. Even the plague had found this isolated community: the elks had carried the mass murderer across the Haff. And the fragile spine of the land itself, when will it break again as it had done once already?

The brooding stillness of the dune land admitted only the rhythmic lapping of the waters, the roar of the wind in the pines and the rustle of birch leaves, the shrill of the gulls and the wafting of wild goose wings. The children played quietly around the boats and the women's eyes were as still and deep as the Haff. But they remained ever alert to the vagaries of weather, the movement of the sand and to any news from the outside world.

Storms, worse than those on either sea or Haff, were brewing and would soon race across the Spit, uproot and kill. It is *man* who destroys and when he does, he destroys utterly. Soon the Curonians' way of life would cease forever. The first dictionary of their language came too late. Today – after catastrophe and cataclysm – only two thousand seven hundred people have made permanent homes on the peninsula. And they are not Curonians. These, along with their distinctive culture, were uprooted and wiped off the face of the earth.

Now the forest is back. What man destroys he can also with intelligence and good will restore. Sturdy grasses were planted to anchor the sand. Conservationists now oppose the cutting down of trees, the saviours of the Spit. So the pines stand tall, row upon row, like soldiers clad in red tunics, a russet red that gleams after the rain's laundry. Their scent oozes goodness. Unimpeded, they stretch to the heavens, up and out of the moss and lichen that cling to the earth; they inspire the eyes of man to look upwards, away from the mundane; they invite him to inhale deeply, to experience well-being; they speak to the listening heart, assuring it that it is safe again: to let go, to open once more to other lands and to other peoples...

And still we are rolling through that tunnel of trees. Trees. Trees. Trees. Where are the dunes? Why do we not stop somewhere? Will we be kept blind behind our smoked-glass? I want to sink my feet into the fabled sands and dip my toes into the enchanting sea like my parents on their honeymoon:

> June days: time to marry.
> White nights: time to make me.
> Like spawning salmon you travelled
> a thousand miles
> by train and steamboat
> to the narrow land,
> that long emaciated arm,
> stretching through
> amber-sand and forest land
> keeping apart
> lagoon and never-silent sea.

> And as you made me,
> did you taste,
> on salty, sun-dried breeze
> under a quiv'ring birch,
> the bitterness?
> Glimpse
> in the flames of equinox
> the bloodied spectre rise?
> Perceive
> the heartbeat of the cannon?
> And feel
> the terror stalk this fragile soil?

Your city toes
dipped into Prussian-blue;
you jumped its waves
that hid from you
their cruel undertow
below intoxicating charm.
Did you, in your embrace
in salty, sun-dried breeze
(ever so faintly) know:
it's not the sea
that is deceiving you,
dragging us under?

...The forest flickers. I am dozing; dreaming. Hubert is just driving, driving.

"Rossitten!" the voice of the traveller with the old map calls down the length of the coach and we all sit up. There is a clearing large enough for the coach to park and its doors swing open. Oh, the scent of the pines! So this is the fishing village of Rossitten hugging the lagoon? No, the low modern building amongst the pines is *not* a fisherman's cottage but a purpose-build Soviet museum. Peter and I are reluctant to be herded inside, only to be greeted by a large showcase displaying a *model* of the Spit. We scan the exhibits on the walls: an educational kaleidoscope of history, geology, zoology, biology, ornithology, ecology...of the *Kursskiy zalis and Kursskaja kosa*, the Haff and the Nehrung. This information is aimed at school children! We have seen enough. Who wants virtual reality when you can inhale the fragrance of earth and pine needles? Unobserved we sidle out of the door.

"The Nehrung is so narrow, we might actually see the lagoon in one direction and the sea in the other," I say, energized by the Child within.

The woodland floor, an aromatic carpet, leads us to a high wrought-iron gate. Chained and padlocked, it bars our way as does a young uniformed Russian who steps into our path. His eyes meet mine and I smile and make a pleading gesture, pointing to the gate. He stares back, unsmiling. I feel my heart racing and my neck flush. I keep raising my hands as if in prayer and plead with my eyes, and the guardian of the gate turns the key. The chains clank and fall away and both iron wings swing open. The Russian motions to us and I walk as in a dream. This is the moment I have long waited for.

The shore of the lagoon lies hidden behind unkempt bushes, weeds and reeds. And then, as if a window had been cut into the shrubbery, there exposed lies the whole expanse of the 'magical' Kurische Haff – grey and entirely empty. Sunlight on tiny waves glints like quicksilver. Nothing but a deserted lake, a large 'gravel pit'! I shudder and at the same time am awed when I realize that it is actually *me* who *at this moment* is standing *here*. Peter respects the encounter; so does the Russian. Then I remember that we had left our party in the museum and they are probably waiting for us at the coach. Peter slips a Deutschmark into a young hand. We return the Russian's smile and mime our thanks. The chains clank; the padlock clicks. Our fellow travellers are still held captive in the museum.

"Let's climb up the other side. Perhaps we can see the Baltic and the dunes from there."

Silver-white sand, seeping through duck boards, fills our sandals. We climb a few more steps. To left and right the sand is stippled with pastel-blue grasses. Broad brush strokes of Prussian blue and azure delineate the edge of the peninsula. It is beautiful but not exactly the celebrated 'Sahara' landscape.

Hubert, bent over his steering wheel, appears to be dozing, and of our party there is still no sign. Have they walked into Rossitten? Have I missed the opportunity of seeing the village, where my parents honeymooned? Have we missed out on the world-famous bird-ringing station? We can now only wait for them to report back. Beneath the pines, flecked with sunlight, a bench invites us to sit. The forest around is filled with birdsong. Here I am, close to Rossitten (a name the Child has always known) *and* on Russian soil! This is surely a suitable place to read from the Scriptures and I look for that one verse that was given me at my confirmation, "*Fear not, I have redeemed you…I have called you by name…you are mine.*" My heart feels warm and thankful.

Chatter and laughter interrupt my meditation. The museum has finally released its prisoners, where, like Elly Wolff's geese in the farmyard, they have been force-fed with information. Satisfied, they climb back on board, unaware that they have been prevented from seeing the *real thing*.

The man had misread his map. This is *Sarkau*. The *next* place is Rossitten. (now called *Rybatchi*). So I have not missed anything. For a moment my hopes that we might visit the village rise, but alas, Hubert is driving on – towards Klaipėda. Does anyone on this bus feel as disappointed as I? We by-pass all the villages and will never know whether the 'typical houses' shown on sepia postcards still exist. The green tunnel seems endless. Someone starts up a song as is usual when Germans travel as a group. And the Child remembers all the lyrics.

We have reached the border. Two very young Russian soldiers, their heads dwarfed under absurdly large military caps, inspect our passports and our visas, take their time and our wad of Deutschmark. From my safe position up high I am looking *down on Russian soldiers*! The barrier is raised but – can you believe this? – here on the Lithuanian side the forest also prevents any view of dune and water. We pass by *Nida* (German Nidden), the resort, made famous by Agnes Miegel and Thomas Mann; once a much sought-after location for artists and writers and thousands of holiday makers. Our road continues straight ahead – walled and roofed – until we reach the ferry terminal. Our group stays huddled around the coach.

Not so Peter. He has spied a fire watchtower. From high above the massed trees he thinks he might *see* the dunes and at least get a photograph. I watch him running, getting smaller and smaller, almost disappearing among ferns and birch saplings. I hope he makes it back in time. Or perhaps I don't want him to: it would be so lovely to stay on the peninsula by ourselves while the others go sightseeing in Klaipėda. I lower myself on to a sun-warmed patch of grass, lean my head against the white trunk of a young birch and try to connect with my beginnings. Sunlight flickers. The sea breeze fans my face. Again I am overcome with gratitude.

The ferry plies the narrow isthmus and we wander around the streets of a multi-ethnic city that has nothing to say to me. My thoughts are in the dunes, on the Castle Road and at a little railway station where small trains stop...

But here in Klaipėda we find ourselves in a sculpture park that had once been the Protestant German cemetery. Modern works are exhibited amongst old iron-ringed trees that have been preserved, those silent witnesses to the events that overran the city when it was still called

Memel. Adjacent to the park rises a vast Soviet concrete war memorial, honouring Russian soldiers.

High-rise flats from the Khrushchevera compete with pretentious new buildings and old houses under restoration. The city seems to have no soul, no identity. Perhaps this melting pot of many cultures never had its own. We follow the tourist trail to the restored theatre and the recently re-erected statue of *Ännchen von Tharau*, made famous by an old German song. We succumb to touting vendors and buy a primitive blue-and-white-stippled jug and an even more primitively executed tiny oil painting which depicts wind-swept pines and a wooden-planked pathway laid across dune sand, reminiscent of the one we climbed up this morning.

I feel restless, vaguely sensing that something has to be completed in the Nehrung-sands. The shadows are lengthening when at last we cross back on to the Spit. Surely now Hubert will take us to the dunes. No, he keeps on driving: we are back in the same green tunnel. Wait, we've stopped! Not in the dunes, but near a cluster of market stalls, stocked with amber and wood carvings and hand-woven linens. Seduced, I buy a T-shirt that bears *'Die Kurische Nehrung'* in Gothic lettering on the front while Peter finds a carved figure of a sad and hollow-eyed Christ who, crowned with thorns, contemplates his Passion, sitting with his head cupped in one hand. Though he looks forlorn, to us he embodies hope: the renaissance of a believing people rising from atheistic oppression. This wooden figure speaks to us of the Suffering Servant who has borne the sorrows of the violent decades. The Child wants three wooden dolls like the ones Mami had made for her dolls' rooms.

We cannot be more than two kilometres from the Russian border and once we have crossed back into the Oblast, we will have missed any opportunity of finding the dunes. So, it is now or never. I lurch forward to speak to the courier.

"Are we going to see the dunes?"

"We can't, I'm sorry. We will be late for dinner."

"We have travelled a thousand kilometres and have to forgo the sight of the dune landscape for which the Nehrung is famous? What? For a Russian supper?" Disappointed and angry I stagger back to my seat. Is no one on this wretched coach interested?

I watch him discussing something with Hubert, and then comes the announcement I had been hoping for.

"We will now make a short detour so that you can see the Nehrung's famous dune landscape. We will be half an hour late for dinner. Is that alright with everyone?" A murmur of approval settles the matter. There are no objections about the dinner. Hubert veers off the road on to a track where there are no trees! And before the door is fully open, Peter and I jump into white sand. How it shimmers under the setting sun. For a moment we stand at the ridge of a wide bowl filled with the same white sand, speckled with blue grasses. An exquisite sight! I start running. No one stops us. No one follows us. At the nadir of the sandy arena…

A high cross! Even from afar it is obvious that it is no ordinary cross. I stumble towards it. Frayed ropes tie vertical and horizontal bar; charred driftwood – timbers that have been through fire and water! "*When you pass through waters, I shall be with you…when you walk through fire you shall not be burnt…*" Around the base of the cross, branches and twigs have been woven into a 'crown of thorns'. I step on to it and hug the sun-warmed bleached timbers, cling to them, feel the rough and the smooth textures and am racked by sobs, feel hot tears flood my face. At last I let go and lower myself into the warm dune sand and sense Someone sitting next to me! Someone I know. Someone who knows me. And it is just like in the vision I had seen some years before: Jesus, the Lord of Life had sat with me, stayed with me, having rescued me from 'shipwreck'.

"You are here, Lord! You are really here!" I cry – and open my eyes. There is an indentation in the sand beside me, a hollow such as a man would leave in the sand – as my parents had made when I was conceived! And I understand – at the deepest level that the Lord of Life – has healed the deepest wound in my life: my sense of abandonment. And I am awed by the profundity of *knowing* that I was conceived for Him and not for a self-acclaimed messiah figure whose photograph had stared out from ebony frames! Jesus had been the Lord of my life from its very beginning! Who can fathom it? Now I know *by experience* that His promise – never to leave or abandon His own – is true. He had 'lured' me into the dunes. Not the tourist trail, not a romantic nostalgic urge have led me to encounter the cross and the Resurrected One, but the Spirit of God had driven me into 'the desert'. In a snatched few moments, between tourist booth and dining room, He had cemented the very foundation of my life with Basic Trust. Sand had turned into a rock-sure foundation. Something no therapy could accomplish.

The slanting sun rests on the undulating sands and from the ridge of the dune bowl there is frantic waving and shouting. Now our fellow travellers are hungry and the Russian dinner is waiting. My face is burning and still wet with tears. I do not wipe them away. Those on the edge will never know what took place by the cross. They may have a photo or two of the sandy expanse where I had – a rendezvous with Life.

3

Bridge over the Memel

Nikolai and I share the same year of birth, but it was another two years before the war reached *his* family in the Ukraine. His little legs could already toddle down his street when tanks and armoured cars invaded his homeland and his young father lost his life in the first week of the German invasion (codenamed *Operation Barbarossa*). Like killer bees half a million soldiers had swarmed out of the East Prussian forests and overrun the Ukraine. Who had sheltered this little boy?

His rosy and well-fed face emanates kindness; his silvering hair and moustache lend it distinction. The battered Lada which he treats with great respect will take us into Lithuania today. I sit beside him but the Child is not comfortable to be so close to "a Russian soldier". Nikolai has struck it lucky: he can taxi German 'nostalgia tourists' in search of their long-lost homes because he has some of their language. I act as interpreter to Peter who has crammed himself into the backseat, his knees under his chin.

"Are you married?" I ask our driver.

"Long time ago. Wife tourist guide. She forgotten me." His laugh is too loud, covers the pain, and I wonder whether the two children he mentions, have also "forgotten" him?

"Have you been back to the Ukraine recently?"

"At mother's funeral. Cost much money."

"What brought you to Kaliningrad?"

"Nineteen when joined Red Army. Sent me to Potsdam. You know?"

"Frederick the Great and Sanssoussi and all that," I say. And he laughs.

"Lived in barracks. Major in army. Twenty five years. When Iron Curtain down, no more soldiers wanted in Germany. Big pension now!" And again his huge laugh. "Won't buy bread."

Kaliningrad had caught him in its net, as it had many soldiers on their way eastwards in search of a home. Outside the safety of barracks walls, he has to scratch for a living along with the thousands of strangers washed into this unfamiliar region. The Black Market (he calls it *Schwarzmarktplatz*) is his playground and he knows all the going prices. Reels them off: petrol, white bread, black bread, tomatoes, bananas...

"Is this your own car?"

He laughs. "Wealthy can buy used cars, can pay repair car. I work for company."

Sarcasm about *Mother* Russia peppers his running commentary but without bitterness or spite.

Nikolai had met us at the hostel and we are on our way to find two villages. We have to rely on the Child who wants to stand again on her daisy-strewn triangle, not far from a house with a grey wall. Do these really exist?

The sun is lighting up the Zelenogradsk villas left from German times. Some window surrounds have been painted white, evidently quite recently, and the century-old stucco is accentuated in pale blue and white. In the out-of-town cemetery the benches stand empty because Kaliningrad's people are at work. On the city boundary, stretching in the direction of the Baltic, row upon row of unfinished houses stare blankly from hollow windows. Between our thoroughfare and the grey concrete high-rise apartment blocks on the outskirts of the city spreads a patchwork quilt of small gardens. Nikolai explains that each plot measures exactly four hundred square metres and is literally 'allotted' to Kaliningrad's citizens to augment the outrageously expensive city food with fresh vegetables and potatoes, chives and radishes. The Black Market, Kaliningrad's way of life, provides shoes and trousers; meat and *good* meat; imported fruit; white bread and black bread; flour and tinned soups; caviar and coffee.

The road bends and veers around the south-western tip of the Haff. Here a sleepy little river, the Djemen feeds the lagoon. Nikolai parks the Lada at the water's edge, in sight of a semi-roofed and dilapidated German farm house. What holds up all those wooden sheds that have tottered like this for decades? Dandelion-spangled grass patches are littered with old lintels and cornerstones. Once Labiau (now Polesk), had had a ferry port from which steam boats crossed over to the Curonian Spit. This morning a few scrawny chickens scratch amongst dock and dandelion. The old fruit trees no longer bear leaves, let alone the mass of white and pink blossom one would expect at this season. Tethered on too short a frayed rope, a shaggy goat nibbles at the grass left over from all its previous meals and quite viciously butts Peter as he approaches. Young self-sown birches redeem this God-forsaken place. Half a dozen canoe-type fishing boats, tied to rotten wooden bollards, rock on still water. Something vaguely familiar...a small black-and-white photo with serrated edges in my parents' photo album...a young man perching on the rim of just such a boat...my newly-wed father...snapped by my bridal mother. So it is *here*, in this small harbour near Labiau, where they had waited for the mail steamer to take them across to Rossitten! No steamer has left from here for a long, long time. We rattle on to a small bridge, giving a wide berth to two head-scarved women pushing bicycles. Our goal is a far larger and infinitely more historical bridge: the *Luisenbrücke*, named in honour of the Prussian queen who had braved confrontation with Napoleon pleading for her country. During a meeting between the Conqueror-Emperor of France and the Tsar of Russia on a raft in the Memel, Luise's husband, the Prussian king, had been humiliated by having to remain on the river's edge. We shall cross the bridge today, that artery connecting nations, having in its time allowed those with good and those with evil intent to cross the river: merchants, travellers and invaders alike.

We are now passing a shabby building that vaguely resembles a church. Loose hay is escaping from open windows in the stump of the bell tower. The East Prussian place of worship, turned into an agricultural store, hides behind young trees that have evidently planted themselves. The trees are sick; they raise their naked winter arms into the laughing May-time blue. Nikolai is pleased to stop anywhere we want him to. He has learnt that these tourists must snap a 'typical' East Prussian house here; a stork nest there; a grey slatted fence, from which time and neglect have peeled all traces of the white paint that had so impressed the Russian soldiers on their arrival; a garden where lilac and chestnut are in blossom; and of course this desecrated church.

And then the forest swallows us up. East Prussian trees – a Russian forest. Spruces (apparently derived from the word 'Prussian') stand densely packed and are still as beautiful and mysterious as they had featured in the Child's fairy tales. While I share the Child's enchantment, I also imagine these very woodlands concealing camouflaged tanks and battalions of propaganda-fed German soldiers...marking time...waiting tensely for the signal to move...east...into Lithuania...Belarus...Ukraine...and the very heart of Russia...to finally end up freezing to death on the steppes or dying like rats in Stalin's gutted city on the Volga. From which of these sandy paths was the fatal operation launched? And had traces of this 'starting line' remained a year later – when the Child and her family arrived in East Prussia?

What is *Nikolai* thinking about, I wonder, driving along this deserted road where the trees almost touch overhead? Without warning he stops and orders us out of the car. He points to a rough wooden bench and motions us to sit there. We are alone in this immense forest. The sun plays on the waving branches and pleasantly warms my arms and face. A bird sings. From out of the quivering grasses and dandelion-gold rises a large tree stump. Our driver is ferreting around in the back of his car. The Child is afraid.

Nikolai emerges with arms laden with bread and cheeses; tomatoes, bananas and a thermos flask. All this food he sets out on the stump and goes back for more.

"*Essen!*" he points to the laden forest table. Am I dreaming?

When we have eaten our fill, Nikolai returns to the car and conjures up a bottle of Russian champagne and two gold-red-black lacquered beakers. "*Zum Feiern*": this occasion deserves to be celebrated. With great care Nikolai removes the foil and untwists the wire. Champagne corks like to enjoy a life of their own and ours is poised for its trajectory flight. With a pop it disappears into the undergrowth. This is serious! Two male bottoms stick up amongst the waving grasses. It is Peter who finds the essential cork and raises it triumphantly. Now the champagne flows. Nikolai drinks Coke from the bottle. (The fines – were the faintest whiff of alcohol detected on his breath – would ruin him financially.) And so we toast: to the past and to this moment. The rest of the precious bubbly is safely corked up. How he did it we will never know, but Nikolai suspects we might need to celebrate again.

The dark trees no longer crowd the straight 'Prussian' road (or is it Napoleonic?). It is seriously rutted. Is this still the damage the tanks caused? The drainage ditches to left and right evoke pictures of exhausted women, children, the old and infirm frozen to death by the icy East winds. *Gauleiter* Koch, responsible for the East Prussian province, had declared it a punishable offence for its civilian population to leave. The delayed evacuation resulted in indescribable chaos. The refugees, fleeing in great panic, were overtaken by the retreating, defending *Wehrmacht* and the vengeful Red Army. The Russian tanks rolled at a greater speed than the horse-drawn carts of the refugees, faster than the old men and women and the mothers with young children could walk. Many were crushed under the tracks. Starvation, slaughter, rape. The trek from East Prussia was the largest ever exodus and perhaps the cruellest. Churchill had advocated a clean sweep and Russia was the broom; the land was swept of Germans but its soil left contaminated with blood and the dead bodies beneath the drifts of snow.

Our little family had been spared all this.

North of the Memel things were different. In the summer of 1944 everyone in the region was panic-stricken as the Front inexorably moved west, coming ever closer to the border. We had seen the red sky in the night and heard continuous thunder throughout the day. Hitler himself ordered the evacuation of Memelland, and it happened in three waves. My father was given special leave in July to help us move during the first wave. By the autumn Memelland had been forcibly cleared of all civilians.

This morning the verdant verges and ditches shimmer with dew; the meadows beyond are a mass of wildflowers. The peaceful beauty helps me to shake off the horrific scenes playing in my mind. Suddenly a massive almost brutal concrete sculpture announces the name of the town: we are arriving in *Sovetsk*.

The now familiar faceless apartment blocks greet us on the outskirts of the former Tilsit. Has it changed at all since the end of the war, since the devastating RAF assaults and Soviet tank invasion? Fifty years on the centre of the town is still a bombsite. We do not linger in the wide bleak streets lined with shell-damaged buildings, and hollow houses, their windows and doors still boarded up. Tomorrow our coach will bring us here again and we shall have time to explore. And fulfil our self-appointed mission. We cross the old market which for centuries had been the meeting place for peoples from many diverse cultures. Traders from East and West, Jews and Gentiles, had met at the Memel and exchanged their wares. The hustle and bustle of that vibrant town has given way to lethargy. Today Sovetsk is still a melting pot, but only for Soviet citizens from their wide-flung empire. And the market is a yawning emptiness. Nikolai heads straight for the bridge. The Child's heart hammers wildly.

Greened twin turrets crown the grey stone gate that still forms the entrance to the re-erected bridge. This portal and a small cluster of houses withstood bombing and shelling. The Lada's wheels mount the incline and for a passing moment the arch throws a shadow across the bonnet of the car. And there flows the Memel. The bridge is empty. I am surprised that Nikolai deems it safe for me to leave the car half-way across, encouraging me to take photographs. Leaden waters are dragging themselves beneath me as if weighed down by pollution and silt and sadness. Defiled by the effluence of the nations through which it flows, the river reflects torn ash-coloured clouds in its waters. Not even the commonest of weeds seems to desire to root into these muddy banks. This brief encounter with the river has made me feel desolate and I wonder whether the Memel's edge had looked like this when the Child had stumbled on the inflated corpse in which maggots had wriggled...

My camera clicks. On the Russian side I capture a few low buildings, and half-hidden by clumps of trees, one dark-brick edifice and a tower looking down on a sad Sovetsk. And on the Lithuanian side? The same bleakness: bare mud, a pylon, metal cranes, a smoking chimney and grey industrial plant that will surely continue to pollute the river. I scramble back into the car. There is no time to dwell on my disillusionment because before us looms the feared toll bar. Will it be lifted? If it does, we shall not be far from the Child's world.

The Russian border guard disappears into his hut. And with him our passports. All we can do is: wait.

Something is wrong.

Our passports carry a *group* visa that is not valid for this private trip! How can we possibly turn back, having come this far? To proceed seems crazy, but the Child insists: travel that road today. Nikolai negotiates. We will be allowed into Lithuania if we leave our passports at the border. The barrier rises and we drive into a foreign land – illegally and without identification.

Can air actually smell of freedom? We reach a historic junction where a huge cross declares that Lithuania is liberated to practise once more its own brand of Christianity. This is our assumption. We do not take the road to the Baltic or the route north to Tauroggen, Riga and Leningrad but the Child directs us eastwards and now we are travelling on the Castle Road, *the Chaussee* of my childhood! How gentle and pleasant are the woodlands. Never more than two cows graze in a meadow. The villages lie tranquil. How this peaceful landscape belies its terrible history. The smooth road surface tells nothing about invasions and desperate flights of thousands of people in both directions. Will we find the village? The Child holds her breath: the signpost reads VIEŠVILĖ.

A beautiful lake lies to our left and the Child recognizes the *Mühlenteich,* the mill pond, where Oma and she had once watched their reflections in the water.

"Will you wait here, Nikolai? We'll walk into the village and see what we can find?" He watches as Peter and I cross the road and disappear into the undergrowth.

Now we have left our last security. Where are we? Just follow the Child's leading. This path is very straight, yes, it must be the old railway track, now disguised by a mass of nettles. This means that we cannot be far from the station. Look. See that empty space over there? Though there is no station building the Child has found her bearings and confidently leads us into the street entirely roofed over by the thick foliage of the linden trees.

"My Kindergarten!" I exclaim.

In the shadow of self-sown birches, set back from the street, its grubby lime-washed rendering flaking, its walls riddled with bullet holes: the Nazi nursery school. In the mud of its 'front lawn' thrives a sea of weed. Stone steps lead to doors that no one has opened for decades. The tall windows that had once filled our playroom with sunlight now yawn behind broken panes. We turn away.

On the opposite side of the road runs a broad flagged footpath in front of a row of dull apartments. *And I am standing over there!* Right there! A large bow grips blond hair...a solemn little girl is watching us...Of course it is not me. She is a Lithuanian child. Maybe four years old. She is pushing a cart twice her size towards a throng of dandelion-lanterns. The presence of strangers alarms her. I smile. She does not. Her little face remains solemn and anxious. She will have been born just before her country reclaimed its independence and began to recover its identity. This little girl will not have to march and wave flags beneath these lime trees; will not be obliged to wear a red neckerchief; will know neither the symbols of a hammer and sickle nor the crooked cross – both black against the same red background. Enjoy your freedom, little one. Use it well.

A solitary house with a grey façade – there it is! It has not changed at all. Framed by the same converging sandy roads, the low house stands as if marooned on an island. And dare I look to the right? Is it still there? Yes, it is! My legs tremble. A pile of logs almost obscures it.

My green grassy triangle! The Child has led us to it.

By the garden gate the old chestnut has lit its white candles and the lilac is still spilling into the garden as it did long ago. A neat flower bed has been freshly planted. The Child scans *her* wall and counts the windows. The wire gate into the garden is locked.

An old woman in faded overall and equally bleached headscarf is eyeing us. I call out to her in German. Cautiously she approaches and answers our smiles with a toothless grin. Her hands slide down the sides of the overall. I try to explain why we are here.

"*Tochter. Tochter.*" She points to somewhere beyond the road, where her daughter evidently lives and leads us across the sandy street - right across the grassy triangle - to the door of an apartment and introduces us to a younger woman with an open friendly face. Dark fine hair escapes from a ponytail; a shapeless cotton shift hangs loosely from her tall figure, the sort of garment which in England we might find as a nightie in a charity shop. In German I explain our unannounced presence and she understands. With a bright and warm smile she bids us come into her parlour. The style of the simple dark furniture reminds me of post-war interiors of German houses: a settee is draped in a brown blanket; a shelf unit holds rows of books. A freshly-picked rose gives life to a room dimmed by heavy net curtains. We shake hands with another lady (respectfully introduced to us as her mother-in-law), whose grey, short straggly hair has been combed back from a wrinkled face lit by a toothless smile. I do not catch the names of either of the old ladies, but it is with *Irena* I can converse and we learn that all three women in this room lost their men under tragic circumstances. Within a few minutes the second banquet of the day is spread before us: home-made bread and jam, fruit and soured milk and some smoked meat and sausage.

"Essen."

And then – for a split second – heaven opens and glory fills the simple chamber. Open hearts – different nations – other cultures – love...in Wischwill-Viešvilė.

I come back to earth. "Our Russian taxi driver is waiting by the mill pond," I explain. "Do you know a village by the name of *Uszballen?*"

"Yes. Not far from here. No signpost. I come with you." Irena goes to change her dress and this one is a little less faded and a little more shapely. Together we find Nikolai who is faithfully waiting where we had left him.

Four unlikely people cram into a Kaliningrad Lada: an ex-Red-Army officer from the Ukraine, a Lithuanian, an Englishman and a German. From the backseat Peter and I watch and listen: Irena and Nikolai are engaged in animated conversation – in classical Russian which both had reluctantly learnt at school. And we are rolling along the Castle Road towards Smalilinkai, once the Prussian-Lithuanian border town of Schmalilingken. A dense forest of spruce hems us in on both sides. When the woods recede and give way to fields, Irena points to the left and Nikolai turns the car up a wide sandy path. The Child's heart is beating wildly: she knows this rising track that snakes between rye fields, meadows and turnip patches. On the horizon the familiar dark forest frames the hamlet of Uszbalai, the Child's Uszballen. While the world was embroiled in war, her little brown legs had danced and dawdled along this path; her sandals had filled with the fine sand; and she had sung about the sun and the moon and the dew rising in gossamer veils from the meadow and the storks rattling on the barn...there it is – the barn! And beyond – a large dilapidated two-winged brick house, the colour of faded pink roses, with hollow windows, set in a yellow sea of dandelion. Elly Wolff's farm!

In front of the half-timbered barn is a good place to stop. The stork nest is no more, nor can I make out farm buildings around a yard where the geese had been fed and the Child had drunk warm milk from her special cup. The pale house is covered in shot wounds. How much fighting had occurred here? Melancholy seems to hang in the air and the place looks deserted.

'Here I herded the geese...Here I helped on the hay wagon...' I know, I know. 'Ronni had laughed like Nikolai...' Our driver has a sense of the importance of this occasion and fetches out the remaining champagne. Together we celebrate: our survival in Europe – all four of us – on different soils. Irena drinks from a coffee cup, Peter and I from our golden-red Russian beakers, Nikolai toasts with Coca-Cola. Time is running out. We cannot entirely dismiss the reality that we are here without our passports. Will the Russian officials hand them back to us?

"My grandfather lies buried in this hamlet," I say to Irena.

"Over there is a German cemetery." She points to a small wooded 'island' in the freshly-sown rye field. "Come and find grave."

Is that possible? No more thoughts of passports. Gingerly we step around the young cereal plants. Nikolai stays with the car.

The clump of trees that had looked minute from the edge of the field is now almost in reach. A deep ditch runs around the perimeter of the old cemetery like a moat. In the tangled undergrowth, overshadowed by elder, pine and lilac, rusty iron crosses and moss-obscured headstones protrude. The inscriptions are difficult to decipher. The three of us push the undergrowth aside and scratch off the moss and lichen – but Opa's grave we cannot find. Who would have chiselled a headstone for an elderly civilian in the middle of war? We bless the tiny island in the rye where the dead sleep and the birds sing. The red dot by a small building tells us that it is a long way back to the Lada.

"*Nimm Erde*. Take some soil", Irena urges. I lift a handful of the grey sand my forebears had tended, letting it run through my fingers. How did my great-grandfather scratch a living from this dust and feed seven mouths? Peter happens to have a small paper bag and all three of us fill it with my ancestral soil. I carry it like a treasure of gold.

"School here, burnt, not long ago." With Irena's help we gather bits of a charred roof tile and find a piece of molten glass, relics of Oma's sole place of learning. 'From right here I sneaked into the rye to pick flowers...' Yes, I know, you were three years old and you were frightened of the *Roggenmuhme*. When now – with adult eyes – I scan the vastness of the field I realize that a child might easily have disappeared among the high stalks. Yes, Child, you were rescued.

Nikolai is eager to leave. Our passports are surely on his mind, too. There is no time to search for Oma's childhood home or for their Snow White's house in the forest where she and Opa had lived happily for a few weeks before the tragic accident happened that brought the idyll to a premature end. I feel the Child's disappointment and promise her that one day we will return here but this afternoon we will climb into the gloomy attic and go into the room that had been her home.

Nikolai bumps along the sandy path and we rejoin the Castle Road. In Viešvilė he stays with his car, this time parked by the grassy triangle. Irena leads us through the heavy scent of lilac and shows us her treasures: four small black-and-white cows in the byre. The wooden steps up into the cowshed on which the Child had loved to sit, have been replaced by concrete ones. '...I want to go into the house...' I know, you do. '...and the room where I heard the great thunder and saw the sky turn red...' Yes, I'll see to it. We follow Irena up the grey worn stone steps. I notice that several windows are covered with torn plastic. Irena's mother, now in a cheerful red and white overall, her wavy grey hair falling freely on to her shoulders, leads us into the ancient kitchen that had been forbidden to the Child, and into the adjacent living room, dominated by a green-tiled stove. '...I want to go upstairs...' Yes, yes.

Hidden behind a pea-green door lies the staircase that leads to the loft. I make a pleading gesture. The old lady nods. Large torn sheets of dirty patterned wall paper hang loose above painted brown treads. Slowly my eyes acclimatize to the gloom: the windows at floor level shed limited light on to the painted floor planks. Several other doors lead off the attic space. The door to the kitchen stands wide open and nothing has changed in there, except it now has a fridge. The one door, the most important one, is locked. 'I want to go in...'

With hands and eyes I plead to be allowed entrance. Please! But the old lady shakes her head.

"Nein."

Have we come all this way just to stand outside a locked door? Why can we not go in? I want to rattle the handle.

"Nein!"

Peter takes a picture of me with my hand on the door handle and with heavy heart the Child descends the stairs again as she had done as a five-year old. I do not look back.

The grey wall bears a red wound: at about two metres from the corner the rendering stops and reveals roughly mortared bricks. A window is set into the fill-in. Above it is fixed a board on which Gothic letters are barely decipherable.

"Yes," I say with unfounded confidence, tilting my head back, "I can read 'Hirsch'. You see, this was a little pub called 'The Stag'."

Handshakes, smiles, thank yous, 'Auf Wiedersehn'. We must get back to the border. In the car I reflect that much has been accomplished, but not everything fulfilled. The bridge is in sight.

Outside the wooden hut we wait for Nikolai to reappear with our passports. This is the Russian border...Yes, I know, but look here comes our driver. He is smiling. He has got our documents. As the engine springs into life a Russian uniform steps in front of the car and beckons Nikolai back into the hut; Peter is to come, too. Alone in the car, I wait. At last the men appear. Both look angry. I see our passports.

"Forty Deutschmark!" snorts Peter, back in the car. "And he would have preferred dollars. I watched the money go into his back pocket." What are forty Deutschmark compared to freedom? Our driver is also angry and apologizes on behalf of his countrymen. Peter's agreement to pay without fuss has secured Nikolai's future: he can drive into Lithuania again.

The landscape has lost the lustre which the sun had lent it this morning. Remnants of villages float by. All feels comfortless. We cross the Djemen; pass the allotments; the building sites; the Orthodox cemetery. Zelenogradsk, we are back. Over there is the German-built red-brick post office, and here the pastel villas. A woman is kneeling by the kerb, clearing the gutter of weeds. The sun is setting over the long beach; the white sand is turning to rose quartz. In a private room we pay Nikolai.

Because of the loss of Deutschmark at the border our tip is much smaller than he deserves. And that I will always regret.

The next day Hubert is retracing our journey right up to the *Luisenbrücke*. The coach also takes a break by the lethargic Djemen. The goat is still tethered in the same dandelion patch but we also have a new arrival. In the dilapidated house with its decrepit sheds someone has hurriedly pulled a T-shirt over her wispy hair. A little girl: her bright yellow T-shirt shouts 'Königsberg' in old Gothic script. Yellow against the side of the black coach. Very photogenic. We all must have a photo of this. Her skirt has deep pockets.

The haybarn-church earns disbelieving head-shakes and loudly expressed disgust; every stork nest is aahed and ooohed over; every old house stroked with every soul's gentle affection. This time there is no champagne picnic in the forest but our rucksacks bulge with thick-cut rough bread filled with a questionable spread. Potholes. Verges. Ditches. The overly-grand sculpture announcing Sovetsk. To fill the emptied East Prussia, the recruitment adverts had lied and lured an ignorant Soviet population into the six hundred year old German town of Tilsit by the Memel, by calling it "the ancient Russian town on the Njemen". A red Lada stands parked in front of a bland apartment block; it is not Nikolai's. Two bow-legged women, their heads swaddled in scarves, hobble along a deserted pavement. And where were *you two* born? From which of the eighty countries the Oblast represents do *you* hail? Were you coerced, deceived or forced to come here?

The approach to the bridge is even emptier than yesterday. Hubert has instructions to wait for us until noon. This gives us two hours in which to explore before we continue our journey into the heart of old East Prussia. Some of our fellow travellers will search for their old homes in the town; others will roam the still cobbled streets, hoping, like archaeologists, to discover some 'Tilsit' features in the Sovetsk cityscape. We are among the first Westerners allowed to set foot in the town. Like the rest of the Kaliningradskaja Oblast, it had been sealed off for over four decades. Peter and I have set ourselves a goal: to find the city hospital. A quick glance at a yellowed map of Tilsit in the Thirties suggests it will be easy to find. The streets we walk are reminiscent of my Ruhr city at the end of the war! A high fence bars our way, behind which building work is in progress. A large structure with empty windows looks seriously ill. This is what remains of the main hospital. No doctors or patients here, but at least I am standing in front of the building in which Opa died fifty years ago.

"What do we do now?"

Out of the ruins steps a woman. Her friendly smile exposes gold teeth and she addresses us in German.

"*Was suchen Sie?*" she asks, seeing that we are clearly searching for something.

"*Das Krankenhaus.*" She evidently thinks that we need medical attention, waves down a clapped-out van bearing a red cross which happens to be passing, talks with the ambulance driver and he assists us into the back of his vehicle. At terrifying speed it rattles along the cobbles, swinging dangerously from side to side. Leafy trees, houses and ruins flash by our dusty windows. Where on earth are we going? We pull into a gateway and are unloaded in front of a blackened-brick building shrouded by the leafage of ancient trees. We enter a gloomy interior. And why should the receptionist understand our German, our English or our mission? I show her our large container, point to the label and try "doctor". She nods and ushers us through double doors – no, padded triple doors – and we come face to face with a large man in a white coat. It would be too complicated to explain our reason for breaking into his world in this unannounced and unprecedented fashion. I simply place the container on to his desk. He turns it with caution, reads *Paracetemol* and eyes us a little suspiciously while cradling the drum in both hands. Like a treasure.

"For you. For your patients." His face betrays no emotion. What do we want from him? We convey: it is a *gift*. He rises to shake our hands, and we return to the dimly-lit reception via the three padded doors, smile at the woman and are back under the deep shade of the trees. I would have liked to have told the doctor our reason for bringing him the gift. Had I been able to speak Russian, I would have said:

'You see, sir, your *German* medical colleagues let my grandfather die in this town. Of a hernia. In unrelieved pain. He was too old to serve as a soldier, you understand. These tablets are intended to relieve *your* patients' suffering. I know it's tempting to sell them on the Black Market!'

For a moment I feel happy. Then panic sets in because the vehicle that brought us and on which we set our hope to return us to the coach, is now squealing out of the gate. What is the use of me jumping and waving? It's not a taxi, Uta, it's an ambulance! The coach will be leaving in ten minutes – and we have no idea where we are. We pray and start running.

"I have a sense, we should keep right," I pant as we enter a park with a lake. The sun stands vertically above us and does not help us to find our bearings. Three times we stop, catch our breath and ask the way; three times like in a fairytale. I remember the Russian word for 'bridge' and the name of the river. And with this abundant knowledge of the language we are helped by kind walkers to find our way back to the bridge, to the coach. It is two minutes past noon when we drop into our seats, red-faced, sweating, out of breath. Our guide points at his watch. We sense the general disapproval. We don't care. Exhausted but satisfied I lean back and close my eyes. Our adventure reminds me of the story of Rohesia, a beautiful Saracen woman, who fell in love with an Englishman when he visited her land. With the only two English words she knew, "London" and "Gilbert", she followed him – and found him and became the mother of Thomas à Becket. By prayer and two Russian words I led us to our bus!

What had been the purpose of all this? It had started when our friend Peter, working in the pharmaceutical industry, handed us a drum of a thousand Paracetamol "for Russia". Who would be the recipient? The only person I *knew* who had suffered in Tilsit was my grandfather. Having survived at least two hundred of the two hundred and ninety-nine bombing raids on Duisburg, he was condemned to die from a hernia in Tilsit! The old bank book shows what his widow had to pay for the hospital stay. In honour of this one German civilian the medication was to be used to relief the pain of a few Russian sufferers in Sovetsk.

Our journey through the Oblast continues into the afternoon. Should we laugh or cry at the waste of cultivation and culture; at the apparent ineptness of building anything meaningful or beautiful? Why had everything been cheapened and treated so carelessly? There had been "better times", we are told; but today, in the wake of the collapse of the Soviet Union and Communist social order, I hurt at the sight of neglect and decay; it pains me that human dignity, personal responsibility and initiative seem to be of little consequence. We give away our Christian pamphlets where it seems right.

Our final destination is *Trakehnen*, the Royal Stud, founded two hundred and fifty years ago, breeding the noble Trakehner horses, unique in the world. Today stable and riding hall are festering shadows of their former glory. In the yard a young woman is whipping a tired nag, forcing it to go round and round, like a circus animal – apparently for our entertainment. We shield our eyes.

Before the Red Army overran the area in 1945, breeders had sought to send the invaluable horses to safety but had been forbidden to do so by the *Gauleiter* who branded such attempts as 'defeatist'. In the end they had just three hours to wrap up 200 years of expertise. They harnessed their stallions and mares (many in foal) to heavy wagons, loaded with their families' belongings, fleeing to the west. The horses (many unshod) walked and trotted a thousand kilometres – across a large expanse of ice, through sand and snow, on frozen and badly rutted roads, often furrowed fields, in sub-zero temperatures without shelter and on a minimum of fodder. They remained in harness day and night and the mares lost their foals. That a thousand horses reached the west is astonishing. Some were requisitioned there; most were immediately used for agricultural purposes. Despite extremely difficult circumstances it has been possible to save the *Trakehner* as a breed. Of all this and the importance of these horses the girl with the whip would have known nothing.

Our journey through Russian East Prussia touches me and challenges my thinking. Who will put a new heart and spirit into these insular people? How long will it take them to develop their own culture (other than that of the Black Market)? How does this conglomerate of ethnic diversity live together? Will the uprooted peoples seek to discover their own identity by researching their own history and culture left behind in the Caucasus, the steppes, the Urals, or will they try to find it in the shards and remnants left by another population driven out not long before their own arrival? Will *their* Inner Children throw up unfamiliar emotions and urge them to begin that search? The sheer need for survival of the eighty ethnic groups will probably suppress such urges. Had not their grandparents and their parents in turn in *their* times been torn from their accustomed life-style and sent all over the Soviet Union to labour? The people we see now from behind our darkened windows have to make the best of what they find left in the four cities and numerous villages, the forests and meadows and the Baltic coast. Meanwhile well-to-do and well-meaning middle-aged Germans will plough aid into the Oblast, while their children know nothing of the mysterious *Ostpreußen* and its history, and will care little about a far-distant land "without culture and where the wolves still howl".

Today I am thankful that the hermetic seal is broken and the taboo lifted and the white patch on the map is coloured in again; that we can stand on real soil rather than glean information from satellite pictures. Maybe one day the soulless capital will shed its grey chrysalis and emerge as a truly "*lovely* city".

For the new settlers ruined cities held no horror. All over the Soviet Union the lives of its impoverished people had been ravaged by starvation, violence, death and the devastation of their land. Many city dwellers and peasants had not lived in proper houses since their Great Patriotic War ended. In dugouts, shell holes covered with metal sheeting, cellars of bombed houses and tiny log huts they had sought to find shelter. Living under such conditions, could they know the meaning of *home*? Perhaps a secretly-held dream of finding space and privacy had persuaded them to come to this foreign province: East Prussia.

Few of the German Inner Children who embarked on this journey found any vestige of what *they* had dreamt to rediscover. Disappointed, the adult travellers vow never to return. Zelenogradsk bids us farewell. The big black bus that came from another planet will return to it. It will cross the great East European rivers Vistula, Warthe, Oder and Elbe disgorge its travellers in a *united* Germany. And from there we will sail the Channel to where *our home* lies.

If only that one door had been unlocked…

4

One locked door

Fourteen years have passed.

Driving up from southern Lithuania we cross the Nemunas on a modern bridge and reach Jurbarkas before sunset. We had chosen the town and Kristina's guesthouse because of their proximity to Viešvilė and Uszbalai, now thoroughly Lithuanian communities. I am honouring my promise to the Child: we *are* returning to the locked room in the attic and her grandparents' homes, and of course to her grassy triangle. We know nothing about Jurbarkas, not even that once its name was Yurburg, a town famous for its beautiful old synagogue. The twin towers of a red-brick church near the river's edge look remarkably Prussian; the concrete buildings that line the quiet main street, very Soviet. We pass small shops, three banks, a restaurant, the tourist information office and a grey *viesbute*, the town's hotel, which, seeing it now, we are glad not to have booked into. According to our stylized map we should almost have reached our destination, when our attention is caught by a row of low dilapidated wooden houses. They contrast with the smart brown and red complex which is our guesthouse. Kristina's German is fluent; her hair jet-black; shiny like the treads of the polished pine stairs that lead to our room. Light streams through a picture window and below us, and as far as the eye can see in both directions, stretches the river. Not far from here, at the border town of Smalilinkai, the river *Nemunas*, for the last hundred kilometres of its long journey from Belarus, had several times changed its name to *Memel*. Today it flows as *Nemunas* right to the Baltic where it fans out into a delta and empties into the Curonian Lagoon. In Jurbarkas its banks are as muddy as I had encountered them from the *Luisenbrücke*. Beneath us the wide, empty waterway stands as still as a lake. Nothing ripples her surface. It serves as a smooth canvas on which the setting sun paints delicate pinks and pale blues.

A towpath leads to the restaurant where we shall have our evening meal. A warm breeze enwraps us and we are surprised that no one else wants to enjoy its mantle. How quiet this world! How empty this river! In the inn by the twin-towered church we find ourselves to be the only guests ordering food. In the dimness of the empty dining room I ring Valda. Her German is excellent. Irena is out of the country and has asked her friend to look after us. She will bring *all* the keys.

The Chardonnay and the anticipation of tomorrow make me feel light-headed. Dusk has fallen and it probably is safer to return to the guesthouse via the main street. Shop windows and the posters displayed in the tourist information office are uninteresting. From a restaurant emanate strains of music, lending a breath of life to the town that feels so strangely dead. We have reached the enigmatic little houses we had passed earlier. Padlocked iron bars barricade the doors, yet *fresh* flowers show from behind dusty panes! Who owns these decaying dwellings? Does anyone live in them? Who puts flowers into vases? Kristina will know. At breakfast we will ask her. But right now, I want to put my head down on that gorgeous fresh-smelling blue-and-white linen pillow.

I doze and the events of the last two days play back…

"Would you like to go away for your birthday, Peter?"

"Where do you have in mind?"

"Lithuania."

"For *my* birthday?" he had grinned.

"There is the matter of the locked door, you see. And we could also stay a few days on the Nehrung, couldn't we?"

Thomas Mann had written about the strong undertow of the Baltic; I feel its pull at my heart. And so we had flown to Kaunas, the second largest city in Lithuania. The first sighting of the white-gold rim of the Curonian Spit, accentuated by the setting sun, had caused everyone on board to cheer. The Lithuanians were coming home. Now the Nemunas delta lay below us and the pilot followed the river's silver course. As the wheels touched the runway of the tiny airport, another great cheer went up and his passengers gave him a grateful ovation. Behind a chain-wire fence a sea of faces and flowers welcomed their people. The luggage carousel, evidently suffering labour pains, eventually brought forth our cases, screaming and squealing; then swallowed them again into a black hole several times before we could retrieve them.

We had hired a car. By the time we rolled on to the highway into the city, it was close to midnight and the windscreen became blurred as a sudden rainstorm unleashed itself. Where was the switch for the wipers? The nightmare had begun. Names of unfamiliar streets were absurdly long and foreign and fixed far too high on walls. They did not seem to correspond to those shown on the small map I was trying to read by the light of the street lamps. We passed and passed again buildings we had already passed, including one that looked like the railway station and finally crossed the river into a dark industrial area. What is that garishly lit building over there? A supermarket? A casino? A club? That knot of lads hanging around outside, are they drug dealers?

"Be careful."

I watched Peter walking towards them. They talked with hands and feet and seemed to get nowhere. I fumbled for the number of our Kaunas guesthouse and to my great relief, the proprietor had not gone to bed. In fluent English he directed us back to the railway station! Did I know where that was? Did I! I was glad when we met, shook hands and were piloted to his *unnumbered* house on a street with *no name*.

The night's rain had given way to a sunny day for us to explore Kaunas. We sauntered along the *Laisves Aleja*, the Freedom Avenue, which claims to be the longest pedestrian street in Europe. The girls looked charming, graceful in whatever 'fashion' they had chosen. Yet the atmosphere in the city struck us as subdued. A lack-lustre waitress brought us drinks, took our lunch order – and walked out! All we could do was to leave as well and try another restaurant. This one, elegant, clad in cool marble, served the perfect salad. In the ladies' toilet I shared my cubicle with a man. A naked man – except for a fig leaf. He stood in a niche and looked down on me. To his fig leaf was fixed a silver hook. I hung my handbag on it.

Who, outside of Lithuania, has ever heard of the artist Mikalojus Konstaninas Čiurlionis since he dedicated all his music and pictures solely to his own people? They in turn honour him with his own gallery where we entered the dimly-lit world of Čiurlionis-fantasies. Instead of canvasses the artist often executed his work in tempera on paper and cardboard. On our arrival in Kaunus a leaflet had informed us of its notorious forts where Jews had been held and murdered. No, let's go to the river, right to the edge of its lazy brown waters...

Loud and urgent knocking wakes me out my reverie. I hear Peter in the shower. Half-dazed I throw off the bedding.

"Open up!" Kristina is shouting. "Water is coming through the ceiling. You have not tucked in the shower curtain."

She has already unlocked the door and barged into the shower room before I can warn Peter who flattens himself behind the door, clutching his towel. Kristina is crawling around his wet feet, feeling around, closely scrutinizing the end of her finger. The floor is entirely dry. The shower curtain had been properly tucked inside the foot basin. Flustered, she leaves and at breakfast we learn that the plumber is on his way – to a different shower room. Now is the time to ask her about the strangely barred small houses with fresh flowers in their windows. Whose are they? It strikes me that Kristina is not entirely comfortable.

"Our young people buy them," she says. "They go abroad to earn enough money to renovate them. They want an inheritance to pass on." Yes, of course. That makes sense. Having lived long under Communist rule, private ownership has become important. That settles the matter.

Valda and I had agreed to meet at the house in Viešvilė at eleven o'clock. I feel happy and expectant as we travel along the Castle Road, following the course of the river, hidden from view by forest and pasture land. At the airport we had seen *everyone* holding flowers, and we need to take flowers to Valda. In Jurbarkas, in Smalilinkai, in Viešvilė – we search in vain for a florist. Along the Castle Road grim-looking farmers' wives are selling very dark, very ripe strawberries. Maybe Valda would enjoy some. Even the purchase of a whole kilo of her produce cannot coax a smile from the vendor.

A huge concrete archway bridges the road to the left which we assume leads into a factory. Backing and U-turns. We are confused. Peter finally drives *through* the archway and I discover that the massive complex has been built on the former station forecourt. Now I know where we are. Turn left. The Kindergarten is just here. Gosh it looks even worse than fourteen years ago; its roof is falling in. The lime trees cast the street into deep shadow but I can't miss the house. How it has changed! Set in a flower garden, it has been freshly rendered and painted. In light drizzle by the once grey wall we shake hands with Valda and give her the large punnet of strawberries, with apologies that we could not find flowers for her.

"No, thank you," she says, "please, no strawberries. I have seen too many this season." She waves a bunch of keys and we follow her into the little garden filled with flowers. The pile of birch logs has been replaced by a gazebo and the cowshed is not the old byre any more. Only the grey stone steps that lead up to the house are as I remember them and the same poison-green door still hides the stairs leading to the loft. I am disappointed that Valda is not taking us upstairs straightaway but into the kitchen. The removable cooking rings on top of the ancient stove are encrusted with rust and grime. A table covered with a crocheted cloth fills the small dining room and on it photographs have been laid out for us to look at. Irena, older now, actually looks younger. Her dark wispy hair has turned blond and is cut in a chic style. She is wearing an elegant outfit. Straggly ponytail and shapeless faded cotton dresses are things of the past. Both her daughters are earning well in Germany. The back wall is covered in old family photos.

"Do you recognize anybody?" Peter asks. When will this man understand that this house and its inhabitants have belonged to another nation - for the last fifty years - and that being *evacuees, we were not related to the German owners?*

In a small chamber on the ground floor beds have been made ready for us; freshly laundered bedding and towels lie in neat piles. I have to explain that we are already staying in a guesthouse in Jurbarkas. The living room furniture we had already seen in Irena's apartment fourteen years ago, except for the modest television which – as everywhere in the world – is the family shrine. The shelves bulge with books and magazines, and piles of typed notes on Viešvilė in English and German have been left for us to peruse. Would Valda like to have lunch with us? Would she choose a nice restaurant? In two hours she will return. In that time, I guess, she might be making jars and jars of jam with her own strawberries!

It feels strange to be in this house by ourselves. As soon as Valda has gone, I run upstairs. We try all the keys on the bunch but not one fits the door we have come to open. This is not possible! I have lost interest in exploring the rest of the attic. Let Peter photograph what he likes, I am going downstairs. Lethargically I leaf through the booklets, distracted by sadness and disappointment....The important door – will it never open for me?

The rain has stopped and Peter suggests we explore the garden: almost all its space is taken up by a strawberry bed where dark-red berries ooze from the dense foliage. A large liquid manure drum lies rusting in the weeds by the fence. I stroke the flaking metal and for a moment lean against it as I had done as a child with Oma, when we had both been wrapped in grief. Behind the gazebo rises a mound with ventilation shafts, entirely grassed over: the air-raid shelter we never had to use. Bombers had invaded this airspace and obliterated Königsberg and Tilsit after we had left for Saxony. But the main attacks on Wischwill would have been launched from the Castle Road. Tanks decorated with *red* stars would have clanked beneath naked lime trees, past the railway station and the Kindergarten, towards the sandy road junction and would have come to a halt by the grassy triangle where the daisies had already gone to sleep for the winter. Shells and bullets had injured the grey gable end. Then the iron monsters left, droning and clanking towards their final goal: Berlin.

'My' wall no longer shows the bullet holes nor the brick fill-in nor the board with the Gothic letters. The new rendering has obliterated the past.

Valda is back and the drizzle has begun again. We are driving along the Castle Road to an inn she knows. The dining room is already filled with a busload of Germans. So we drive on beyond the large wayside cross which, we had previously assumed, celebrated the end of a Godless regime. If with Nikolai we had stopped here, on these historic crossroads, we would have learnt that this cross stands as a *memorial* to honour thousands of German civilians who died of starvation, in the terrible cold or by violence. We would have discovered that it also stands for the

25,000 *Wolfkinder*, those waifs and orphans who, having lost their parents in the chaos, roamed the forests in search of food and shelter. The older ones jumped the freight trains into Lithuania to find work. Few received an education and most of the despised *Hitler children* were exploited as slave labour.

"Where are we going, Valda? At this rate we'll be having lunch overlooking the Baltic," I joke. The restaurant she has been aiming for is the converted barn of a German manor house; its courtyard decked with flowers; its interior tastefully timbered; the menu bilingual; the waitresses swift. The salmon dish is gorgeous and we celebrate our meeting with a glass of wine. Valda does not show the slightest interest in us but I am curious about *her* childhood and teenage years in Viešvilė. When Peter embarks on another subject, Communism, and wants to know whether she has visited *Gruto Parkas* and what she thinks of it, it turns out that she had never ventured far from the village where she was born. To make her laugh Peter paints a hilarious picture of the 'sculpture' park that exhibits rows of statues of Stalin and Lenin and Engels and Marx that had once stood prominently in every Lithuanian town square. Now redundant, a mushroom-entrepreneur had bought up much of the Communist paraphernalia before it would be destroyed and displayed it all in a replica of a labour camp, complete with watch towers and martial music. But Valda is not amused.

"That was *my* youth," she says defensively. "We were told that everything was good and we believed it."

I nod. Only one generation separates us both. Two little girls, who in the same village had received their first rudimentary political education. Both of us had been told that all was good and we believed it. Two little girls: one indoctrinated by Naziism, the other by Communism. Today the two grown-up girls, sipping wine together, do not have to turn their heads furtively, watch and listen intently and guard their tongues. This place and time is free of informers. Here and now we are allowed to think for ourselves. Yet I sense that Valda does not trust us. Only as the wine begins to loosen her tongue, does she speak about her life.

"Under Communism working life was not as complicated as it is now." With one hand she shackles her wrist to illustrate how bound she and her husband feel in their independent country running an independent business. "Nothing but regulations," she complains. "Innovations are frowned on and our taxes are very high."

Under the Soviet regime her husband, a trained carpenter, had played the Black Market successfully and things had gone well for them. Now his furniture business, legally registered, employs six men and life is very difficult.

"A carpenter," I say, "that seems an apt Lithuanian trade. You have a long tradition of working with wood. You have so much forest in your country."

"We do not use Lithuanian wood. All our wood is imported from Siberia."

"From Siberia?"

"It's better quality timber because in the very low temperatures the wood grows more slowly. It is also far cheaper to fell it there. Finnish workers cut it on site using their machinery and it is still cheaper for us to import than to use home-grown wood."

What a world! So this has nothing to do with the ancient Lithuanian belief that trees are too sacred to be cut down. Yet another of my assumptions. And yet, the vast Viešvilė forest does stand under protection as a nature reserve.

"We are seeking markets in Denmark and Germany," Valda continues. "We can supply well-made cheap furniture." Is she fishing for business?

"Do you supply to IKEA?" I ask.

"I think so." Now she sounds evasive.

The afternoon wears on and I become inwardly impatient. I want to get back to the house.

"I would very much like to go into the room where I lived as a child. It is the one room we have not yet seen." I try to conceal from Valda the urgency I feel. She explains that Irena has tenants living upstairs but thinks it might be possible to get the key.

As we arrived at the house in the morning I had noticed a tall young woman in tight jeans and clingy low-cut top, getting into a car with three men. It turns out that it is her grandmother who occupies the room behind the locked door and she may well have a second key. Although neither of them is at home, the hope of a key has buoyed me up into exploring the rest of the loft. The same peeling wallpaper, crumbling plaster, exposed electric cables, spiders and filth. From one small dusty window I can see it: my grassy triangle.

We duck under a low door frame into a dismal crate-like elongated room. Its single window is laced with cobwebs. The sun will have to make an extra effort to pierce through these layers of dust.

"This is the room where my Oma slept for a whole year after Opa's accident and death. Only quite recently Mami told me that Oma had been so depressed she did not want to leave her bed. That helped me *understand* the ever-present grey veil that has been the backdrop to my inner life. This miserable cell would have depressed anyone, let alone someone in shock and bereavement in the middle of a war. Whenever I thought of this attic, it had always seemed black. Here in this dirty box room I understand even better why I had lost my mother's presence: had she not lost *her* mother to the darkness of grief and depression?"

We examine the metal bedstead, lifting cover after cover until a rusty wire-mesh base is exposed. The bed is old. It was here before the war. It is Oma's bed!

And what about this wardrobe here, hidden beneath layers of dusty cloths? The long 'piano hinges' on its three doors again tell us: pre-war. So it was ours! And we left it all behind in 1944 when we fled westwards. All this is disturbing me and I am glad to lock the rough timber door behind me.

The door to the kitchen stands ajar, a light room where Mami had cooked and where I remember Opa shaving. There is no bathroom or toilet up here. I had not realized this. However did we manage? In the centre of the loft squats a big chimney, its door painted in yet another shade of hideous green. I hesitate before opening it. Behind it hang meat hooks covered in soot and filth. What had been smoked here? When was it last used?

I have seen enough. Downstairs I idly thumb through the leaflets left for us when my attention is arrested by the following lines, written in English:

You have stepped into Lithuania.

Small is this land, but great is its truth:
To exist.

To survive.
To testify to the many and varied nations of the world
About the value of a man's life in freedom in his own homeland.

Painful is this land:
Each blade of grass sprouts
From a drop of blood
Or a tear.

Fruitful is this land:
In the sandy soil of a small hill it grows grain and
Graves marked with crosses.

Brave is this land:
It went from uprising to uprising,
From exile to exile,
From deportation to deportation.
A great number of people were laid to rest
In the permafrost of Siberia,
Some of their bones were flown back to their native soil,
The survivors lost their health in slave labour, but returned home.

Let's bow our heads and show respect to these victims,
Let's kneel down before Lithuania's unappeasable pain.

Beautiful is this land:
Each hillock, each forest, each lake
They look the same yet different.
Like our folk song.
Across the Nemunas it seems to be sung in a different way,
Yet filled with the same longings and poignant emotion.

The bonds between land and people here are more enduring
Than anywhere else.
More often people here pray to earth than to heaven.

A happy land is the land of a happy man.

I am still copying these lines into my notebook when I hear the front door opening. The young woman in tight jeans is back. Now is our moment. We follow her upstairs and I put my palms together in a pleading gesture: please may we see *this* room. She nods, seems to understand, but instead of unlocking the door, she runs down the stairs and disappears altogether, while we are waiting in the gloom.

What is this mysterious rustling *inside* the room? Someone is clearly moving about in there. A key turns...the door handle tilts...the door stands wide open...

...I am inside the room of my childhood, the room that had haunted me for so long. Have we stepped into a gypsy caravan? Every wall space is covered with hangings, carpets, rugs, posters, pictures. Every surface is laden with ornaments and knick-knacks. ...I want to go over to that window where I made friends with the stars...on which my breath made ice flowers...from where I could see the grassy triangle... where Papi had stood in uniform... from where I had seen the red sky glowing and heard the big thunders... but I cannot.... Even the windows are draped with hideous pink damask table cloths that give a rosy tint to the whole room. The green-tiled stove that had greedily consumed my mother's birch logs all winter long is half hidden by a shrouded bed shoved up against it. Why is the bed standing in the middle of the room? And the wardrobe, too? There are no frying pans and cooking pots poking from under the bed. No, of course not. I am so shocked and confused that my brain refuses to think. Go on, look around. Observe. Compare. Remember. Feel. But I cannot. I am numb. It is someone else's bedroom and out of politeness I must not stay in it any longer.

"Thank you," I manage to say. The young woman in tight jeans locks the door from the inside and a few moments later comes running up the stairs, passes us who are still standing outside the door, and without a word or gesture disappears into her own room. I can't make it out.

So, that's it then. I hand the keys back to Valda and ask her to convey our thanks to Irena. I am about to climb into the car...

No wait! There is something I need to do first: I must cross the sandy road to stand on the small grassy triangle – and love the Child and thank my God for having led me back to my roots and foundations. The grasses bear droplets and the daisies have opened their faces after the rain.

"Little green grassy triangle, be happy because 'a happy land is the land of a happy man.'"

I am happy. And I shall not have to return.

5

Surprised by horror

A kilogram of overripe strawberries cries to be eaten. All we need is cream. Why do they camouflage supermarkets in Lithuania? At last we find one in Smalilinkai. Which of these many plastic tubs holds cream? Each label is written in four languages; but neither Lithuanian nor Latvian, neither Estonian nor Russian gives us the slightest hint of the content. I leave Peter studying the small print. High up a ladder a young shop assistant is arranging tins.

"Do you speak English," I whisper up to her.

"A little," she calls down.

"Is this cream?" I hold up a pot.

"Yes."

Peter is still bending over the display of pots, puzzling…

"This here is cream," I say confidently.

"How do you know?"

"I just do."

In our room, looking out over the river, we gorge ourselves on mushy strawberries and cream.

"There must be another door leading into that room…" I muse, red-lipped.

"Yes, there has to be. That wardrobe standing in the middle of the room… Strange!" Peter wipes juice from his chin.

"There is another staircase, there has to be. My big bed must have blocked a door I never knew about."

At breakfast we tell Kristina about the house.

"Oh," she becomes enthusiastic, "I know a man in Viešvilė who runs his own museum. He is the mayor of the town and knows all there is to know about it. I'll ring him right away and ask him to see you today."

And so we drive to our private appointment, in the one-time Prussian Magistrates' Court of which I have a fifty year old black-and-white photograph. Algis is the headmaster of a large boarding school for children whose parents cannot have them living with them. Algis is like a father to a hundred children. After a conducted tour through the school he takes us to his museum under vaulted ceilings. It holds a collection of documents, publications, pictures and artefacts of a settlement which probably began with the Baltic crusades of the Teutonic Knights. In the mid-sixteenth century under Prussian influence a Protestant church was built. Catholicism did not take root in the region for another two to three hundred years. Prussian initiatives included several mills, powered by water. The narrow-gauge railway that I remember had run for five decades before it was demolished after the war. When my family arrived in Wischwill, a central dairy had still been producing cheese; a telephone line had been laid beneath the Memel; every household had running water. I ask about the huge Forester's House of which I possess a sepia photo. It is not clear whether it became a prison. It burnt down.

It is Algis' own story that awakens my real interest. His German father who "had been with Hitler", served in the *Wehrmacht*, and in the chaos at the end of the war had been declared "missing". Algis' Lithuanian mother had gone in search of him south of the river and had made it as far as the Polish border. Once there, she decided he might have gone back to Viešvilė to look for her and his little son. So she returned to her village.

"That was her mistake!" Algis smiles wryly, "because now we found ourselves trapped in the Soviet Union." So he grew up fatherless and in great hardship. His present position has sprung from his own experience.

I show him my photo of the grey house as we had found it on our first visit. Yes, of course he knows the house. And Irena had been his deputy mayor! I point out the scarred gable end, the rough brickwork around the window and the lettering above it. Barely audible he whispers,

"It was a Jewish shop."

A party of German visitors now demand his time and we turn back on to the Castle Road. Our car labours up the sandy track to Uszbalai, the path along which my great-grandmother, my grandmother, my mother and I had walked.

Undulating fields fan out in every direction until they are met by the dark forest framing meadow and standing rye. Today in the midsummer sun the land is still as magical as I had experienced it as a child. I am standing in a field full of wildflowers, a sea of yellow and pink and orange and blue. Even wild lilies rise amongst sparse and coarse grasses. I drink in the scene, this dazzling near-empty land, and I know that it has shaped my soul. How could such poor sandy soil bring forth such exquisite beauty? This patch of eastern soil that had birthed my grandmother, bewitched my mother and taken away my grandfather has made a deep and lasting impression on me. Below us, just visible by its roof, lies my great-grandparents' smallholding. The Simoneits had farmed this land and I am standing on ancestral ground.

I know nothing yet about the hardships these smallholdings had to endure; nothing about the devastation of the plague, nor of indentured servitude to the big landowners. In 1813 serfdom was abolished. It did not lead to the expected freedom, but slowly the old social order of the village communities eroded. Farmers, no longer supplying the landowners' markets, were now forced to compete and use means of transportation. Many fell into debt. Later again farms faced bankruptcy. In many cases the farm went to the eldest son who had to look after the parents and to pay out his siblings. Did this pay for Oma's fare to the Ruhr?

To the left lies a small clump of trees, a green islet in an unploughed field, preserved over decades within an ocean of Russian and Lithuanian cultures. We had of course visited it before – with Irena: the German Lutheran cemetery that had survived Catholicism and Communism, a miracle, since ninety percent of grave sites in East Prussia were destroyed. Carefully we cross the fragile meadow, lest even one flower that has bravely pushed itself out of the dust, be crushed. Around the circular cemetery runs a ditch, spangled with buttercup and forget-me-not. Our feet squelch in our shoes. The sun stands high and insects hum. Suddenly, out from behind the dense shrubbery, emerges a brown man, stripped to the waist, approaching us slowly and wielding a weapon. Keep walking. Just keep walking. And smile. The weapon, we can see more clearly now, is a rusty toothed implement. Resolutely Peter strides through reeds and stinging nettles and I am thankful that he is a big man. I follow at a distance.

"Hello!" shouts my husband – in English of course. "We want to visit the cemetery." As if this man understands a word!

We point to the overgrown mound to make our intentions clear, but the little thin brown man keeps thrusting the rusty thing into the air and does not budge. Just keep walking. Finally he lowers his arm with the sinister implement, answers our overconfident smiles with a shy grin. There is not a tooth in his mouth. He leads the way up into the graveyard, thrashing at the undergrowth, to the right and to the left. *So* that's what it is for, this serrated tool! With gesticulation, grimace and German words I try to tell him that my Opa is buried here. He keeps on slashing to uncover the grave we might be looking for. Here and there a rusty iron cross appears that bears a German name and a few stone grave-surrounds lie dishevelled. As we had done with Irena, we scratch away moss and peer at every Gothic letter that reveals itself. Today time is on our side and our passports are safely in *our* pockets! Though we search and search, I know that we will never find Opa's grave. A rough wooden cross would have been all that had marked this "useless civilian's" final resting place in the summer of 1943.

"How life tosses us about," I muse. "My Rhenish grandfather lies here in an eastern grave and his East Prussian wife in a Rhenish cemetery."

We have grown tired of scratching and searching. A scythe lies idly in the high grass and we ask the little skeletal man to hold it and pose for a photograph. We all laugh and shake hands, but we do not learn each other's names. He can neither read nor write.

At the entrance to this minute burial place a board has been erected which fourteen years ago had not stood there. It reads

USZBALIU II

KAIMO
KAPINĖS

So there are *two* (German?) cemeteries in Uszballen? *Kapines* is a word I shall later recognize.

The sand lies deep on the track towards the barn. Hope we won't get stuck here! Peter stops where Nikolai had parked the red Lada; where we had drunk Russian champagne with Irena; where four people from different lands had marked the moment by toasting to "the unity of the nations"; where four adult 'children' had celebrated their survival from the great slaughter.

Today we have time to walk up to Elly Wolff's farmhouse, its bleached brick, stark and sad in an emptied space where a few poor vegetables struggle. Since we last saw it, the once stately manor house has suffered even further dilapidation. Yard, byres and stables have long gone. I am clutching my family album and as we near the house, a young woman scurries away. The brickwork is crumbling and pock-marked with bullet holes; in empty window frames shredded plastic sheeting flaps where double glazing once had kept out the bitter eastern winds. Is Elly Wolff still alive – somewhere in Germany? I hope so with all my heart. Had the Red Army tanks humming up the sandy path found the hamlet entirely empty? I hope so.

"Guten Tag." I greet the elderly woman at the side entrance.

"Guten Tag," she answers, and that concludes her knowledge of the German language. I smile, open my album with the black-and-white photos my mother had taken, point to house and barn and feel a fool. Beneath the headscarf forms a shy smile. As we evidently do not pose a danger, the young woman, her daughter, reappears, grins at the pictures – and then there is really nothing else to say. Peter, the perfect English gentlemen, shakes hands with the ladies and I follow his example. What do these two Lithuanian women make of these strangers with a picture book? I have no need to look around the house. The golden bed knobs will not be there. Nor anything familiar. In any case my little world had been the Great Outside. The fairytales were integral to this forest. In my little world, the sun and moon and the stars, the storks and the wildflowers were my friends.

The barn has survived the terrible century, though its upper timbers built on a brick base have cracked with weather and age. Once there was a wagon wheel fixed to the ridge of the roof to welcome the storks to their summer home. It has gone. Who today has a spare wagon wheel? The empty barn stands as a silent witness that world events had not spared even this secluded hamlet. Yet on this summer day, meadow and rye field and forest breathe peace again. I am so grateful to the Lord of Life for having given happiness to a child on this secure 'island' in the midst of war-turbulence. The short bluish stalks of the rye stand straight, share the same field with cornflower, poppy and marguerite and still lure the eye. But the *Roggenmuhme* has been scared away. Our sandals collect warm sand from the path which leads into the forest. Further and further we penetrate. Where is the little house where Opa and Oma lived?

"It's gone," I say sadly and we turn back.

"Wouldn't you expect a little wooden house to be at the edge of the forest and not *in* it?" We search at the edge where the footpath enters and there – is a mound, blanketed by moss and grass.

"This could be the site. Either it was destroyed or has simply collapsed with age and rotted away. If we could dig down we might find the foundations." We clamber all over the green knoll, looking for any clues.

"Come over here and have a look at this! It's a fire brick. Part of a chimney?" Peter is poking a branch into the moldering vegetation. I look with tenderness at this lone blackened broken brick, as it lies there in the moss.

There is one more place to visit: my great-grandparents' house. Into the gable end a date is chiseled: 1904. It marks the completion of an extension. Oma had gone west by then and married Opa in Duisburg four years later. Her eldest brother had inherited the farm and had continued to plant rye and keep a cow or two.

I feel a little shy but Peter has already unlatched the wooden gate. *Wölfchen*, the farm dog, had once guarded the entrance. A dog squeezes itself through a hole cut into the bottom of the wooden barn and barks at us viciously. Its chain is also long but not long enough for the angry animal to reach us. Two women are watching from the door step, one dressed in sea-green, the younger one in red; both wear headscarves and look well-fed. I notice new doors and windows; it looks as if their little farm pays. With my album under my arm I address mother and daughter. Why do I speak in broken German? What do they make of my cradling movements? I am trying to indicate that my grandmother was born in this house. They smile broadly. The little garden lies open to view. May we go in? They nod.

No apple tree casts dancing shadows. But the well is there, now a grey concrete circular wall in the centre of the garden. The two women leave us alone. For a few moments I linger where the Child had once played, then turn and close the slatted gate of my ancestral home behind me.

Along the Castle Road the magicians' sleeves of the spruces wave to the right and to the left as we head towards Jurbarkas. I feel so happy. The fairytale forest stands unchanged. I would not be surprised to meet Little Red Riding Hood. Even the wolves are back, having drifted unimpeded from central Russia into the neglected western regions. The midsummer sun broods over the forest. We are hungry.

"It's so lovely here. Let's have a picnic. We have a few snacks left. "

Peter spreads out his jacket and we forage in the bag. All around us the forest floor is dotted with little red jewels amongst small ternate leaves. The familiar odour of soil, needles, and fungi excite my senses. We gather a handful of the wild strawberries and let them glide into our mouths. Some leave a bitter taste. How peaceful it is here. A deep blue tent spreads above the tree tops, a lone car rattles by, and then only the music of birds and insects interrupts the stillness. No deep-pile carpet could feel softer than this springy ground. Reluctantly we rise to leave, shaking twigs and needles from our clothes.

We are not far from Jurbarkas when a low black marker set at the edge of the forest catches my eye. It reflects the sun… We turn back for a closer look. A golden Star of David on black marble! A short distance down a sandy track we come to a stone sculpted to resemble a torn page, bearing an inscription – in Hebrew and Lithuanian. Only this much can I read: 500. Jurbarkas. 8th September 1941. Behind the stone row upon row of young birches stretch upwards from a mound on which lies a white veil spun from fine woodland grasses. Delicate heart-shaped leaves quiver in dappled sunlight that has dried the morning's dew drops. We have stumbled on a mass grave! Pebbles have been placed around the rim of the memorial. Five hundred citizens of Jurbarkas... What happened here? I notice another mark on the memorial. A bullet hole. Who would have shot at it?

It is our last evening in the guesthouse. Below our window the Nemunas looks weary from her long journey. Languidly she stretches under a pale blue and apricot sky, mirroring it back without distortion. What became of the merchants' ships that had plied the river and made this town a rich community? Where are the steamboats that once conveyed hundreds of passengers? Where are the rafts that brought the logs downstream? There is no sign of a fishing boat. No one rows, no one paddles a canoe. No rod plays over the water. No children make pebbles dance.

Heavy rain wakes me. It is getting light. I pull the armchair close to the window and watch rivulets run across bright red tiles and misted panes. The river is being whipped into a frenzy and ferocious currents, entirely hidden last evening, are now revealing their presence, retorting angrily to wind and rain that have disturbed her trance. No longer placid, her waters have swollen like a vein in a fit of rage. The river races and gulls plunge vertically into the wild vaulting waves. The rain keeps drumming and demure *Fräulein Memel-Nemunas* is displaying her menacing side. She has donned the rough grey shawl of a hag.

Suddenly it is all over. Tiny glistening pearls roll lazily off the roof tiles. A small stream gently trickles down the sloped garden; it waters a weeping willow. The Nemunas has folded up her ugly wrap and flows peacefully again, a silver band flecked with the sweet pastels of morning. Even the smallest ripple has been ironed out. But did I not witness a violent drama?

"A violent drama? No, of course not. There has been nothing disturbing here," the river assures me, "nothing disturbing... nothing at all..."

She is lying.

6

Two shoots out of a hollow tree

Tonight we shall sleep on the *Kurische Nehrung*. For a long time I have wanted to *stay* on the Spit. We will again follow the Castle Road right to the sea and catch the ferry at Klaipėda. Now that the forests hug the thoroughfare again, I feel they could strangle me. Five hundred Jurbarkas citizens – that can only mean five hundred Jews – are lying beneath friendly birches. And so close to this road! And so close to the Child's innocent summer paradise! I shiver.

In Viešvilė we stop because I want to take a closer look at my former Kindergarten. I walk around the large boarded-up building, and take photographs. Why has such a big building been allowed to fall into decay? Not far away, a group of youngsters is loitering in the street, watching us narrowly. It is probably wise to move on.

Having passed the restaurant where we dined with Valda, we are now on new ground. This is Lithuania Minor, the watery lowlands formed by the Memel Delta. Most of the tiny fishing villages that hug the lagoon lie on the Russian side and are inaccessible to us without visas. I had read in a German magazine that after the ethnic cleansing of Germans, émigrés from Russia had settled in Gilge (where my mother had worked in the Labour Service) and the other fishing villages in the once again waterlogged land. Into the near-derelict houses moved the *Volga-Germans* who, even after a long time in the heartland of European Russia, have retained their Swabian dialect. Whether they have the know-how and tenacity of those hardworking Mennonites who in former generations had wrested the land from the waters in order to farm it, only time will tell. War and post-war neglect have turned the hard-won meadows and arable land back to marshes, into a paradise – for wildlife.

We are about half-way on our journey through Memelland. There are no forests here, only the wide horizons of the wetlands that had been so inspirational to Lithuanian and German writers alike. A lane veers off the Castle Road towards the river. We follow it and to our surprise the asphalt gives way to perfectly preserved Prussian cobbles.

Melancholy hangs over this landscape, as if it were close to tears. Our road snakes along the eastern shore of the Curonian Lagoon; shrubbery and undergrowth hide the water from view; the car park of a restaurant at last allows access to the Haff: again no keel disturbs the galena-like surface. The entire floor of the lagoon is said to be littered with war debris and explosives. The restaurant advertises *Authentically Cooked Fish* but the Haff no longer maintains the fifteen different species of freshwater fish illustrated on the wall chart. Pollution has almost decimated the fish population. How safe is it to eat the "authentically cooked fish"? In the warm wood smoke-laden atmosphere – well, let's take the risk. We make our choice and the salvaged old grill, suspended over an open fire, cooks it to perfection.

The leaden waters of the lagoon lap lazily on to the shore, wash unremarkable boulders and dispense pebbles and empty snail shells which I gather as mementoes. A lone stork amuses the visitors. The bird, however, looks depressed and it is no wonder. Its wings have been clipped. Never again will this mutilated creature join its companions on their annual flight to Africa. We climb the lighthouse here at Viante (Windenburg) from where the outline of the Nehrung is clearly traceable. I feel as if all the mystery of the *Kurische Haff* has been dispelled. Let's go.

A sign points to a *Homeland Museum*. It is worth delaying our ferry crossing to visit the old farmhouse. An ancient willow guards the entrance. Age and weather have eaten out its core, but the wind has filled it with enough silt and soil for a small apple tree and a baby elder both to grow inside the hollow. New and entirely different lives emerge from the battered gnarled trunk. An old man, equally battered and gnarled, beckons us to join the small knot of visitors gathered around him. With tears shimmering in his sunken eyes he alludes to terrible events and suffering that had swept across his homeland. Inside the farmhouse we wander through kitchen and parlour and bedrooms, linger by painted furniture and inspect old kitchen utensils, agricultural tools and fishing implements. Embroidered pictures bear witness to the lowlanders' strong faith and desire for godliness.

We reach the outskirts of Klaipėda. How the city has grown! Amongst the numerous sea-faring cargo ships it is difficult to find our small ferry port. The crossing is very short. This time we are not bound to a tourist schedule, either to hinder or hurry us. I dream of romantic solitude...and then a huge queue of cars? We are not at the Russian border, are we? No. *Hundreds* of visitors are buying their entrance ticket to *Kuršių Nerija*, the nature reserve.

A pine-needle carpet leads to the guesthouse. Sculptured russet trunks raise my eyes upwards to dark olive umbrellas silhouetted against a rose-coloured sky. We may well become "heady on the scent of pine and ozone" as the guidebook boasts.

Birdsong fills the warm morning breeze as we amble on soft, shade-dappled paths towards the Baltic, drawn on by the sound of the waves. And there lies the *Ostsee* of my dreams: white-crested waves roll on to a dazzling beach where I know the amber hides.

We climb the dunes and from high vantage points scan the undulating sands but I see no sign of the driftwood cross. Perhaps wind and rain have reclaimed it and its splintered, scattered wood is already buried beneath the sand. It does not matter. It was *then* that I knew His presence and I know it now – every day. At one with Him, at one with myself, I stand on a sure foundation, with neither excruciating need nor unrealistic romantic notions. Mid-summer on the *Kurische Nehrung*: yes, it is beautiful, but I have divested myself of the effusive words I had imbibed as a child; shaken off the manufactured romanticism that had shaped me; all that sentimental kitsch that clung to my German soul. I am sure that true creativity does not ask for the soul to be overwhelmed by deep emotion and magic symbol. The undertow of strong feelings has been shown to be dangerous. I have learnt how easy it is to be washed out of one's own depth and carried into wild waters that have power to destroy.

Summer-heat gives way to sudden torrential rain and a fierce gale. The umbrella I buy from a nervous female street vendor at an exorbitant price lasts minutes. An austere *kavine* serves mediocre food at bare tables. We search the streets for Nida's post-office and seek shelter in the local museum. Its interesting exhibits throw light on Curonian, German and Lithuanian lifestyles but of the long Russian occupation of the Nehrung nothing at all is shown.

Back on the Castle Road, I recall that we are on the amber trade route of antiquity; the crusader trail carved out by the Teutonic Knights; highway for mail coach and merchant's wagon; for horse-drawn conveyance to wedding and funeral; for hay and straw-laden farm carts; warpath for French, Lithuanian, German and Russian soldiers; the tanks of the twentieth century; refugees' handcarts loaded with belongings; fleeing Estonians, Latvians, Lithuanians, Jews and Germans. Once river and railway had also shared in the transport of goods and people, now the river flows empty, the rails have been dismantled and traffic on this main artery is very thin. Peter and I travel in freedom, unhindered and unobserved. The wetlands' horizons are extinguished by the forests which again frame and darken the *Chaussee*, these stoic woods, these silent witnesses that kept their dreadful secrets from the Child. Poppy field and, meadow, gloomy attic and her daisy-strewn triangle had shielded her from terrible knowledge. Soon I will learn that our peaceful travel in a hired car still shields me against awful truths: of swift armoured cars filled with men charged to carry out horrific orders; of the hiding places of marauding partisans who stole from Memelland's population; of the terrible screams of the Jews, herded together for execution in many places; and of the homeless parentless children, a number so great it would fill five thousand Primary Schools, many roaming and scavenging in the forest. Were my fairytale woods really the scene of mass murder? Was my enchanted summer paradise a witness?

There is no need to stop again in Viešvilė or drive up the sandy track to Uszbalai. After we have passed the preserved Prussian oaks of Smalininkai I am dreading the moment when we will reach the black marble marker with the Star of David. Memories, reflections, thoughts...

In Jurbarkas we pass the Prussian church and the Soviet hotel; the empty, barred dwellings; and our guesthouse on the outskirts. The large sign at the road side cannot be overlooked: GENOCIDO AUKŲ KAPINĖS.

Through a modern brick archway we enter an old Jewish cemetery and wander amongst the graves. Most headstones are standing upright, the Star of David, names and dates are all decipherable. The last interment occurred in 1939. Interesting. Time is running out. We really must go now to catch our plane. No, wait. There is a memorial. Look at the long list of Jewish names. Evidently Jurbarkas honours the victims of the Holocaust. We lay a pebble where others have placed theirs and I barely notice the two unplanted flower beds.

Under the shadow of Panemune, the only remaining castle on the Castle Road, we spread our picnic by the river. I have little appetite.

The small airport is buzzing. Many young people are leaving for England: I presume to earn enough money to renovate small wooden houses "so that they can have an inheritance". By the time the plane reaches the Baltic it is too dark to make out the long white curve of the Nehrung dunes below. My farewell is without emotion. The Baltic "undertow" has lost its power. I have no need to return.

7

Discoveries

The Child had urged me to undertake a mission and I have completed it. I have walked her paths, opened her doors and verified her story. I have a deep sense that the uprooted child, the evacuee, the refugee has been made whole and that my empty places are now filled. Maybe I needed such solidity before I could cope with the nauseating historical events I had only begun to discover.

There had been the wistful ambiguous poem about Lithuania, a marble tablet in a birch grove bearing the number 500, appearing to mark a mass grave, the whispered words "a Jewish shop" and a row of small empty barred wooden houses with fresh flowers in their windows. The placid river had briefly shown me its violent propensity and, having reverted to its still beauty, totally denied its raging. The newly rendered house wall now hides the 'wound', the crude brick in-fill, as well as the enigmatic name above a small-paned window. And then there had been the locked door which had mysteriously been opened from the inside.

Back in England, I embark on research into all these discoveries. I need to know and understand. Apart from opening my eyes, I am about to learn how easily I jump to conclusions. The unfolding story is not only sickening but complicated as it changes with each discovery.

Had we lived above a *Jewish shop*? Was there a *separate staircase* leading into our room? The grave in the birch grove and the memorial tablet by the Jewish cemetery – what happened in Lithuania, just across the border from where we had lived?

I had taken a photograph of the grey wall on our initial visit. The name sign is hard to read; perhaps the gothic lettering was superimposed on an earlier designation. In any event I had read "*Hirsch...*", connected it with the vague impression of drunks singing beneath our window one night and had emphatically concluded that the room below us had been a small pub. German inns are often called '*Zum Hirschen*' (The Stag), I had been sure that the sign would have read *Hirschschenke* (*Schenke* being an old word for a drinking establishment). It had made sense fourteen years ago. I scan the picture into my computer and zoom in on detail. Yes, it could easily be a traditional shop window. A wooden architrave, painted green and bearing a simple corbel, suggests a door.

It is at the tip of Africa I gain more insight. In the Jewish Museum in Cape Town I find replicas of small wooden houses, Jewish houses, closely resembling those on the High Street of Jurbarkas! One is a shop. It has a *separate* staircase leading to the upper storey. This is how the Lithuanian Jews who found a new life in South Africa remember their homes. *The grey house opposite my green triangle had been a Jewish shop.* In this light I re-examine the lettering: I now read *Hirshverk*, surely a Jewish surname. It also becomes clear that a small board had been nailed over the original forename. ROSA has been painted on it in non-gothic capitals. *Rosa Hirshverk:* that was the name of the Jewish shopkeeper. Somewhere she must have taken over from her husband. What had become of him?

My desk fills with pictures and reports, stories and documents. I read and read, my mind confused, my heart saturated with the horror of it all. Every day I make new discoveries.

As Hitler and his party grew in power many Jews in the Lithuanian Klaipėda Region (the Memelland) read the warning signs and sold their houses and businesses to Germans. Many crossed the border into main Lithuania. Since the gates into European countries were closing to them, many emigrated to America, Australia or South Africa or followed the Zionist call. Perhaps Rosa Hirshverk's husband had joined the Red Army, as many Jewish men did, leaving her to run the shop. Maybe he had died. She may have *sold* her house and business and emigrated or simply moved from her isolation across the border to Jurbarkas, where the Jewish community thrived.

When, days before I was born, the Führer arrived in Klaipėda (which he renamed Memel) and announced 'liberation' to the population, bringing the Lithuanian region "home into the Reich", the remaining Jews fled for their lives, leaving everything behind. Along the *Chaussee*, the Castle Road, they *ran*. Had Rosa Hirshverk, the German Jewess, left it too late? Did she have to *abandon* her property to run with the others to the safety of Lithuania? Had the secretive German family downstairs simply moved into the vacated house? Or had the Party allocated it to them? Had my grandmother and my mother been aware that we had moved into a *Jewish house* and that goods and chattels had been 'taken over' from Rosa? Emotional turmoil: my world view is being turned upside down. My grassy triangle had called me to truth, but this is truth I had neither expected nor sought. From now on the thought haunts me that Rosa Hirshverk might lie in the mass grave in the forest! I need to find out more.

Jurbarkas' tourist information office is silent about the town's former name (Yurburg) and forgets to mention that it was the most Jewish on Lithuanian soil and possessed a famous beautiful synagogue. Instead the official leaflet draws the tourist's attention to the modern bridge across the Nemunas, extols peaceful parks and sculptures and even a medieval castle from the time of the Teutonic Knights of which *in reality* no trace remains.

In 1939 a Jewish citizen had written about Yurburg's long beautiful wide street, pavements and nice houses. With sadness the writer had noted that in his beloved *shetl* some of the old buildings, *small affordable houses*, were being demolished, thus robbing the Jewish poor of their homes and means of earning an income. (Those padlocked wooden houses with fresh flowers in the windows!)

Reputedly invited into the town by one of Catherine the Great's lovers to act as a buffer between aristocracy and peasantry, the Jews became the affluent educated middle class. Jewish chroniclers write of the town's Jewish citizens as having been well-to-do, well-dressed and well-shod, exhibiting a highly developed self-esteem. They worked efficiently and profitably and made their mark. Jews owned the steamship company plying on the Nemunas; owned sawmill and flour mill; were proprietors of the power station and the bathhouse; merchants and exporters; hoteliers; shopkeepers and artisans. They also were the academics: doctors, lawyers, teachers and bankers. Were the town's amenities accessible also to the Lithuanian peasants who farmed the surrounding land and brought their harvests to market to trade with the Jews? There had certainly been neighbourliness between the Lithuanian and the Jewish population, particularly at the time when the Nemunas flooded the town. That cooperation all stopped – in Jewish words – "with Hitler's politics". But until the late thirties, the Jews, living close to their sacred synagogue, felt secure and in charge and found rest and relaxation in the surrounding forests.

Did Rosa Hirshverk live in Yurburg in the summer of 1941?

When Hitler's attention was turned towards his Western front, Stalin saw his opportunity for extending Soviet influence on Lithuania. In one year of occupation the internal politics changed. Jews, who had been increasingly discriminated against, both politically and economically, were now given responsible posts in local government and in the police force. Yet Russian nationalization of private enterprises brought hardship to Lithuanians and Jews alike. Since a sizable number of Jews had Communist leanings and felt safer under Soviet administration, Lithuanians viewed them as siding with their enemy. Within a short time the Soviet Union showed its uglier side. In the *second week of June 1941* forty five thousand Lithuanians were executed or transported in cattle trucks to Siberia. (Amongst them were also many Jews.) The Lithuanians were in a state of shock, reeling and raging helplessly. Their rage, seeking an outlet, would soon turn on the Jewish community.

Only days after this trauma, *in the third week of June 1941* before the early dawn breaks, German tanks pour out from their cover in the forests across the Memel and on to the Castle Road. *Operation Barbarossa*, the planned conquest of the Soviet Union, has begun and the Memelland is the first to experience it. Lithuania lies in the war path and its Jewish population becomes the first target. In the wake of the tanks follows a sinister group. Sent from Tilsit, they, too, cross the *Luisenbrücke*. Their distinctive mission is to 'clean' a 25-kilometre strip of all Jewish life. It is an arbitrary radius. The *Einsatzkommandos* (EK) are racing along the Castle Road, though Wischwill and Schmalleningken, crossing the border, and into Jurbarkas. The Jews have had warning and many seek refuge in the bathhouse. They are quickly discovered and rounded up together with all other Jewish citizens. They are forced to wear a yellow patch on their clothing, are forbidden to leave the town, ordered to stay away from all contacts with non-Jews and to submit to a nightly curfew.

If Rosa Hirshverk is in Yurburg, she is forced to witness or participate in the destruction of the synagogue and the valuable books. As a helpless bystander she is made to watch the sordid humiliation of the rabbi. Rosa in Yurburg hears the tumult as three hundred Jewish men are beaten and driven along the Castle Road towards the Jewish cemetery. There they are ordered to dig deep pits and attack each other with their spades. Then they are shot and pushed into the trenches. Rosa in Yurburg tries to stop her ears to shut out screaming and shouting and the shots and – later that night – the noise of the drunken brawl as the executioners celebrate their 'achievement'.

The *'unplanted flowerbeds'* by the Jewish cemetery! When I placed my pebble on the Holocaust memorial I was unaware that I was standing at the very place where these executions had taken place; that I had glimpsed the very pits, the mass graves.

Rosa in Yurburg is herded into a yard with many other women and children and kept there, not fed for four days. Weakened and terrified, she is marched along the Castle Road towards the German border, in the direction of her former house and shop, into a clearing close to the edge of the forest. A place well reconnoitred: remote enough to shield from the world what is about to happen, yet easily accessible from the road. The copse of young birches and fine grasses we saw is known as the "Smalininkai Grove". Here Rosa is one of five hundred women and children (the latter regarded as "useless eaters") who are mown down by rifle or machine gun fire or pushed alive into the ready-dug pit.

In the frightened brains of the citizens of Schmalleningken (and possibly Uszballen, though it lies a little further from the border) the "screams and screams and screams" and the horror will be indelibly recorded, as they surely will be in the minds of those German initiators and Lithuanian collaborators and all the gunmen who had been forced or enticed or volunteered to become executioners.

Birch leaf had rustled and grasses had danced on the mass grave for many years until research began and unearthed the terrible details of the executions at the cemetery and in the forest. The murdered women and children were exhumed and re-buried beside the cemetery through which I had walked.

On that balmy night when Peter and I strolled hand in hand on the tow path by the river I had no inkling of the cruel taunting and torturing Jews had suffered on the very spot. Our experience had been an eerie silence and a strange emptiness. The deserted long main street had not impressed *us* as "beautiful". Today, as far as I know, not a single Jew lives in Jurbarkas.

The official report of the *Einsatzkommando* reads:

> *I can confirm that EK 3 has achieved the goal of solving the Jewish problem in Lithuania... The Jews were transported in detachments of five hundred to the execution area, with a distance of at least two kilometres between them.*

My story takes another twist. My surmise, however logical, is overthrown when I find two documents amongst my mother's papers. They are witness statements – one signed by Elly Wolff who has survived the war and found a new home in Berlin – and stamped as correct, attesting that my grandmother for a stated period in 1943 had lived in "her own accommodation" in a house owned – by a *Frau Hirschbeck*. Such documents were required by the Federal Government of post-war Germany to pay some compensation for property lost in the east.

H-i-r-s-<u>c</u>-h-<u>b</u>-e-c-k. Again I zoom in on the faded lettering. Yes, that's right! A German name. So the woman downstairs (the mother of the raw-potato-eating girl) was Rosa Hirschbeck? It is from her that my grandmother had purchased the rooms in the attic, possibly with the intention of making a permanent home in Memelland when the war had ended.

Much later I find out that few Jews lived in Memelland. About nine thousand resided in Klaipėda, *none* in rural areas. But Viešvilė was of course a small town. If Herr and Frau Hirschbeck had their names painted over an existing one – a Jewish one –, experts with the appropriate technology today could possibly make it out, had not the wall been newly rendered. And who would remove *that* to find the truth?

So, only God knows.

In October 1944, under the threat of death by the Nazi administration, Frau Hirschbeck and her child would have been forced from their home, in the third and last evacuation wave from Memelland. Where did *they* end up? In West or East Germany? They might have died on the flight. Maybe they re-crossed the Memel in search of food in Lithuania. Several families did so and make up that small German population who watch over the little cemetery where my Opa lies.

For a time Uszballen, Wischwill and the other communities in Memelland became 'ghost villages', after German and Russian soldiers had moved on. Who lived in our rooms? Who slept in my bed? Who trampled my grassy triangle?

I am no eyewitness to the terrible events and can only recount what I have read. But I *have* seen the flowers by the rendered wall.

They were planted neither by Jews nor by Germans.

They are planted by Lithuanians.

8

A farmyard west of the Elbe

Our flight from the most north-eastern part of Germany must have taken several days and nights, travelling by narrow-gauge railway across the *Luisenbrücke* to Tilsit, changing for Königsberg and from there – most probably circumventing Berlin – to Saxony in central Germany. My inner film of that journey is lost; I have not retained a shred of memory. We were in the first wave of the human flood from the *east* to swamp Glesien, an unremarkable village, tucked under the arms of an autobahn junction, just west of the river Elbe. It already served as a collecting point for refugees from the destroyed *western* cities.

A large farm on the outskirts was obliged to allocate rooms to us. The Red Army raged into Eastern Europe, East Prussia, Silesia and Pomerania and drove before it a multitude of refugees. The Allies agreed on the necessity of the ethnic cleansing of all Germans from those areas. The Great Spoon – another *Völkerwanderung*, migration – stirred more and more strangers into the village. Glesien became a kind of waiting room, a transit camp without barbed wire, where the prevailing atmosphere would soon change from hope to doom, from relief to terror.

In 1993 Peter and I traverse the village by car. I cannot find my bearings and have to ask an elderly man if knows the street that had changed from Adolf-Hitler-Straße to Roosevelt St. He points us in the direction "where the well-to-do-farms used to be". The village streets are lined with post-war trees. And then I recognize it.

"The gateway!"

It stands wide open as it always had and I am back in the farmyard where the Child, the five-year old had roamed unsupervised. The dirty-red brick byres and the pig sties appear even grimier and more dilapidated than I remember them. No farm noise from anywhere: no rooster crows, no pig squeals and no cattle low. The high barn, where the great threshing machine used to thud, stands silent, and its gates that had swallowed the carts laden with rye and wheat are locked. The window frames of the farm buildings have lost their panes. Someone has started to concrete the rutted and potholed yard but abandoned the work. Does anyone live here?

"Look! That was our window, above the slaughter house."

I knock on the familiar door. When a woman opens to us and I explain who we are, she invites us to see the upstairs rooms. The brown linoleum on the curving staircase and the shiny handrail are the same. The room that had been my home for nine anxious months looks so small, the same yellow-tiled stove takes up most of the space. The adjacent bedroom is even tinier than I had imagined. And here in so little space we played when the American soldier had looked down on my little brother and me. Had he come further than the door, he would surely have trampled on us.

This is really all I need to see. On our way down I remember the bottom step where Mami sat with us children while the bombs fell close by. Today there is peace.

Through this corridor the soldiers had dragged the farmer, the regional Nazi official. And it had been a great tumult. Today no one shouts and wails. The Americans left and the Russians came and an Iron Curtain divided the land. Now Germany is reunited.

'I want to see the meadow. Today there is not time. But we will be back

A few years later the village shows signs of growing prosperity. The dark brick of the farm buildings has collected yet more grime but the concreting has been completed and there are no more potholes in which puddles and small ice rinks can form. Again the farmyard appears deserted. Are there still no animals? I make straight for the small gate at the far end to look for ditch and meadow. To Peter I point to the spot from where I could see the American tank blocking the farm entrance and where the Child had experienced the triumph of liberation and the terror of the conquered: a Frenchman's joy and a German woman's fear. But the meadow is no more. A new housing estate has erupted where harebells, marguerites and clover had bloomed. Someone is calling to us from the yard.

A woman is coming towards us. She looks wan and haggard, her clothes poor. I explain our unexpected presence.

"Are you the owner?" I ask.

"Oh no," she waves her hands, "I just live here. We came as refugees." The Great Spoon had stirred her out of Bessarabia, the land between Dnestr and Prut, north of the Danube Delta. She had fled with her mother through Romania, Hungary, Czechoslovakia and south-east Germany to escape the Russians to end up in Glesien. We discover that in May 1945 we had both lived here! But I was already on the way to the Ruhr, when she and other children strolled along the Autobahn, accepting sweets and chewing gum from American soldiers. That bliss had not lasted long. The Russians overran the village. In the end they had caught up with her! So she went to school in Glesien and was indoctrinated with Communist ideology. Of those years she does not speak to me.

The weeks preceding our departure had been terrible. The village fell within a radius of less than fifty kilometres from the cities of Leipzig, Halle and Madgeburg, Gotha, Aschersleben and Bernburg. The region was responsible for the construction of one third of all Messerschmitt planes. In nearby Delitzsch anti-aircraft batteries were based. In the summer of 1944 the historic city of Madgeburg had been reduced to rubble but at the end of February 1945 the RAF and a thousand US bombers and their escort planes came again and hit a dozen targets in central Germany during "Big Week". Bombs went astray more often than not, since US planes bombed by radar which was not very accurate. Low-flying aircraft strafed the countryside, keeping us indoors.

In mid-April the bombing stopped. Ground troops approached the Elbe: the Russians from the east; the Americans from the west. For the US soldiers the river was the finishing line. There they shook hands with their Russian counterparts. In the vacuum which followed capitulation, the brief lull before the American withdrawal and the Russian surge toward Saxony and Thuringia, we made our escape. Glesien came under Soviet rule and one totalitarian power replaced another. And then the Iron Curtain!

The die was cast. One six-year old girl travels into freedom, one is trapped. If *her* mother had lifted *her* little daughter on to one of the few trains travelling west, how differently would have run the course of her life.

A page found recently in my mother's notebook gives the account of our flight from Glesien in her own words. No one knows when she had written it nor for whom.

The war had ended. We were evacuated to Saxony. The first trains were running west. We also travelled: I with two small children and my mother. On route we had to get off the train because a bridge had been destroyed. It had been very difficult to get to the station by horse-drawn cart. Then the trains arrived. We were standing there with so much luggage that we could not get on. The crowd's jostling was so strong that we were left behind. That happened several times. So I went to the front of the train, where the engine had stopped, and talked to the driver. I told him that we had been standing a long time and had not been able to get on to a train. How did he respond? He drove the train backwards until a door was right in front of us. The conductor helped us to get on the train.

Later, in a different-coloured biro, she had added:

It sounds unbelievable. I have to explain that all trains started from that station and that the doors were opened only just prior to departure.

To me she had never told this dramatic story.

9

Tears for my cities

In the country I find my sense of well-being while cities sap my energy. I relish the moment I can leave a big city behind me. Yet I spent only three childhood years in a rural environment and most of my youth in two cities which I need to revisit. I am ready.

Wuppertal, my birthplace, where the red *Schwebebahn* screeched above roofless, burnt-out buildings, had given me a new life: a kaleidoscope of play and friendship; an understanding of social class and betrayal; religious awe and aggression; thieving and lying; shared imagination and the beginnings of formal learning. Best of all, here I found a sense of belonging.

My visit today will be brief. It does not take long to walk the one street up to my primary school and down to the station set in a rocky embankment. The unique hanging railway, now painted in cheerful orange and blue, glides above new houses and busy streets. I come away from my city grateful that my childhood had *not* ended when the grown-ups tore me out of my treasured world. Rather, life had widened out and become fruitful.

Duisburg spells coal and steel. Sitting at the confluence of Rhine and Ruhr, it is home to Europe's largest inland port and stretches for over twenty kilometres along the Rhine, the Continent's most travelled shipping route. When I arrived there at war's end, all lay in ruins and had nothing to offer but debris and water-filled craters. And when the city rose from the ashes and its industry revived, smoke and grime turned it even uglier. How my young eyes had searched for beauty, yearned for good forms, for aesthetics, for clear clean design! And somewhere it could always be found. The plane trees growing alongside the Ruhr Road could hold on to their greenness no longer than a week before turning grey. But in winter, silhouetted against the evening light, they had made a lovely picture. And in the evening, when 'Lantern Pete' had lit the gas lamps, a golden sheen transformed their dust-laden branches.

In the basements of bombed-out houses we children created rooms, furnished them, cooked in them, and placed the ubiquitous milkwort into shards we found, creating flower arrangements on tables made from charred bricks.

Back in Duisburg I am actively seeking for positives. I want to love the revived city with its cleaner air. We book into a hotel on the Rhine where the Ruhr joins it and the two busy rivers become one. It is here where we had held our wedding reception. It had been a one-storey restaurant in the lee of the new Rhine bridge; now it is the highest building around.

It is Advent. The shopping streets are tastefully decorated. The Christmas market stretches along the entire *Königstrasse*, the one kilometre-long main street. Myriads of lights glitter.

Our first port of call is my grandparents' house built at the turn of the twentieth century. With a new coat of paint, it looks impressive. I glance up to the kitchen window where as a teenager I had lamented the end of my school days as the "end of my life". Again I had been wrong! I give my home and the flat-faced houses a last loving look. Prosperity has come back to *Lakumer Straße*.

The severe blocky Reformed church where we sealed our marriage with a simple '*Ja*', is firmly locked. In the adjacent cemetery Oma's and Papi's graves have served their purpose and have been sold. It comforts me that on one visit we had pulled up a sapling linden tree and replanted it outside our cottage. It is enough to connect me with my father and grandmother. Opposite the cemetery gate the small *Gemeinderaum*, the old parish room, has not changed from the time I attended confirmation classes there.

A memorial tablet fixed to the wall of the air raid shelter bears a long list of names but not those of my paternal grandmother and cousin. They were buried in the Protestant cemetery because both bodies could be identified. From the air-raid shelter leaning against the railway embankment we go to find the site of my father's family house. A new building fills the gap where the burnt-out ruin had stood, from which Gert-Dieter and I had extracted bricks, had knocked off the blackened mortar and sold them for others to rebuild their homes. The few Deutschmark the driver of the pick-up lorry had handed us in payment for the bricks - were our only inheritance.

I just *had* to spend an evening in my beloved theatre. In the dazzling foyer I think I can still hear the rustle of my long pale-blue taffeta dress and almost expect to see myself in it in the large mirrors. In the orchestra pit many more women are now playing instruments. We settle in the stalls. All around us well-behaved children sit spellbound by the magic of Humperdinck's opera *Hänsel und Gretel*.

Duisburg has built a new art gallery, dedicated entirely to Wilhelm Lehmbruck's works. The city's talented son is being honoured. How the Nazi regime had despised his art, mocking it as *"entartet"*, degenerate. In cool lofty halls and in the surrounding park we wander from sculpture to sculpture.

Peter drives me along the industrial roads that took me to school and to the swimming baths. The steelworks and mines that flanked them are closed. Today no owl-faced miners meet us and the coking plant no longer sprays warm ill-smelling water. The heavy industry lies silent; much of it already demolished. On their ugly sites nature and leisure parks are planned.

The long corridors of my old school are deserted and no one forbids me peeping into the classrooms. Nothing has changed. Desks and chairs and even the wall maps, everything looks exactly as it did the day I left school! In the *Aula*, the big hall, the school choir is rehearsing. Leaving, I feel no pain or nostalgia. Only gratitude.

Dawn is about to break on this, the shortest day of the year. Cuddled into my dressing gown, I creep out on to the balcony of our hotel room. An icy wind slaps my face. Slowly a red fire ball rolls up from behind roofs and steadily climbs above the city. Rhine and Ruhr are aflame. Below, container ships bearing Dutch, German, French or Swiss flags, are plying the crimson waters in both directions. It's a new day – it's a new hour.

Travelling into town the trams no longer screech, but glide smoothly cross the bridges that span the many waterways. They still stop at the *House With A Thousand Windows* and the *Rathaus*. The tower of the *Salvatorkirche*, the Church of the Redeemer, has been capped and no longer resembles the rotten tooth that had once served as a grim reminder of the destruction wreaked on this city. Reluctantly I follow Peter inside the church.

Silvery soft light reflects on lofty plain white walls. The sounds from street and Christmas market do not intrude. Two tall spruces frame a simple lectern on which a Bible lies open. Only white candles and hundreds of straw stars decorate the trees whose simple and beautiful majesty do not obscure the elegant Gothic windows. They stretch upwards, muting the morning light as if through grey shards. No, not shards. Not broken glass. New glass: tiny silvery panes. All traces of the medieval interior have gone and only its fine bone structure has been respectfully preserved into the twenty first century. Hushed, hand clasping hand, we stand in the aisle, allowing this simplicity, this unpretentious beauty to touch us. Spruces and silver windows draw our eyes upwards.

"Lift up your hearts."

"We lift them to the Lord."

And suddenly the silence is broken. Clean and commanding the organ swells with Widor's *Toccata*. We receive it as a wedding gift. Awe turns to joy and thankfulness that the Lord of our lives has led us together. This church, wounded and all but destroyed by British bombers, has been resurrected and redeemed. It confirms us in our calling to form small bridges to span national divisions; to heal the enmity between our countries. It's a new hour, it's a new day. The two 'bridge heads' – named so at our wedding by a citizen of the lost Königsberg - both know that they have been rescued by the One who holds the keys to death and hell...

The last chord leaves a faint echo. The organ lid falls shut. It is time to move on.

Outside, under the clear sky, Duisburg's winter air is good. The glorious smells of roast chestnuts and burnt almonds, stone-baked pizza and spiced biscuits invite us into the colourful and festive world of the Christmas market. *Glühwein*; wood carvings and crystal figures from Bavaria; candle-powered carousels from Thuringia; *Bratwurst*; German carols and the bells from the *Salvatorkirche*, full and deep. The crowd carries us from stall to stall.

And kindness meets us everywhere. Help comes in the underground car park and at the ticket dispenser; a photo shop mends my camera without charge; the saleswoman in the shoe shop, with patience and good humour, helps Peter to find the right kind of slippers. How different German people are today. No longer humourless and officious as I had known them throughout my childhood. Nowhere do we find a trace of xenophobia. No one is afraid of an ever-present informer. This new generation has *not* emerged dazed and terrified from the ruins nor woken from a long nightmare of trauma and deprivation.

An incomprehensibly large number of humans - all over the globe - lost their lives in horrendous circumstances. Too many - to really engage the heart. Numbers. Numbers. Not entirely so. Over a period of time I had therapeutically accompanied a survivor of the bombing raid on Coventry. Molly and her mother had been pulled from the rubble. Her mother had succumbed to agonizing injuries. Molly was four years old at the time. With *her* pain, bereavement and loss of childhood happiness my heart had engaged. Never with mine. I had *not* been pulled from beneath bricks and dust and my mother *is still alive*. Now at last the fate of my two cities is coming into focus. Jörg Friederich's book *The Fire* opens my eyes – and my heart. The author draws on eyewitness accounts, personal stories. The very first chapter describes in detail the effects of the firestorm unleashed in the narrow Wupper valley - in *Wuppertal-Barmen* - just a few steps down the hill from our flat.

It had taken not much more than ten minutes to unload over 300,000 bombs. Like a huge 'crate' the formation of six hundred planes had rumbled towards the city. Barmen had been a labyrinth of narrow winding alleyways and half-timbered houses, typical for the area. Bomber Command had dropped blockbuster bombs to destroy roofs, followed by incendiaries to create self-igniting fires. The wind fanned the flames into a firestorm that pulled everything into itself and from which there was no escape. The city was completely wiped out, its people charred to doll's size or asphyxiated in their cellars. In one clinic – was it the one in which I was born? – thirty mothers and their newborns were incinerated. Even in the waters of the Wupper there was no relief because phosphorus floats. So *that* is what happened in my city! If this terrible holocaust had happened one year earlier I - we - might have been among the 3,400 victims. Instead I played with my dolls on a green grassy triangle under an 'un-invaded' blue sky and sang to the daisies! And when we returned to the devastated city I took the ruins for granted.

Duisburg. Two hundred and ninety nine. What? Air-raids on that one city. I try to imagine what life was like when again and again the people looked up and saw the sky blotted out with formations of dark mothers birthing murderers and tried to hide from the thousands of tons of explosives and incendiaries that would rain on them. And then it is the sheer *number* that suddenly evokes my sobs, for the very first time. Amongst my mother's papers I find a letter she had kept all these years. It was written in February 1945 by one of my grandmother's tenants in answer to her enquiries about the house and would have arrived in Glesien while I roamed the farmyard.

Worthy Frau Nehles and daughter!

As you have written to us twice already, I want to write to you immediately.

You have heard that we escaped death. I do not want to write about that because I never want to experience it again. There were fifty four dead and fourteen survivors; we were the only family who came out of it all – together. I have always said: either everybody or none at all. If I was to write to you about everything it would fill several pages.

Now, worthy Frau Nehles and daughter: concerning your house. The whole house is occupied by strangers, but as long as I have lived with you, these are the most difficult people I have ever known. The one thing we need is that the war would end, then you could say, yes, this is a peaceful house community.

We have all been hurt, but perhaps God wanted it that way. Well, the house has suffered much under the bombs, but no repairs are done.

Everyone is responsible for the roof and the flats. The worst rooms are on the top floor. The laundry stove (copper) *can no longer be used. The lower part and the heating are totally destroyed, but we will see to it that it becomes usable again; we will buy the material if we can get it, and then I shall repair it myself. Let us hope that your house is saved from a bomb and after the war it will be made beautiful all the way through. And there is nothing more lovely as when the tenants are united and understand each other, and not as it has been up to now. I have sent the rent for the month of February. RM157.50.* (A breakdown of rents paid by six families follows.) *I do hope it arrives.*

Now I will tell you the names of those who died in Lakumer Straße (there follows a long list of people my grandmother had known: couples, families, visitors.)

I will stop now because of the tears in my eyes. My own family was sent into safety by the National Social Services two days later. Hopefully all this will come to an end soon so that I can live together with my wife and children again.

Stay healthy and happy and let us hope that we shall meet again soon.

Warm greetings

from

Johann Heinen and all the tenants

I put the letter down and I feel tears falling, falling... My heart is finally engaged.

On arrival at our hotel I ring my brother. "Thank you for our early Christmas present," I laugh down the phone. "Thank you for the snow."

"Snow? " exclaims my brother, "It has not snowed in the whole of North Rhine Westphalia!"

"But it has snowed here! Everything is white and slippery. At least three centimetres of snow!"

"I don't want to disillusion you," Gert-Dieter laughs, "but all that white stuff is frozen fallout from the petroleum industry."

The young chemist is sweeping up the "snow" that her customers had trodden into her pharmacy. I ask for an ointment to relieve a minor complaint.

"What do you use in England?" I tell her the trade name.

"I am sorry," she says, her voice warm and caring, "this we do not have in Germany...but we also have something good."

Her ointment proves effective. Even more healing are the words she dispenses.

We also have something good.

Coda

We wake in the cottage, having closed the doors on parish ministry. The autumn sun is already streaming through the window. The diary is blank. The wind of freedom blows in our small garden. Over the years it will expand and stretch up the hillside. It will take a long time to reclaim from the brambles and self-sown trees the terraces which the lead miners created a century ago; to rebuild the many walls; to enrich the sapped soil; to hack out the rocky foundations for the summerhouse in which one day I will write this book.

"How are you surviving?" There is concern in the bishop's voice, when he rings.

Yes, how? We have come out of parish life without savings, have to wait yet a while for a pension and Peter does not qualify for dole.

"You resigned?" questioned the official.

"Yes."

"Was pressure put on you to resign?"

"Pressure from whom?" Peter asked.

"From the Bishop for example?"

"No. Higher than that."

"The Archbishop?"

"No. From the very top."

"Well, that doesn't count, I'm afraid," the lady replied.

Morning by morning cards and letters from many places land on the doormat: they contain encouragements and often a cheque or a wad of notes!

Three months after leaving the parish we feast in New Orleans at the table of a shipping magnate. Peter is taking his daughter's wedding. On the Mississippi steam boat plays a jazz band, and days later we are rolling through the frozen prairies, the Rockies and the Nevada desert. Amtrak takes us to San Francisco and along the Columbia River. In Boise we hire a 4x4 and travel through Idaho to visit old friends, are caught in a blizzard in the Cascades and arrive on Vancouver Island to lead a healing mission in an Anglican church. We are discovering a Father who not only feeds sparrows.

And the vision of a therapeutic community? Finally it is fulfilled. Peter and I *are* that community, providing accommodation and counselling. We are surrounded by The Shadow Trust, a group of committed friends and also fifty intercessors who pray for us for wisdom and safety. In the next ten years four hundred people from twenty two countries will have come to the house we call Lower Springs. No appeal and no advertisement will be necessary. The Father brings whom he calls. But before the real busyness begins there is much time for reflection on what Jesus has done in our lives.

The picture of Hitler never 'graced' my parental home, but it hung over my life, from clinic to Kindergarten; from birth to playtime. Somewhere deep down it held a power over me, emanated a darkness in my soul I could no longer tolerate. An English clergyman, formerly an officer in the British Army, prayed for me. In his Vicarage living room I lost consciousness and for several minutes descended into a dark night. Coming back into awareness I 'saw' to the left of me a shattered picture; its glass splintered. I felt utterly exhausted and so did the priest, having prayed "...and deliver us from evil..." Inside me is light.

In her hundredth year, shortly before she dies, my mother has lost all conception of family relationships; even her husband of 47 years is a vague memory; and she no longer understands that I am her *daughter*. Old age simplifies life. Yet it was her (and her mother) who brought us two young children safely through the war-torn land: a thousand kilometres east; a thousand kilometres west; in terror; through suffering and deprivation.

Before the Second World War the Königsberg-born Käthe Kollwitz created a bronze she called *Tower of Mothers*. Using their own bodies, arms raised high, faces attuned to danger, a group of women form a stronghold, a place of safety for their children. The sculptor's work was removed from its Berlin gallery and mocked. Hitler asserted that German mothers did not need to protect their children; that was the task of the State. The State? What did the State care about any children within its borders? What did the State care that they were burnt to death, gassed, shot, suffocated, drowned, driven from their homes, separated from fathers and mothers, orphaned, starved, became fugitives and victims of rape? My mother and my grandmother were integral parts of the protective *tower* for me. They guarded their two young charges so well that for a long time afterwards I asserted that the war had not harmed me in any way. But it had. The prevailing circumstances *had* deprived me psychologically of adequate maternal care, of attachment and also of an inner freedom. Not bonded, yet bound. Bound by guilt and anxiety. To make my mother aware of my perceived lack of personal freedom, I wrote for her a short fable about a fledgling that wanted to fly unencumbered. She understood the meaning. For my birthday she sent me a letter, releasing me from all her expectations and demands. I was free to fly. Maternal deprivation with all its debilitating consequences no longer clipped my wings.

Over the years I carried a sense of injustice. Had my father not beaten me for writing a 'naughty word' in the bathroom? I remained convinced that it was not my little hand that had formed the word. One day in a quiet room God himself brought up the subject. *Take a pen and write the word.* Confidently I pick up my biro and begin to form the capital letter S, try to add a 'c'...the biro refuses to obey. Slowly and deliberately I connect h and e and i and ß and finally the last letter. There: *Scheiße*, shit. Not adult handwriting, but the painstakingly drawn letters of a seven-year old. I *had* written it after all? So I had lied to my father? And accused him of injustice? Then came the divine, the redeeming explanation. *Your father habitually used the word himself – but he needed you to be a good and pure girl.* Justice and mercy met. I understand and desire – with that same mercy and understanding – to embrace all those Christian leaders who in their dealings with me had gone beyond justice and insight. It is not difficult to step out of God's wisdom. It is difficult to truly listen. They are my brothers and sisters. A minus can be as much a marker in one's life as a plus. Each encounter, positive or negative, brought me ever closer to entrusting myself to Jesus alone.

We fall and are picked up.

We are lost and found.

Out of danger we are rescued.

Dividing walls remain only for a season.

Roots are torn from their soil by ourselves and others. God carefully replants them.

The clump of violets in the Vicarage lawn! I *had* to extract it carefully with all its roots – to be replanted in a different place.

That dream image is strongly evoked in an unexpected setting. We are travelling in Eastern Germany, close to Weimar. On the map a name, on the hillside to our right at the forest's edge rises a high edifice, a memorial. Buchenwald.

The large car park has emptied. The museum is about to close but the entrance gate is still open. Multiple strands of barbed wire. The large clock has stopped. The phrase *Jedem das Seine* (To each his own) is worked into the design of the wrought iron gate. We move into a vast bleak space: row upon row of rectangular 'plots' of blackish aggregate, the foundations of the barracks. Slowly, prayerfully we walk amongst them. We are alone. A cart has been placed by an upright post, the two symbols for the camp's 'ethics': labour and punishment. 56,545 human beings were worked to death or murdered here. "To each his own. – Each gets what he deserves!"

Amongst the survivors is the Dutch psychiatrist Conrad Baar. His therapeutic model for the *healing of the unaffirmed* had significantly contributed to my recovery. At the time I did not know that he had been incarcerated in Buchenwald!

Cruelty and death in this place had not ceased with the Nazis but continued for another five years in a Silent Camp, a ready-made secretive Russian gulag for East German men of whom only a small percentage had belonged to the party.

Peter and I can look up to the watchtowers with impunity. They are no longer manned and I doubt that the barbed wire is electrified.

At the rail terminus I imagine the wagons spilling out their doomed human cargo, the prisoners herded into cold wooden huts to be starved, worked and destroyed. And we are walking free, passing a small grassy area. (A triangle?) The last rays of the sun highlight a patch of blue: violets.

They have no right to grow here! Did they flower when the prisoners passed by? *They* would not have been allowed to stoop and look more closely as we are doing right now. We admire this quiet unassuming beauty growing outside the barbed-wire.

And on the woodland walk above *our* cottage, there grow violets in great profusion. Each year the Creator adds more and more. In time, light will shine into a darkness that does not and will not comprehend it. Beauty will replace ugliness. Humility will conquer barbarity. Prison gates will be flung open.

Life is waiting to meet with us.

Integration

Heart of my child
Come home.
Your laden dolls' pram
Clatters in unfamiliar streets.

Heart of my child
Come home.
Comfort in fantasy
Leads you away from truth.

Heart of my child
Come home.
No one will listen
To your stamm'ring story?

Heart of my child,
Come, find
Me. I am your home.
Here someone understands.

BALTIC SEA

LITHUANIA

Memel
(Klaipėda)

MEMELLAND

Tilsit
(Sovetsk)

POLAND

Kurische Nehrung
(Curonian Spit)

Rossitten
(Rybachi)

Kurisches Haff
(Curonian Lagoon)

Cranz
(Zelenogradsk)

Königsberg
(Kaliningrad)

EAST PRUSSIA

Danzig
(Gdanski)

GERMANY

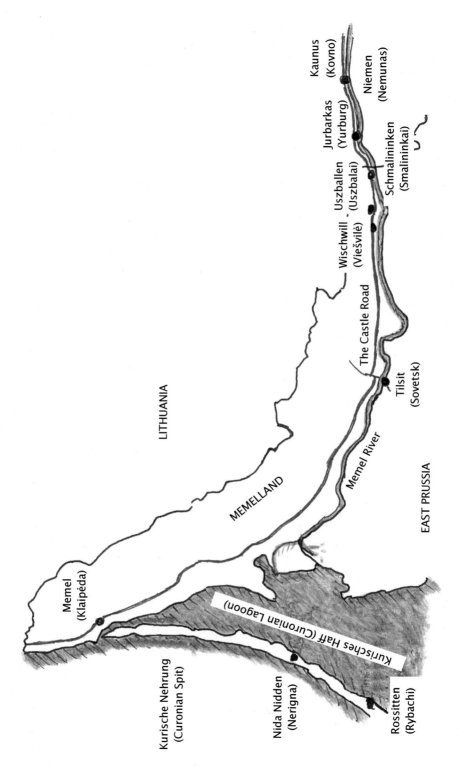

LITHUANIA

Memel (Klaipėda)

Kurische Nehrung (Curonian Spit)

Nida Nidden (Nerigna)

Rossitten (Rybachi)

Kurisches Haff (Curonian Lagoon)

MEMELLAND

Memel River

Tilsit (Sovetsk)

The Castle Road

Wischwill (Viešvilė)

Uszballen - (Uszbalai)

Schmalininken (Smalininkai)

Jurbarkas (Yurburg)

Niemen (Nemunas)

Kaunus (Kovno)

EAST PRUSSIA

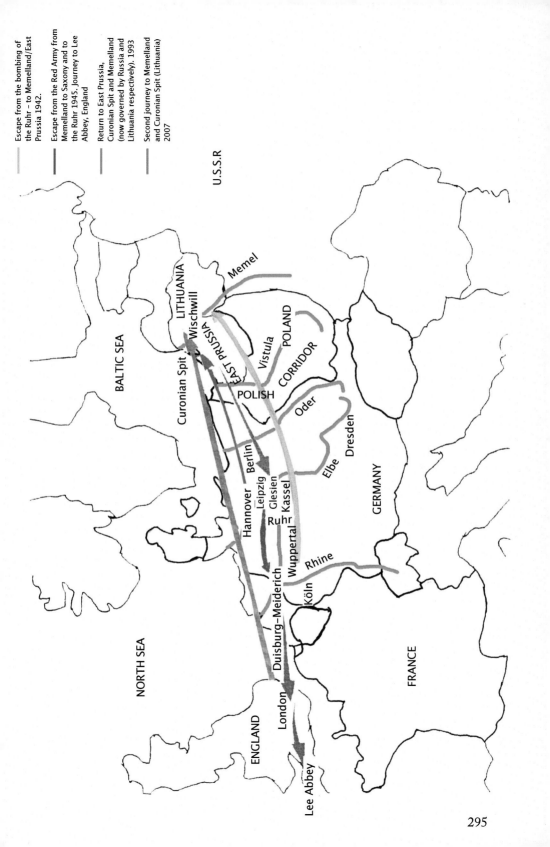

Escape from the bombing of
the Ruhr – to Memelland/East
Prussia 1942.

Escape from the Red Army from
Memelland to Saxony and to
the Ruhr 1945. Journey to Lee
Abbey, England

Return to East Prussia,
Curonian Spit and Memelland
(now governed by Russia and
Lithuania respectively). 1993

Second journey to Memelland
and Curonian Spit (Lithuania)
2007

U.S.S.R

Memel

LITHUANIA
Wischwill

POLAND

Vistula

BALTIC SEA

Curonian Spit

EAST PRUSSIA

POLISH

CORRIDOR

Oder

Dresden

Berlin

Elbe

Leipzig

Hannover   Glesien

Ruhr   Kassel

GERMANY

Wuppertal

Rhine

NORTH SEA

Köln

Duisburg-Meiderich

London

FRANCE

ENGLAND

Lee Abbey

295

Bibliography

These books and publications helped me piece together a jigsaw puzzle.

Dan Allander, *The Wounded Heart* Revised edition. 1995

Conrad Baars and Anna Terruwe, *Healing the unaffirmed – Recognizing Deprivation Neurosis*. A Shand Publication. The society of St. Paul. 1976. Revised and shortened version of *Loving and curing the neurotic*. New Rochelle, NY. Arlington House. 1972.

Gerda Erika Baker, *Shadow of war*. A Lion Book. 1990

Melody Beattie, *Codependent no more*. Hazelden Foundation. 1987–1992

Earl R. Beck, *Under the bombs – The German home front 1942-1945*. The University Press of Kentucky. 1986

Anthony Beevor, *Stalingrad*. Viking. 1998

Christabel Bielenberg, *The past is myself*. Corgi Books. 1988

Sandra Bloom, *Creating Sanctuary*. Routledge. 1997

John Conway, *The Nazi Persecution of the Christian Churches 1933-45*. Weidenfeld and Nicholson. 1968

Michele Elliott ed., *Female Sexual Abuse of Children*. Longman. 1993

Helmut Euler, *Die Entscheidungsschlacht an Rhein und Ruhr 1945*. Motorbuchverlag. 1981

Jörg Friedrich, *The fire – The bombing of Germany 1940-1945*. Columbia University Press. 2008

Robert Gerrard, *The battle of ISandlwana & the fugitive's trail*. Series Anglo Zulu War. 2007

Sebastian Haffner, *Defying Hitler*. Weidenfeld and Nicholson. 2002

Sebastian Haffner, *The meaning of Hitler*. Phoenix. 2003

Stephen Howarth, *August '39*. Hodder and Stoughton. 1989

JewishGen websites. 2011

Guido Knopp, *Die Befreiung – Kriegsende im Westen*. Econ. 2004

Andreas Kosset, *Damals in Ostpreußen. Der Untergang einer deutschen Provinz*. Pantheon Verlag, Random House GmbH, 2010

Ulla Lachauer, *Die Brücke von Tilsit – Begegnungen mit Preußens Osten und Rußlands Westen*. Rowohlt. 1996

Ulla Lachauer, *Paradiesstraße – Lebenserinnerungen der ostpreußischen Bäuerin Lena Grigoleit*. Rowohlt

Frank Lake, *Clinical Theology*. Darton, Longman & Todd. 1966

Hans Graf von Lehndorf *Ostpreußisches Tagebuch. Aufzeichnungen eines Arztes aus den Jahren 1945-1947*. Biederstein Verlag, München. 1961

James Lucas, *The last year of the German Army. May 1944–May 1945*. BCA. 1994

Elizabeth Moberley, *Psychogenesis – The early development of gender identity*. Routlege & Kegan Paul Ltd. 1983

Donald Morris, *The washing of the spears*. Sphere Books. 1973

Robert Norton, *Secret Germany*. Cornell University Press. 2002

Ostpreußen – Ein Lesebuch. An anthropology of East Prussian writers. Heyne Bücher. 1990

Leanne Payne, *Restoring the Christian soul through healing prayer*. Baker Books. 1996

Cornelius Ryan, *The last battle*. Wordsworth Editions. 1966

Rainer Maria Rilke, *The notebooks of Malte Laurids Brigge*. Penguin Classics. 2009

Wolfgang Ulrich, *Uta von Naumburg – Eine deutsche Ikone*. Verlag Klaus Wagenbach, Berlin. 2005

John and Paula Sandford, *Healing the wounded spirit*. Victory House. 1985

John and Paula Sandford, *Transformation of the inner man*. Charisma House. 2007

Jacqui Saradjian, *Women who sexually abuse children*. John Wiley and sons. 1997

Fritz Schilke, *Trakehner Pferde*. BLV Verlagsgesellscaft, München. 1982

Nijolė Strakanskaitė, *Klaipėda – Curonian Spit – Königsberg: a guide*. R. Paknio leidykla.

J.P. Stern, *Hitler – The Führer and the people*. Revised edition. Fontana press. 1990

Paul Tournier, *Creative Suffering*. (transl. from the French). SCM Press Ltd. 1982

Estela V. Welldon, *Mother, Madonna, whore*. Free Association Books. 1988

Charles Whitfield. *Healing the child within*. Health Communications. 1987

Charles Whitfield. *Codependence*. Health Communications. 1991

Charles Whitfield. *Boundaries and relationships*. Health Communications. 1993

World War II, Time-Life Books, Alexandria, Virginia. 1997

Rose Zwi, *Last walk in Naryshkin Park*. Spinifex Press Pty. 1977

~

Max Egremont, *Forgotten Lands*. Picador. 2011 fell into my hands after I finished my manuscript and makes fascinating reading for anyone who would like to know more about East Prussia.

~

For further study of Attachment Theory I recommend:

Jeremy Holmes, *The search for the secure base. Attachment Theory and psychotherapy*. Brunner Routledge. 2001

Valerie Sinason ed., *Attachment, trauma and multiplicity*. Brunner Routledge. 2002